"Although the ecumenical movement and brought Christians of different traditions munion remains as elusive as ever. This collection of essays by scholars from diverse backgrounds not only helps us understand why the Eucharist continues to divide us but also offers sensible suggestions on how to continue the conversation toward better mutual understanding. For the perplexed, these essays should offer more than a glimmer of hope."

Simon Chan, Trinity Theological College, Singapore

"These essays offer unflinching honesty, surprising humor, keen insight, and possible ways forward as they wrestle with the hard questions about why Christians are and remain divided over what should unite us: the sacraments of baptism and the Lord's Supper. This book richly rewards thoughtful reading."

James R. Payton Jr., professor emeritus of history, Redeemer University College, author of *Getting the Reformation Wrong: Correcting Some Misunderstandings*

"This book, a collection of essays from leading mainline and evangelical Protestant, Roman Catholic, and Orthodox theologians, offers fascinating and helpful insights into traditional and contemporary reflection on the sacraments as they relate to issues of Christian unity. Here we see honesty about the divisions among us and the challenges before us as well as serious theological reflection on the reasons for those divisions. And with these probing and sober reflections on the faith, we also see hope and charity."

Thomas H. McCall, professor of biblical and systematic theology, Trinity Evangelical Divinity School

"Nowhere does the evil of division come to the fore more poignantly than in the celebration of unity at the Eucharistic table. This volume's plea to 'come' and 'eat together' calls on believers East and West, Catholic and Protestant, to refuse to accommodate our empirical divisions. George Kalantzis and Marc Cortez place us in their debt with a volume of essays that represents a dialogue that is honest, rigorous, and open, yet conducted in the recognition that we belong together at the Table of the Lord."

Hans Boersma, J. I. Packer Professor of Theology, Regent College

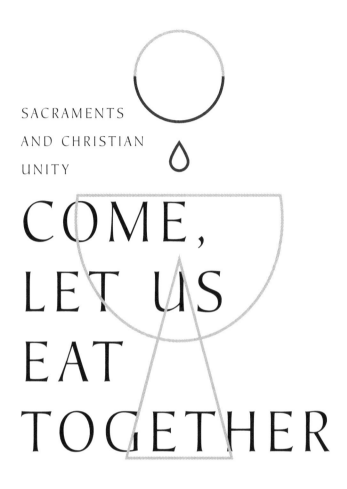

SACRAMENTS
AND CHRISTIAN
UNITY

COME, LET US EAT TOGETHER

EDITED BY
GEORGE KALANTZIS and MARC CORTEZ

IVP Academic

An imprint of InterVarsity Press
Downers Grove, Illinois

InterVarsity Press
P.O. Box 1400, Downers Grove, IL 60515-1426
ivpress.com
email@ivpress.com

InterVarsity Press® is the book-publishing division of InterVarsity Christian Fellowship/USA®, a movement of students and faculty active on campus at hundreds of universities, colleges, and schools of nursing in the United States of America, and a member movement of the International Fellowship of Evangelical Students. For information about local and regional activities, visit intervarsity.org.

Cover design: David Fassett

Interior design: Jeanna Wiggins

Images: Forerunners of Christ: © The Forerunners of Christ with Saints and Martyrs by Fra Angelico (Guido di Pietro) at National Gallery, London, UK / Bridgeman Images.

> *Cover illustration: Graphic element by David Fassett.*
>
> *Figure 8.1: Lucas Cranach the Elder (1472–1553), "Law and Grace," 1529, Stiftung Schloss Friedenstein, Gotha. Wikimedia Commons.*
>
> *Figure 8.2: Wheaton College Art department. Photo by Matthew J. Milliner.*
>
> *Figure 8.3: Unidentified subject with women, children and two elderly men (study for the "Benediction of the Seed of Noah"), ascribed to Jacopo Pontormo, 1518–1572, © The Trustees of the British Museum.*
>
> *Figure 8.4: Photo by Matthew J. Milliner.*
>
> *Figure 8.5: Lucas Cranach the Elder (1472–1553), "Law and Gospel / Damnation and Salvation," 1529, National Gallery in Prague. Wikimedia Commons.*
>
> *Figure 8.6: Lucas Cranach the Younger (1515–1586), altarpiece in St. Peter and Paul, Weimar, 1555, National Gallery in Prague. Photo by GFreihalter, CC BY-SA 3.0, Wikimedia Commons.*

ISBN 978-0-8308-5317-5 (print)
ISBN 978-0-8308-8728-6 (digital)

Printed in the United States of America ∞

InterVarsity Press is committed to ecological stewardship and to the conservation of natural resources in all our operations. This book was printed using sustainably sourced paper.

Library of Congress Cataloging-in-Publication Data

A catalog record for this book is available from the Library of Congress.

P	25	24	23	22	21	20	19	18	17	16	15	14	13	12	11	10	9	8	7	6	5	4	3	2	1
Y	37	36	35	34	33	32	31	30	29	28	27	26	25	24	23	22	21	20	19	18					

TO

Jill Peláez Baumgaertner

CONTENTS

ACKNOWLEDGMENTS

THIS VOLUME HAS BEEN MADE POSSIBLE because of the longstanding partnership between Wheaton College's Department of Biblical and Theological Studies and InterVarsity Press. The 2017 Wheaton Theology Conference was also sponsored by The Wheaton Center for Early Christian Studies, whose mission to promote historical and theological engagement with the early church's witness complemented the vision for this year's conference particularly well.

The editors are grateful to Bob Fryling, Dan Reid, and the whole IVP team for their unflagging support of the conference. David McNutt deserves special recognition for bringing this volume to completion. Lynn Cohick, Wheaton College's interim associate dean of biblical and theological studies, provided leadership and encouragement at every phase of this project. Paula Anderson and Judi Nychay were the administrative gurus who made the conference possible, Daniel Hall and Justin Zahraee played a critical role in all stages of editing, and Aaron Hill labored over the indices.

We dedicate this volume to Jill Peláez Baumgaertner, the indefatigable dean of humanities and theological studies at Wheaton College, whose witness to the faithfulness of God and legacy of inclusion and ecumenism will continue to guide us for many years to come.

INTRODUCTION

THE LATTER PART OF THE TWENTIETH CENTURY witnessed a tremendous surge of interest in the unity of the church. Ecumenical conversations proliferated as theologians, ministers, and lay people from every Christian tradition wrestled with what it means to be the "one" church of Jesus Christ in the midst of such undeniable diversity and disunity. Despite such efforts, questions of church unity remain among the more pressing theological issues today.

The sacraments have played an ironic role the story of the church's unity. People often tell that story as a movement from the fundamental unity experienced by the earliest Christians to the fractured reality that characterizes modern Christianity, a tragedy of fissure and fragmentation from which many see no real hope of recovery. Yet such stories neglect the fact that early Christians faced their own struggles over the issue of Christian unity. Scattered throughout the Roman Empire, separated by geography, culture, language, and experience, and often differing in how to understand and articulate fundamental features of the Christian faith, these early Christians faced a broad range of issues that contributed to their own divisions and discord. Given these conditions, it would not be difficult to imagine a scenario in which these early believers began to envision themselves as autonomous local bodies, largely separated from the others by their distinctive beliefs and worship practices, and only loosely related through their shared commitment to Jesus—many churches rather than one church.

In the midst of this potentially fractious environment, the liturgical life of the church—primarily expressed in baptism and the Eucharist—played a fundamental role in facilitating the church's commitment to the catholicity (in the sense of *universality*) of Christianity. Eventually, Christians recognized that the common worship life of the church served as a visible expression of the underlying theological truth that all true Christians are part of the one church of Jesus Christ.[1] Christians in this era thus manifested a keen interest in maintaining

---

[1] See Paul F. Bradshaw, *The Search for the Origins of Christian Worship: Sources and Methods for the Study of Early Liturgy*, 2nd ed. (Oxford: Oxford University Press, 2002). See also Andrew B. McGowan, *Ancient Christian Worship: Early Church Practices in Social, Historical, and Theological Perspective* (Grand Rapids: Baker Academic, 2014).

common liturgical forms throughout the Christian world. This common liturgy and the sacraments these Christians shared tangibly demonstrated that every gathering of believers participated in the same liturgical action, the common worship of the one body of Christ. Indeed, more than merely expressing the unity of the church, the common sacramental life of these early Christians helped establish and maintain that unity despite the many centripetal forces that could have pulled it apart.[2]

By the time of the Reformation, however, the story had taken a notably different turn. Although the Middle Ages witnessed their own share of debates regarding the nature and function of the sacraments, before the Reformation they continued to serve predominantly as markers of Christian unity. With the Reformation, though, radical differences developed in both the theology and practice of the sacraments. Theologians on every side of the various debates accused the others of undermining the graciousness and efficacy of the sacraments and endangering the well-being of God's people. Even if we set aside disagreements about whether things like marriage and ordination should properly be viewed as sacraments and the strong criticisms raised by the Protestant Reformers regarding confession and penance, the differences surrounding the Eucharist and baptism alone were sufficient to cause significant disunity in the church. This was true even among the various Protestant groups, as clearly demonstrated at the Marburg Colloquy (1529) when disagreements about the Eucharist precluded institutional unity between the various Reformers. And we can see these differences as well in the wedge driven between the magisterial Reformers and the various Anabaptist groups at least partly over the nature of baptism. Throughout this period, then, rather than holding the church together in the midst of its manifold diversity as in the earlier periods of the church, the sacraments had now become one of the more prominent forces pulling it apart.

Even now, five hundred years after the Reformation, the sacraments remain one of the more challenging issues involved in understanding what it might mean for disparate Christian groups to develop closer ties. Many view the sacramental beliefs and practices of other ecclesial bodies with skepticism, concerned that they undermine firmly held convictions about grace, salvation, the church, the natures of Christ, and other important theological issues. Indeed, George Hunsinger has

---

[2]Indeed, the emphasis on having a common liturgy was so strong that some have worried that these early Christians failed to recognize and celebrate legitimate diversity and that localized expressions of Christian identity were unnecessarily minimized (see Bradshaw, *Search for the Origins*, 118-43).

recently argued that the sacraments in general and the Eucharist in particular stand as one of the clearest obstacles to ecumenical dialogue in theology today.[3]

Even the very terminology used in the discussion is potentially divisive. We have already referred in this introduction to the "Eucharist" and "sacraments," terms that will sound to some like a capitulation to theological views they find objectionable. Many Christians choose to refer to the former as "the Lord's Supper," emphasizing the fact that the table belongs to and is overseen by Jesus himself, or "Communion," highlighting the centrality of fellowship. And some Protestants have tended to prefer the term *ordinances* when referring to this aspect of Christian worship, focusing on the idea that these rites have their origin in the commands of Jesus. However, others would raise questions about adopting such alternate terms, worrying that they suggest a tendency to downplay their own commitment to these rites as real sacraments, that is, visible signs of an invisible grace that God makes available in and through the ritual action itself. None of the language involved in the discussion is entirely neutral, and yet *some* language must be used. For the title of the volume and for this introduction, we thus chose terms like *Eucharist* and *sacrament* because this is the language most commonly used by Christians throughout the centuries to express a variety of views regarding these central aspects of Christian worship. Consequently, the intent behind such terminological decisions is not to privilege a particular perspective on the sacraments so much as to root the discussion in the long history of Christian reflection on these issues.

As we recognize the five-hundredth anniversary of the Protestant Reformation, this is a fitting time to explore these issues in greater depth. The essays in *Come, Let Us Eat Together* thus seek to discuss the topic of Christian unity specifically as it relates to the sacraments. Although that issue could be addressed from many directions, a central question is the extent to which Christ's church can and should be unified through the sacraments today. What is sacramental unity? Can we really achieve sacramental unity today? If so, what issues must we address, and what practices must we embody to make progress toward that end? Originally presented at the twenty-fifth annual Wheaton Theology Conference held at Wheaton College in Illinois, these essays represent a theological dialogue across a variety of Christian traditions, including Roman Catholic, Eastern Orthodox, and numerous Protestant perspectives (e.g., Methodist, Lutheran, Anglican, Episcopalian, Baptist, and Pentecostal). The goal is not to bring together scholars from various Christian traditions

---

[3]George Hunsinger, *The Eucharist and Ecumenism: Let Us Keep the Feast* (New York: Cambridge University Press, 2008).

simply to present a variety of viewpoints on sacramental theology. Rather, the hope is that these essays will allow us to explore more deeply the theological basis and practical expression—and therefore implications—of the unity that is "the body of Christ." Although the title of the volume highlights the importance of the Eucharist in this conversation, which is reflected in a number of the essays to follow, the subtitle correctly reflects the volume's focus on the sacraments as a whole.

The volume rightly begins with Amy Peeler's discussion of "the supper of the Lord" (κυριακὸν δεῖπνον) in 1 Corinthians 11:17-34. This chapter not only serves to analyze one of the key texts involved in any discussion of the sacraments, but it also addresses at least two fundamental questions. First, Peeler takes a close look at the text to determine what it teaches about the theology and practice of the Supper as well as to discern what dependence (if any) Paul's comments have on the teachings of Jesus. Here Peeler offers an important analysis of the problems that had arisen in the Corinthian church and the resulting divisions and spiritual danger. With this textual ground in place, Peeler then focuses on identifying some of the implications this passage has for our own practices, particularly as they relate to the ways in which this celebration of God's goodness and grace should inform our compassionate embrace of those around us.

With chapter two we continue this focus on how sacramental theology should inform the ways in which we engage one another, but this time from a more international perspective. Drawing on his experience as a social justice activist in Africa and an assistant bishop of the diocese of Kampala, Church of Uganda, D. Zac Niringiye discusses sacramental unity by looking specifically at the ecumenical challenges facing the Roman Catholic and Anglican churches in Uganda. Niringiye argues that the fact that these two bodies have traditionally failed to achieve unity can be traced to an underlying tendency to focus more on "other-ness" than "oneness," which is itself grounded in social-political rivalries and power structures. Much of the essay thus offers a close reading of the cultural context in which the relationship between these two groups has developed, avoiding a tendency toward theological abstraction that often plagues ecumenical conversations. Ultimately, Niringiye contends that any attempt to move toward greater unity around the sacraments needs to focus first on fostering an atmosphere of mutual respect and the pursuit of the common good.

With the third chapter, Fr. Thomas G. Weinandy raises the challenge issued by the Roman Catholic understanding of the relationship between Eucharist and the nature of priesthood. As Weinandy rightly points out, Roman Catholic theology maintains that there is an inseparable link between the sacramental nature of the Eucharist and the sacramental nature of ordination. Throughout the essay, Weinandy offers exceptionally clear summaries of Roman Catholic views on the nature of the sacraments, offering invaluable assistance to those seeking to understand this important perspective. From there, Weinandy focuses specifically on the nature of ordination and what it means for a priest to operate *in persona Christi* (i.e., as Christ's representative) as Christ's sacrifice is made present to the church in the Eucharist. On this view, then, a true sacrament requires one who has been properly ordained as a priest. This clearly raises questions about how Roman Catholic theologians understand the sacraments offered in other Christian traditions, which Weinandy addresses toward the end of the essay. He also explains why he thinks that this view of the relationship between ordination and the Supper makes it difficult to envision a scenario in which Protestants and Catholics could share the same table.

Shifting ecclesial gears, chapter four takes us into D. Stephen Long's reflections on baptism and ecclesial unity through his experiences in the Brethren and United Methodist churches. Using his own narrative as the backdrop for understanding the rite of baptism, Long draws on Rowan Williams to contend that every Christian tradition must be able to articulate how the local church fits with the universal church, how the universal church is somehow present in every local church, and the manner in which every local church is open to admonition from other ecclesial bodies. Long contends that these three provide the non-negotiable starting point for any adequate understanding of ecclesial unity, even though each tradition will offer different ways of addressing these issues. He then offers an explanation of how these can be addressed from the perspective of United Methodist theology, how this relates to other ecclesiologies, and why he thinks that the pursuit of the "true church" is ultimately misguided.

Cherith Fee Nordling turns our attention in chapter five to what she argues is a theological issue that has been sadly neglected in this discussion: the ascension of Christ. According to Nordling, the New Testament authors present the ascended Christ as the lens through which we must understand the entirety of the new creation, including the sacraments. She thus offers a theological framework comprising seven principles drawn from the ascension that should inform our understanding of the Eucharist as a fundamentally political act that culminates primarily in the call to manifest the self-giving character of God.

Bradley Nassif offers the first of two Eastern Orthodox contributions in chapter six. Nassif focuses on the Orthodox contention that ecclesial unity requires "full agreement in faith." In the twentieth century, a number of Orthodox began focusing more specifically on "Eucharistic ecclesiology," contending that the Eucharist lies at the center of Christian worship and is the sacrament that constitutes every local church as a true church in and through the Spirit. Consequently, to participate in the Eucharist is to participate in the eucharistic community, which in turn involves participating in the very faith of that community. According to Nassif, this means that there can be no intercommunion but only either full communion or lack thereof. Although this might seem to preclude any meaningful unity between Orthodox communities and other ecclesial groups, Nassif concludes the essay with some helpful thoughts on how a greater emphasis on the gospel in Orthodox theology might facilitate increased partnership in mission.

In chapter seven, Katherine Sonderegger addresses the issue from the perspective of "Christ the *Ursakrament*." Sonderegger takes as her starting point the words of Paul in 1 Corinthians 2:5, "God made Christ, who knew no sin, to be sin for us, that we might become, in him, the righteousness of God." According to Sonderegger, the idea that the sinless One became sin for us is grounds for affirming that he is the "primal sacrament." In an extended engagement with Schillebeeckx's theology—which Sonderegger views as a vital dialogue partner for thinking about the sacraments as "personal and person-forming"—Sonderegger contends that the person of Christ is the primal sacrament and should be the focus of any discussion of sacramental unity. This does not mean that we should downplay the very real importance of things like baptism and Eucharist, but Sonderegger contends that such a "strongly Christocentric" view of the sacraments is the proper avenue toward sacramental unity.

The eighth chapter offers a notably different contribution. Drawing on his expertise as an art historian, Matthew J. Milliner explores the idea of a "visual ecumenism," or the possibility that we might be able to find greater unity across ecclesial differences by focusing on the theological truths expressed in and through the visual arts. Milliner examines an impressive range of art expressions, offering close analyses of the theological ideas embedded in medieval icons, Reformation wood carvings, and more. Although at first glance this might seem like an odd essay to include in a discussion of the sacraments, Milliner's essay reflects on the possibility of expanding the scope of the sacramental beyond traditional categories to include such artistic formulations and the ostensibly more hopeful form of ecumenical dialogue they represent.

Matthew Levering takes us on the road to Emmaus in chapter nine, asking about the possibility that we might come to know the resurrected Christ in the very Eucharist itself, not just through historical study. The first part of the essay engages the views of several New Testament scholars on the significance of "the breaking of the bread" in Luke 24:35, ultimately concluding that we should see this as having Eucharistic connotations. This suggests that the risen Jesus is present, though unseen, in both the Old Testament Scriptures and the Eucharist. The second part of the essay focuses on the question of what exactly the Eucharistic experience adds to our knowledge of the risen Jesus. Finally, Levering draws on the experience of Gertrude the Great to explain what the Eucharist can add to our knowledge of the resurrected Christ. In the end, he suggests that affirming that Christians in many ecclesial traditions all meet the resurrected Jesus in their own Eucharistic experiences might be one avenue toward greater sacramental unity.

Our second Eastern Orthodox contribution comes from Paul Gavrilyuk in chapter ten. Gavrilyuk begins by noting the prominent role that Schmemann and other Orthodox theologians have played in the modern ecumenical movement, despite significant reservations among certain more isolationist parties. Gavrilyuk then draws on a distinction made by Sergei Bulgakov between "dogmatic minimalism" and "dogmatic maximalism" to outline different perspectives in Orthodox theology on what is required for ecclesial unity. Although the latter requires significant agreement on a broad range of theological issues, the former stipulates only certain commitments relative to the Trinity and the incarnation. In the final part of the essay, Gavrilyuk argues for an eschatological reorientation of the discussion, one that recognizes the ways in which all Christians are *already* in partial intercommunion as an anticipation of the ultimate communion that will be achieved in the final state.

In chapter eleven, George Kalantzis offers an essay that interweaves personal story, historical dialogue, and theological analysis to shift the focus of the discussion from whether we can achieve sacramental unity to whether we should even presume that we have a right to "come to the [same] table." He thus interrogates a number of important tendencies that often corrupt theological discussions on this issue. He focuses first on a tendency to oversimplify the history of the church and to idealize certain aspects of the story, thus failing to appreciate the messy particularities of the history of God's people. Instead, we must appreciate that this history points to the *ecclesia reformata semper reformanda*, a messy and complex story that is always in progress. Second, Kalantzis warns against a tendency to focus on experience above conviction, highlighting "spirituality" for the sake of unity at the expense of historic Christian faith. Finally, Kalantzis draws on Cyprian, Calvin, and John Milbank to highlight the importance of the church in God's plan for his people against a tendency toward individualism in Western Christianity. Ultimately, Kalantzis warns against all of these tendencies if we are to develop healthy ways of thinking about ecclesial unity around the Lord's table.

In chapter twelve, Marc Cortez seeks to speak to and for those who may have felt underrepresented in the preceding essays. Recognizing that many will have found the language of "sacrament" and "Eucharist" disconcerting, especially those who have grown up in largely Baptist contexts, Cortez explores the possibility of a "Baptist sacramentalism" that can appreciate the real power of the sacraments without denigrating other historic Baptist commitments. Cortez first analyzes the meaning of the term *sacramental* as an adjective, with the goal of discerning a baseline by which we might determine whether a particular perspective qualifies as sacramental. He then draws on a number of Baptist confessions and hymns from the seventeenth and eighteenth centuries to demonstrate that there has always been a robustly sacramental stream in the Baptist tradition. Finally, he utilizes several more recent Baptist theologians to explain how such a sacramental view of baptism and communion can be integrated with other Baptist commitments. However, although this argument might seem to suggest that Baptists can and should be open to the possibility of sacramental unity with other ecclesial traditions, Cortez also points out that long-standing debates about "fencing the table" suggest that Baptists face their own challenges in this area.

Finally, Veli-Matti Kärkäinnen concludes the volume by casting a bold vision in which all Christian traditions can recognize the "full ecclesiality" of the other traditions by emphasizing the church as a "communion of communions." After first noting the three main perspectives on ecclesial unity that led to the current impasse, Kärkäinnen contends that the real issue is whether and how we can discern the presence of Christ in other ecclesial assemblies, which is the ultimate marker of a true Christian church. He then appeals to the Lutheran Augsburg Confession as providing a "middle" way through the debate, affirming that we ground ecclesial unity in the preaching of the gospel and the right administration of the sacraments. After dealing with some possible objections, Kärkäinnen concludes the essay by offering some resources and tools for thinking further about his proposal for sacramental unity.

It would go far beyond the intent of these essays, or the potential of any single volume, to claim that we have resolved one of the most intractable problems in modern theology. We haven't. Nonetheless, by bringing together an array of voices from various ecclesial traditions and disparate Christian experiences, these essays offer an important dialogue on the nature of the church, its sacraments, and the unity of God's people. Regardless of whether we have solved any of the problems involved in the discussion, we think you will find the ongoing conversation stimulating, challenging, and fruitful.

George Kalantzis and Marc Cortez
Feast of the Transfiguration, 2017

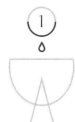

THE SUPPER
OF THE LORD

Goodness and Grace
in 1 Corinthians 11:17-34

AMY PEELER

IT SEEMS FITTING TO BEGIN with a focus on the biblical witness for the supper of the Lord (κυριακὸν δεῖπνον, 1 Cor 11:20), which could comprise the story of the exodus and the first passover meal, or a close comparison of the various accounts of Jesus' last meal with his disciples. I have decided to focus on Paul's instructions about the Eucharist to the Corinthians because it is the earliest example of believers in Christ following Jesus' commands to keep this meal and because, as Richard Hays says in his commentary, their "trouble serves for our instruction."[1] We can learn much about the meaning of this practice from Paul's excoriation of their missteps.

In this chapter of 1 Corinthians, Paul is on a tirade against contentiousness (φιλόνεικος), or a party spirit, where one group is pitted against another; this, he says, has no place in the church of God (1 Cor 11:16). In the first part of the chapter Paul has been seeking to repair the gender divide, helping men and women to see the necessity of their mutual interdependence because of the creative glory of God manifest in creation and in the church.[2] In the second half of the chapter, he turns his sights on the divide of class. God's kingdom functions differently

---

[1]Richard B. Hays, *First Corinthians*, Interpretation (Louisville: John Knox, 1997), 203.
[2]Amy Peeler, "Imaging Glory: 1 Corinthians 11, Gender, and Bodies at Worship," in *Beauty, Order, and Mystery: The Christian Vision of Sexuality*, ed. Todd Wilson and Gerald Hiestand (Downers Grove, IL: IVP Academic, 2017), 141-53.

than the kingdom of the world and its ways; while the haves might acceptably distinguish themselves from the have-nots in society, Paul will not have that in the church.

My task in this chapter is two-fold: first, to describe as best as possible what interpreters can ascertain about the Corinthians' practice of the Lord's Supper and its dependence (or not) upon the words and life of Jesus. Second, I will suggest a few ways in which Paul's exhortations for a meal that embodies Christlike compassion might inform our own sharing of the table. In these words of Scripture and the tradition, we realize both the cultural distance and the christological bond between the church in ages past and ourselves as we hear the call for faithful love and the promise of undeserved grace. My focus will admittedly be personal and local, but I hope to provide common commitments on which global and inter-denominational conversations could build. Paul's admonition to the Corinthians remains true, I think, for all of us: this is the Lord's Supper, and we rightly participate in it by remembering his goodness and grace.

THE LORD'S TABLE IN CORINTH

Paul approaches the Corinthians' keeping of the supper of the Lord based on oral reports. He has learned this information neither by observation nor from the letter they have written to him but by hearing; someone has come to him and described a Eucharistic situation that Paul finds dismal (1 Cor 11:18). Whereas Paul had multiple instructions and explanations to give to them concerning gender distinctions during prayer and prophecy in the first part of this chapter, he opens that section by praising them (ἐπαινῶ ὑμᾶς) for keeping his traditions (1 Cor 11:2). But here in the next set of instructions, he says he will not offer any praise (οὐκ ἐπαινῶ, 1 Cor 11:17). Even if the first promise of praise is perfunctory or even ironic,[3] the situation with the Lord's Supper is such that even irony is not appropriate. He cannot praise them even in jest. For, he says, when they gather, people leave worse off than when they came (1 Cor 11:17), and he finds that true for both sides of the divided social structure: the poor leave shamed, and some of the rich leave—well, if I might speak as boldly as Paul—dead.

The problems occur when they come together "upon the same" (ἐπὶ τὸ αὐτὸ, 1 Cor 11:20). Commentators suggest that this kind of gathering is not the typical

---

[3]Hans Conzelmann, *1 Corinthians*, Hermeneia (Philadelphia: Fortress, 1975), 182; Alan Padgett, *As Christ Submits to the Church: A Biblical Understanding of Leadership and Mutual Submission* (Grand Rapids: Baker Academic, 2011), 121.

occurrence.[4] They might gather in smaller groups in multiple houses on a more regular basis, but they come together as a whole group "upon the same" less frequently. No matter what they *think* they are doing when they have this big gathering, Paul is very clear that they are not eating the supper of the Lord (1 Cor 11:20).

His issue of first concern here—which is the issue of first concern in the letter as a whole as well (1 Cor 1:10-13)—is that when they gather, they remain divided.[5] He believes this report about fracture because he has already talked about the divisions that exist among them (e.g., 1 Cor 1).[6]

In the following verses, he gets more specific about the nature of these divisions. Their practice is not *communion* but rather each person for him- or herself. Everyone, he says, consumes their own meal (1 Cor 11:21). This statement could be a reference to the practice of *eranos* meals, where guests would bring their own picnic.[7] Other first-century authors such as Plutarch recorded debates about taking individualized portions or sharing.[8] A primary concern revolved around equality. Hesiod is quoted as saying, "But where each guest has his own private portion, companionship perishes." Plutarch's conversationalists assert, "This is true where there is not an equitable distribution."[9]

Paul's concern also seems not to be only with a rampant individuality but also inequality. He says that when they eat their own meals, someone goes hungry and someone else is drunk (1 Cor 11:21). It seems to have been a common and acceptable occurrence for owners of large homes to entertain their equals in their dining room, a smaller space called the *triclinium*, which on average would hold seven to nine people. Those below them in social class would have had to gather in the atrium, the grand entry room holding thirty to fifty people.[10] There is also attestation that those outside the main dining room would have been served different, lesser food

---

[4]Jerome Murphy-O'Connor, *St. Paul's Corinth: Text and Archaeology* (Collegeville, MN: Liturgical Press, 2002), 183.

[5]Hays, *First Corinthians*, 194.

[6]Bruce W. Winter, *After Paul Left Corinth: The Influence of Secular Ethics and Social Change* (Grand Rapids: Eerdmans, 2001), 161.

[7]Panayotis Coutsoumpos, *Community, Conflict, and the Eucharist in Roman Corinth: The Social Setting of Paul's Letter* (Lanham, MD: University Press of America, 2006), 21-28; Barry D. Smith, "The Problem with the Observance of the Lord's Supper in the Corinthian Church," *BBR* 20, no. 4 (2010): 517-43.

[8]Plutarch, *Moralia: Table Talk* 2.10, 642F–644D, in Plutarch, *Moralia: Volume VIII*, trans. Paul A. Clement and Herbert B. Hoffleit, LCL 424 (Cambridge, MA: Harvard University Press, 1969), 182-95.

[9]Plutarch, *Moralia: Table Talk* 2.10, 644C.

[10]Murphy-O'Connor, *St. Paul's Corinth*, 180-82.

and would have even had to see and smell the more succulent dishes as they were carried into the triclinium.[11] This is not a picture of unity.

Moreover, Paul's words here show an interesting contrast. He does not say someone is hungry and someone is full. Paul certainly describes the difference in levels of consumption, but it is worth asking why he chooses food and drink rather than food and food. Possibly it is his way of previewing the discussion of the body and blood of the Lord, the bread and the wine, but could it also be that in addition to an inequality of food there is also an inequality of drink? This possibility adds to the widespread shame occurring at this meeting.

In verse 22 Paul begins a series of questions, signaling a slight shift in audience. Whereas he seems to have been discussing the situation with the whole church, the content of these questions indicates that he is now talking to the small group of elites: do you not have houses in which you can eat and drink? This seems a bit ironic because they are eating and drinking in house churches. This becomes an especially ironic comparison when he asks next: "or do you despise the *ekklēsia* of God?"—the *ekklēsia*, which must meet in one of the elites' houses.[12] Are you shaming those who don't have food or such houses? The answers are clear. Those of you who do have houses in which you can eat and drink are despising the gathering of God because you are shaming those who do not have as much as you do. There are multiple suggestions for the specific situations here, but they all reach a very similar conclusion.[13] The rich Corinthians have enough space, food, and wine when they gather for this meal, and the poor Corinthians do not. Therefore, Paul's interrogating questions reach a climax in verse 22: "What should I say in such a situation? You think this deserves praise?" He says it again: "about this gathering, I will not praise you" (1 Cor 11:22).

Imagine for a moment the level of shame when this letter was read. He is calling out their divisions. Many contemporary audiences would be uncomfortable with

---

[11]Ibid., 184-85.

[12]David L. Balch and Carolyn Osiek, *Families in the New Testament World: Households and House Churches* (Louisville, KY: Westminster John Knox, 1997).

[13]Each of these scholars presents a possible recreation of the dinner situation in Corinth: Gerd Theissen, "Social Integration and Sacramental Activity: An Analysis of 1 Cor 11:17–34," in *The Social Setting of Pauline Christianity: Essays on Corinth* (Philadelphia: Fortress, 1982), 145-74; Murphy-O'Connor, "House Churches and the Eucharist," in *St. Paul's Corinth*, 178-85; Coutsoumpos, *Community, Conflict, and the Eucharist*, especially 25-27, 31-64, 99-138; Stephen Richard Turley, *The Ritualized Revelation of the Messianic Age: Washings and Meals in Galatians and 1 Corinthians* (New York: T&T Clark, 2015), 133-72; Bruce Winter, "'Private' Dinners and Christian Divisiveness (1 Corinthians 11:17-34)," in *After Paul Left Corinth*, 142-63; Smith, "Problem with the Observance of the Lord's Supper," 517-44.

the exposure of the fact that not everyone is in the middle class. Their economic situation is different. Maybe they would not be uncomfortable with the reality of divisions; that was an accepted part of their lived reality. To call out divisions would not be to name an uncomfortable unspoken reality, as it would be in many contemporary settings, but to do so is still a source of shame because Paul has to correct their misperception that what they are having is the supper of the Lord. They think they are having the supper of the Lord. Moreover, it might expose the hurt of some of the have-nots in the congregation who reported the divides but were not being heard by the haves. He is saying that these kinds of divisions that seem so normal are not commensurate with the Lord they confess. The owners of the houses are not sharing, and they are shaming their guests. In the process of becoming drunk on their own wine, they are bringing shame on themselves. The least of these are getting the least, and the rich do not seem to care. That is not how the church of God, the table of the Lord Jesus Christ, works.

THE LORD'S SUPPER

In light of this problem, Paul needs to go back to the basics to remind them of what he has already taught so that they can follow the pattern of this supper not just in form but also in content. Typically, scholarship gravitates toward the word *received* in verse 23 and asks, "How did Paul receive the instructions about the Lord's Supper? Directly from God or through other Christians?"[14] That invites a comparison with the Gospel traditions.

Differences certainly exist among the four evangelists. John has Jesus discussing the eating of his flesh and the drinking of his blood with the Jews, who puzzle over his exhortation toward what seems to be cannibalism (Jn 6:52), and that gives Jesus the opportunity to proclaim the eternal life found in this meal. Even among the Synoptics, all three of which portray this as a meal shared during the celebration of Passover (Mt 26:17; Mk 14:12; Lk 22:8), there are variations: Luke includes a cup before and after the bread, and only he (like Paul) has Jesus say that the bread is given for them. While noting these differences, we should nevertheless not forget that the similarities are what dominate. The bread is designated as his body, and the wine is associated with his blood and (by the Synoptics and Paul) the covenant.

[14]For a discussion of this debate see Jerome Murphy-O'Connor, *Keys to First Corinthians: Revisiting the Major Issues* (Oxford: Oxford University Press, 2009), 207-8; Gordon D. Fee, *The First Epistle to the Corinthians*, NICNT (Grand Rapids: Eerdmans, 1987), 548; Anthony C. Thiselton, *The First Epistle to the Corinthians* (Grand Rapids: Eerdmans, 2000), 866-67.

Overall, the New Testament witness of Matthew, Mark, Luke, John, and Paul shows an incredible consistency.

In addition to the word *received*, it might be equally important to pay attention to the word *Lord*. Whether supernaturally, eccesially, or a mix of both,[15] Paul says that this information came from the Lord. He, the *Lord* Jesus Christ, is in charge of this meal and sets the paradigms by which it should be conducted.

Paul then sets up an interesting chiasm in verse 23:

I took from the Lord (παραλαμβάνω)

I gave to you (παραδίδωμι)

the Lord was given (παραδίδωμι)

The Lord took (λαμβάνω) bread

Using forms of the words λαμβάνω and δίδωμι, Paul's actions of taking and giving echo the Lord's. But, even more interesting, these words show that he mediates to the Corinthians the Lord's self-offering. When Paul receives from the Lord, he does receive this story, but the story is not just about an evening meal in the past. The body of believers takes the second-person plural "you" to refer not just to the disciples but to them. This would have been natural to do since the Passover meal was an invitation to all Jews to consider how God's actions toward an ancient generation of Abraham's children in Egypt redeemed them as well (Exod 12; 34:25; Lev 23:5; Num 9:2-14; 28:16; Deut 16:1-6; see also *m. Pesahim*). When Paul takes from the Lord, he takes the story; in taking the bread, Paul also takes the body and then gives that over to the Corinthians. This was possible because the Lord, the one in control, allowed himself to be *given* by his act of taking the bread and designating it as his body (1 Cor 11:24). When they eat the bread of the Lord, it is to be for the remembrance *of him*.

After the meal, Jesus took the cup. He designated it not as *his* blood but as the *new covenant* in his blood, thereby recalling the establishment of the covenant by blood when the people had left Egypt (Exod 24) and Jeremiah's hope for a new covenant in which sins are forgiven forever (Jer 31). Jesus said the same thing.[16] It was to be consumed in remembrance *of him*. Remembrance (ἀνάμνησις), used here and in Luke's account, is a beautiful and powerful word. I seek only to make a

---

[15]Murphy-O'Connor articulates this both/and solution beautifully (*Keys to Corinthians*, 207-8).

[16]Ellen Aitken, "τὰ δρώμενα καὶ τὰ λεγόμενα: The Eucharistic Memory of Jesus' Words in First Corinthians," *HTR* 90, no. 4 (1997): 359-70; Jane Lancaster Patterson, "1 Corinthians: The Community that Keeps the Feast," in *Keeping the Feast: Metaphors of Sacrifice in 1 Corinthians and Philippians*, SBL Early Christianity and Its Literature 16 (Atlanta: SBL Press, 2016), 117-58.

simple point about it: this meal is supposed to point their memories back to Jesus and therefore should be done in a way that reflects Jesus. This is precisely what Paul says next: whenever they eat this bread and drink this cup, they proclaim in word and deed the death of the Lord until he comes. Note that he says the *death*, not (explicitly) the resurrection. Resurrection is understood, of course, since he is the Lord, and for Paul the Lord is clearly risen and seated at the right hand of the Father (Rom 8:34; 1 Cor 15:25; Eph 1:20). Yet the focus of this meal is on his death, and it makes total sense that Paul would say only θάνατος here and not also ἀνάστασις: his focus has been on the giving of the Lord—the giving of his body and blood in his death for his disciples past and future. This meal is all about the Lord and his selfless act for others in death. Eating and drinking say something, namely, that this Lord is a Lord who has given himself in death.

Herein lies the problem with their practice. The way the Corinthians "celebrate" the supper of the Lord does not look anything like Jesus' selfless, others-focused death. Because of some of the Corinthians' selfishness, it simply cannot be the supper of that Lord. So Paul transitions back from tradition to their situation. They *should* eat the bread and drink the cup to proclaim the Lord's death (1 Cor 11:26), but if anyone eats the bread and drinks the cup in a manner unworthy of him (as Paul has said they are doing), they will be liable for the mishandling of the body and blood of the Lord (1 Cor 11:27). Paul makes a parallel statement in verse 29: anyone who eats and drinks without discerning the body eats and drinks judgment to him- or herself. An "unworthy manner" seems to be partaking without discerning the body, and when one is responsible for mishandling the body and the blood, judgment results.

This judgment is intense. Because of this—because some of them are doing what Paul refers to in verses 27 and 29—many of them are weak and sick, and a sufficient number have died. Mishandling of the body of the Lord results in a judgment on one's own body.

This section casts light upon one of the more confusing verses earlier in the chapter. Near the beginning of this discussion, in verse 19 Paul says, "It is necessary for sects (αἵρεσις) to be among you in order that those among you who have stood the test might become manifest." Is he changing course here in saying divisions are acceptable? That suggestion seems to fly in the face of the rest of this chapter as well as his calls for unity throughout the letter. The best way through this confusing verse is to imagine that he is mimicking them first and then following with his own comment. "It is necessary for divisions to be among you" is not a quote from a letter, or even necessarily what some of them have said orally, but the *message* of their actions. He acknowledges that some of them are acting in such a way that might as well say "sects are necessary." This is how the world works, they might say; you do things differently for the haves than the have-nots. Paul uses this word αἵρεσις negatively, as evidence of the works of the flesh in opposition to the fruit of the Spirit (Gal 5:20). But even if it simply means one group portioned off from another, as in the sects of the Sadducees, Pharisees, or Christians (Acts 5:17; 15:5; 24:5, 14; 26:5; 28:22), Paul has made it clear that such division does not belong in the church.

The next word for divisions, δόκιμος, carries quite different connotations. This is a positive word, used for passing the test or being approved by God (Rom 14:18; 16:10; 2 Cor 10:18; 2 Tim 2:15; James 1:12). Later in this section it is used as an admonition for people to test themselves (1 Cor 11:28). I think Paul would approve of the proven ones being made manifest.

It seems then that Paul is saying it this way: You think that it is necessary to be divided. I agree, but not along class lines. Instead, divisions are necessary to show who has been approved by God or not, and who has really gotten the message of his Son the Lord. Those who you think are superior and maintain divisions will be divided out in judgment. Paul is not opposed to distinctions per se. He wants it to be clear who is following the way of Jesus and who is not.[17] He is opposed to the way in which the Corinthians have been dividing themselves. It is actually their divisions that are prompting the divine distinctions of judgment.

Yet even in this judgment Paul finds the grace of God. In verse 32 he says, "But if we are judged, we are being disciplined (by this very same Lord whose supper we are shaming), then we will not be condemned with the world." Paul can think of punishment—even the punishment of mortality—as distinct from eternal judgment.[18]

The Corinthians are pursuing the wrong path in how they are sharing the meal, so Paul also offers the right path. In verses 28 and 31, he states: Let a person test him- or herself, and if we evaluate ourselves (διακρίνω), then we would not be judged. There is both an individual and communal dimension here: a person needs to assess his or her own actions, but those actions are the ones that affect others and contribute to the functioning of the group.[19] To be guilty of the body

---

[17]As seen in his willingness for the man living in sexual immorality to be divided out for a time (1 Cor 5:5-13).

[18]Fee, *First Corinthians*, 566; Joseph A. Fitzmyer, *First Corinthians*, AB (New Haven, CT: Yale University Press, 2008), 448.

[19]Fee, *First Corinthians*, 566.

(1 Cor 11:27) or to fail to discern the body (1 Cor 11:29) seems to point to a mishandling of the elements of bread and wine in the midst of the body of Christ—the group of believers or the ἐκκλησία, the same way he refers to the body in chapters 10 (1 Cor 10:16-17) and 12 (1 Cor 12:13-15). The proof for this communal focus of σῶμα comes in his concluding comments: Here is the point, my brothers and sisters—when you do come together to eat, welcome one another (1 Cor 11:33). This could include the rich waiting for the poor until they get off work as well as a more general call "to receive" by correctly entertaining one another.[20] Have a meal during which everyone is really together: everyone waits, shares, and has the same quality and quantity of goods.

Then Paul adds, "If anyone is hungry, let that one eat in a house" (1 Cor 11:34). Many interpreters take this as saying if anyone is hungry, let that person go home to eat,[21] which raises certain problems. Can the wealthy have lavish meals at home as long as the poor do not see? That does not seem to solve the problem of division but hide it. Moreover, if this is heard by the poor who are hungry, Paul's instructions could be nothing less than cruel: "Go to that nice home you don't have and eat that food you don't have." Might it be better to remember the association between the ἐκκλησία and the οἶκος, the church and the home? If anyone is hungry, let that one eat in a house, namely, the house in which you are gathering for the meal. In other words, when you come together, feed the hungry. If you do so, then you will not be judged. This seems to be the correct discernment of the body: making sure the needs of the body are met.

The rest—which indicates there must have been other, less-pressing problems—Paul says he will address when he comes. We will have to wait until glory to hear the other things he wanted to say. Nevertheless, if God is sovereign over the giving of the biblical word—providing what we need for our instruction—then there are lessons Paul's instructions to the Corinthians offer to us who also share at the table of the Lord.

GATHERING AROUND THE TABLE TODAY

First, it must be acknowledged that it is exceedingly challenging to make any kind of direct move from the situation in Corinth to our own Eucharistic practices.

---

[20]I find Bruce Winter's more comprehensive meaning of ἐκδέχομαι, "to receive, to entertain," convincing (*After Paul Left Corinth*, 181).

[21]Theissen, "Social Integration," 151; Coutsoumpos, *Community, Conflict, and the Eucharist*, 111; Smith, "Problem of the Observance of the Lord's Supper," 531; Hays, *First Corinthians*, 197.

Although I realize there is a debate on this point,[22] it seems to me that Paul's congregation would have followed the pattern of a Passover meal in memory of Jesus. The Synoptic Gospel tradition, where the christologically designated bread and wine were part of a celebratory meal, makes this explicit. This seems especially to be the case because (1) they likely did not gather as a large group on a regular basis, and when they did, it would be normal to have a meal together. Also, (2) the problem that arises has to do with the consumption of too much versus too little food and wine. For many contemporary churches, our sharing of the Lord's Supper—in miniscule quantities of bread and wine or juice—is completely separate from the church potluck. And at the church potluck, we would never sit apart by social class and designate different quantities and qualities of food for the different groups. I have been struck anew by that great cultural gap between us and the communities of the New Testament.

I am also struck by the narrow but miraculously enduring bridge between us. Just as there are differences between the accounts of the Lord's Supper in the New Testament but also unmistakable similarities, so too in the midst of the completely different settings—just like that rag-tag, passionate, but misdirected group of confessors that "Jesus Christ is Lord" in Roman Corinth in the early 50s CE— we too hear and say these words: "This is my body, this is my blood of the new covenant which is given for you and for many for the forgiveness of sins. Whenever you eat and drink this, do so for the remembrance of me." We have all done this quite odd thing in which we take common elements and, through the proclamation of Jesus' life and words, experienced these elements as means of grace. Therefore, because we share this, Corinth does have something to teach us about the supper of the Lord.

First, this meal is powerful. As Paul attests to the Corinthians, the mishandling of this meal brings judgment upon the collective body and individual. *Anamnēsis*, remembrance, is not simply, "Remember that time when Jesus had that last meal with his group of disciples? Wow, what a night!" Instead, *anamnēsis* involves participation and being invited into the reality of which the words speak.[23] This need not demand belief in any particular Eucharistic mode, for from commemoration to transubstantiation, communities believe that when they share this bread

---

[22]Thiselton traces the major positions of this debate as it relates to 1 Corinthians (*First Corinthians*, 871-74).

[23]W. J. Grisbrooke states, "It is an objective act, in and by which the person or event commemorated is actually made present, is brought into the realm of the here and now" ("Anaphora," in *The New Westminster Dictionary of Liturgy and Worship*, ed. J. G. Davies [London: SCM, 1986], 18a).

designated as Christ's body, they are Christ's body. As Paul himself said in 1 Corinthians 10:17, "The bread which we break—is it not the fellowship of the body of Christ? Because in one bread, we, the many, are one body, for we all share from one loaf." Hence to enter into this meal is to enter into Christ. This is holy ground, since he is the image and glory of God, and it should not be approached with flippancy or disdain.

The focus on Christ leads to the second applicable principle. As Paul said to the Corinthians, this is the Lord 's Supper, not yours. The way they were celebrating it, even though they might have been saying the right words, looked nothing like the life and heart of the Lord they were invoking. Therefore, Paul said to them: when you gather it is not to eat the supper of the Lord (1 Cor 11:20). Nevertheless, the Lord is still sovereign over this mispracticed meal because they are being held accountable for partaking of it unworthily. He is ever sovereign over this supper even when it is practiced without appropriate consideration. How then might we practice this meal in such a way that it looks like his? This, as I mentioned, is the most challenging question. There is no easy way, it seems to me, to be mindful of social and economic equality in the distribution of small quantities of bread and wine in a church setting.

Are there other ways that we could proclaim the selfless death of the Lord in this meal? Paul's overarching concern revolves around meeting needs and avoiding shame. Everyone would be left hungry if the Eucharist were the only thing we ate, but sharing this meal binds us together and gives us both the responsibility and blessing of knowing one another and sharing one another's burdens. If this is really going to be a supper that honors the Lord it names, then we need to be mindful of the needs in our congregations. Is anyone hungry in mind, body, or spirit? Then we should be the body of Christ to one another by meeting one another's needs. This demands a certain vulnerability, investment of time in relationships, and sacrifice. But that is how our Lord lived: knowing those around him and giving of himself to meet their needs. This necessarily is a very local and small-group vision of the Lord's Supper. It will not be possible to know the needs of everyone with whom you share the supper, but there should be some knowledge. Moreover, if you know of a need and aren't willing to assist with it, that would at least call into serious question your proclamation in this meal that Jesus of Nazareth is Lord.

John Chrysostom, the fourth-century Greek preacher and bishop, read the meal in this way:

"Wherefore whosoever shall eat this bread and drink the cup of the Lord unworthily, shall be guilty of the Body and the Blood of the Lord." Why so? . . . Seest thou how fearful he makes his discourse, and inveighs against them very exceedingly, signifying that if they are thus to drink, they partake unworthily of the elements? For how can it be other than unworthily when it is he who neglects the hungry? who besides overlooking him puts him to shame? . . . Thou hast partaken of such a Table and when thou oughtest to be more gentle than any and like the angels, none so cruel as thou art become. Thou hast tasted the Blood of the Lord, and not even thereupon dost thou acknowledge thy brother. Of what indulgence then art thou worthy? Whereas if even before this thou hadst not known him, thou oughtest to have come to the knowledge of him from the Table; but now thou dishonorest the Table itself; he having been deemed worthy to partake of it and thou not judging him worthy of thy meat. . . . Wherefore I beseech you that we do not this to condemnation; let us nourish Christ, let us give Him drink, let us clothe Him. These things are worthy of that Table.[24]

Paul wants the needs of the congregation met, and his related concern is about the shame that arises in their practicing of the meal. Some of them are made to feel less than the others. He is obviously thinking of a social dynamic, but it causes me to reflect on the particular feelings of shame that could arise with our practice of the meal. I wonder if by now some readers are feeling nervous. I know I did as I worked with this text. How can I ever really do this meal justice? How can I ever address the needs in my parish, let alone the sufferings and needs of the global church? In my spiritual history I have a tendency toward anxiety over the Lord's Supper. This probably began in my late teens when I was visiting the church of the young man who is my now husband. This church had communion only once a year, and it was preceded by a week of fasting and revival to ensure that people were worthy to receive the meal.

I am not the only one in the history of the church to have such concerns. In his sermon on "The Duty of Constant Communion," John Wesley takes up the same verse:

[People say,] "I am unworthy; and 'he that eateth and drinketh unworthily, eateth and drinketh damnation to himself.' Therefore I dare not communicate, lest I should eat and drink my own damnation." The case is this: God offers you one of the greatest mercies on this side of heaven, and commands you to accept it. Why do not you accept this mercy, in obedience to his command? You say, "I am unworthy to receive it." And what then? You are unworthy to receive any mercy from God. But is that a reason for refusing all mercy? . . . In this very chapter we are told that by eating and

---

[24]John Chrysostom, *Homilies on First Corinthians* 27.6-7, NPNF[1] 12:161-63.

drinking unworthily is meant, taking the holy sacrament in such a rude and disorderly way, that one was "hungry and another drunken." But what is that to *you?* Is there any danger of *your* doing so,—of your eating and drinking *thus unworthily?* However unworthy you are to communicate, there is no fear of your communicating thus. Therefore, whatever the punishment is, of doing it thus unworthily, it does not concern *you.* You have no more reason from this text to disobey God [i.e., to not take communion], than if there was no such text in the Bible. If you speak of "eating and drinking unworthily" in the sense St. Paul uses the words, you may as well say, "I dare not communicate, *for fear the church should fall,*" as "for fear I should *eat and drink unworthily.*" If then you fear bringing *damnation* on yourself by this, you fear where no fear is. Fear it not for eating and drinking unworthily; for that, in St. Paul's sense, ye cannot do. But I will tell you for what you shall fear damnation;—for not eating and drinking at all; for not obeying your Maker and Redeemer.[25]

What then is it? Is the situation so far removed that we could never eat or drink unworthily, as Wesley argues? His point about the Lord's command and God's grace is compelling. We are told to participate in this meal, and we are always unworthy of God's gifts. Or is Chrysostom correct, that right living is a necessary feature of coming to the table?

I see value in both a dependence upon grace and a call to knowledge and compassion (with which I actually think both of these eminent preachers would agree), but it is John Calvin whom I find to articulate so well this particular balance.

If you would wish to use aright the benefit afforded by Christ, bring faith and repentance. As to these two things, therefore, the trial must be made, if you would come duly prepared. Under repentance I include love; for the man who has learned to renounce himself, that he may give himself up wholly to Christ and his service, will also, without doubt, carefully maintain that unity which Christ has enjoined. At the same time, it is not a perfect faith or repentance that is required, as some, by urging beyond due bounds, a perfection that can nowhere be found, would shut out for ever from the Supper every individual of humankind. If, however, thou aspirest after the righteousness of God with the earnest desire of thy mind, and, trembled under a view of thy misery, dost wholly lean upon Christ's grace, and rest upon it, know that thou art a worthy guest to approach the table—*worthy* I mean in this respect, that the Lord does not exclude thee.[26]

[25]John Wesley, "Sermon 101: The Duty of Constant Communion," in *John Wesley's Sermons: An Anthology,* ed. Albert C. Outler and Richard P. Heitzenrater (Nashville: Abingdon, 1991), 505-6.
[26]John Calvin, *Commentary on the Epistles of Paul the Apostle to the Corinthians,* trans. John Pringle, CC 20 (1848; repr., Grand Rapids: Baker, 1999), 388, emphasis original.

We can't come flippantly without any thought of what we are doing. We can't come rightly, it seems to me, if we know a need of one of our brothers or sisters and are unwilling to meet it. But if we know our state, that "we are not worthy so much as to gather up the crumbs under thy table," and if we know our Lord, "whose property is always to have mercy,"[27] and if we bring faith, a desire for repentance, and a hunger for a life of selfless giving, God will meet us at this table with his gracious presence.

Jesus' words from John should have the final word: "Those who eat my flesh and drink my blood have eternal life, and I will raise them up on the last day; for my flesh is true food and my blood is true drink. Those who eat my flesh and drink my blood abide in me, and I in them" (Jn 6:54-55). When we partake of his meal, he changes us. We are graced to do his good will and feed the hunger of souls and bodies, our own and those of our siblings, because this is the supper of the self-giving Lord.

---

[27]As the prayer of humble access, taken from Jesus' interaction with the Syrophoenician woman (Mt 15:26-27; Mk 7:27-28), so provocatively articulates (*The Book of Common Prayer* [New York: Oxford University Press, 1979], 337).

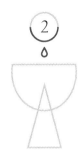

2

CHURCHES
AND THE POLITICS
OF THE SACRAMENTS

Rethinking "Unity of the Church"

D. Zac Niringiye

THE "UNITY OF THE CHURCH" as a subject of theological discourse is very broad and multi-dimensional—historical, theological, sociological, political, and cultural—and all these dimensions are interwoven. Although the focus on sacramental unity helps to delimit the conversation, nonetheless one has to admit that the other aspects of "being church" have to be taken into account in order to engage meaningfully even with specific questions around the sacraments. Moreover, "sacraments" itself is also a very broad subject.

The choice of the title of this chapter has been informed by research I have undertaken over the years on the biblical narrative of the people of God,[1] the story of the Church of Uganda (Anglican),[2] and my current work in Uganda as a civic-political activist working for the common good. I therefore begin the essay with some autobiographical notes because it would be disingenuous to posture objectivity without acknowledging my vantage point. More importantly, however, I have become persuaded over the years that all theology is biographical and contextual—it is located in personal narratives as well as in particular historical, social, cultural, economic, and political contexts. Thankfully, gone are the days when theologies

---

[1]David Zac Niringiye, *The Church: God's Pilgrim People* (Downers Grove, IL: IVP Academic, 2015).

[2]David Zac Niringiye, *The Church in the World: A Historical-Ecclesiological Study of the Church of Uganda with Particular Reference to Post-Independence Uganda, 1962–1992* (Carlisle: Langham Monographs, 2016).

from European and North American perspectives were considered "theology proper" while other theologies were relegated to the category "ethnic." All theologies are "ethnic" and contextual. Thus all theology is partial, tentative, and provisional. We are incapable of grasping and articulating the whole picture. We see in part! We see dimly! The value of a space such as the 2017 Wheaton Theology Conference, gathering us from diverse contexts, is that it affords us the opportunity to think together as a hermeneutical community.

After the autobiographical notes, the essay then outlines what I call "contours of a theology of the church"—an outline of an ecclesiology, and the place and role of the two sacraments: baptism and Holy Communion.[3] This sets the backdrop for the next section of the essay in which I discuss how, with the emergence of Christendom, sacraments became part and parcel of Christendom's narrative of being church. This narrative is grounded in ecclesiologies of territoriality and public power, as illustrated by the story of two churches in Uganda—the Church of Uganda, a church that stands within the broader Anglican tradition, and the Roman Catholic Church.[4]

The thesis of this chapter is that the critical question of the failure of the two churches to find common ground on the sacraments of baptism and the Holy Communion is primarily due to their sense of "otherness" rather than "one-ness." This is manifested in their social-political rivalry, because their ecclesiologies are grounded in a theology of conquest and domination rather than unity, catholicity, and apostolicity. By their failure to find sacramental unity they have shown that they have no ontological unity. Thus unity cannot and should no longer be based on "being united in Christ" but rather on other grounds. I propose that efforts should be geared towards mutual respect, cooperation, and the pursuit of the common good rather than discourse on the unity of the churches steeped in ecclesiologies grounded in social-political rivalries.

---

[3] I use "Holy Communion" in this text for that is what we call it in the Church of Uganda (Anglican), while other traditions prefer to call it "The Lord's Supper," "The Eucharist," and many other variants.
[4] The Church of Uganda is a member of the world-wide Anglican Communion, a theologically diverse communion of national and regional autonomous churches. Currently, the Anglican Communion has thirty-eight national and regional member churches in 165 countries, according to www.anglicancommunion.org/identity/about.aspx. My parents were first-generation Christians, and my father served as a church planting evangelist and lay pastor (catechist) in the church.

AUTOBIOGRAPHICAL NOTES

There are at least two angles from my story and context that are relevant to this subject: first, my own experience of "church" as one born and bred in rural Uganda. Mine is an account of feasting on a *katogo* meal—a Ugandan version of a casserole meal or mixed grill. I am a bishop in the Church of Uganda, from the "low" end of the Anglican tradition. My location is made even lower by my formation, first, in the spirituality of the East African Revival movement—a renewal movement that emphasized repentance, fellowship, and evangelistic mission.[5] Second, I was part of the evangelical student movement (Scripture Union in high school and the Christian Union at university). During the latter season, as a young man I sampled a whole range of church options available at the time in Uganda out of a sheer desire to know more—especially options of the Pentecostal-charismatic flavor. Later, during the prime of my adult life, serving in a nondenominational student movement made me appreciate unity in diversity of the children of God.[6] We found a formula of sharing in Holy Communion without bothering with which church the communicants belonged to, provided they confessed Jesus as Lord. My theological education and ministerial formation also reflects my penchant for *katogo*.[7]

The second angle is the nature of "being church" in the polarized church context in Uganda—a situation of conflict and rivalry between the Church of Uganda (Anglican) and the Roman Catholic Church. The first missionaries from the Church Missionary Society set foot on Ugandan soil in June 1877. They were followed nearly immediately by French Roman Catholic missionaries of the order of the Society of Missionaries of Africa, otherwise called the White

---

[5]The East African Revival is a movement reckoned to be the most important development in the church's life in Uganda in the twentieth century. It was a movement of protest, renewal, and reform in the context of a church that had become nominal. It originated among the indigenous laypeople of the church in Uganda, Rwanda, and Burundi, and missionaries from the Ruanda Mission, a small mission formed out of the Church Missionary Society (CMS) in the late 1920s. The movement spread to the eastern African countries of Kenya, Tanzania, and Southern Sudan and is still alive today.

[6]I served as the staff team leader of the Fellowship of Christian Unions (FOCUS), the evangelical student movement in Uganda, and later the International Fellowship of Evangelical Students (IFES) for a total of twenty years.

[7]I did an MA in theological studies (systematic theology) in the Graduate School at Wheaton College—a college that stands within the broader American evangelical tradition; an ordination certificate at Bishop Tucker College Mukono, today the Bishop Tucker School of Theology and Divinity at Uganda Christian University, Mukono—the Church of Uganda's premier Seminary; and a PhD in theology and mission history at New College, Edinburgh University, a college within the Church of Scotland tradition.

Fathers, in February 1879. The two sets of missionaries brought with them baggage of historical conflict and rivalry,[8] setting the stage for a future of social and political rivalry in an emerging Uganda. Violence has characterized all transitions in Uganda from the colonial period, except for the transition from colonial rule to independence.[9] Both churches are not just participants in the story of turbulent Uganda but its very roots.[10] In spite of the fact that sacramental theology is in the DNA of both churches, they have been unable to arrive at sacramental unity.

CONTOURS OF A THEOLOGY OF THE CHURCH: THE ONE, HOLY, CATHOLIC, AND APOSTOLIC CHURCH

The creedal statement "one, holy, catholic, and apostolic church" expresses in a succinct manner what I call contours of a theology of the church.[11] A cursory reading of the exposition of these concepts by various theologians, however, shows that there is no unanimity on how they should be understood, because different assumptions, ecclesiastical traditions, and theologies have determined their meaning. Consequently, they are used differently and assigned varying content.[12] Calvin, in addition to affirming "one, holy, catholic and apostolic" as the true marks of the church, asserted, "Wherever we see the Word of God purely preached and heard,

---

[8]The two missionary groups belonged to rival Christian traditions, Roman Catholic and Anglican, and hailed from two traditional enemies, France and Britain, whose relationship had been embittered by their imperial interests. In addition to the Anglo-French rivalry, the nineteenth century was marked by a recurrence of ecclesial-theological disputes between Catholics and Protestants in Europe, occasioned not least by the first Vatican Council (1869–1870), which decreed the doctrine of papal infallibility, thus completing the process of "counter-Reformation" that had begun several centuries earlier at the Council of Trent (1545–1563).

[9]Except for the first independence government of Milton Obote (1962–1971), all subsequent political transitions were violent and often preceded or followed by civil war: the Idi Amin years (1971–1979); Uganda National Liberation Front (UNLF) (1979–1980); Milton Obote's second term (1980–1985); the Military Commission (1985–1986); and the National Resistance Movement (NRM) Government (1986 to date). It is estimated that well over one million people have died as a result.

[10]For a detailed account of the story of turbulent Uganda, see Niringiye, *Church in the World.*

[11]They are otherwise called "marks of the church," "notes of the church," or "dimensions of the church." See especially Avery Dulles, *Models of the Church* (Garden City, NY: Image, 1978); Anthony Hanson, *Church, Sacraments and Ministry* (London: Mowbray, 1975); Hans Küng, *The Church* (London: Burns and Oates, 1967), 263-359.

[12]In his *The Church: Its Changing Image Through Twenty Centuries* (London: SPCK, 1977), Eric Jay outlines some of the content assigned to these marks by the different generations of theologians and churchmen from the time of the early church fathers, when the Apostles' Creed was framed. Colin Gunton has made this point as well in his "The Church on Earth: The Roots of Community," in *On Being the Church: Essays on the Christian Community*, ed. Colin E. Gunton and Daniel W. Hardy (Edinburgh: T&T Clark, 1989), 48.

and the sacraments administered according to Christ's institution, there, it is not to be doubted, a church of God exists."[13]

I take it as evident, as the Reformers did, from the Gospel accounts of the life and teaching of Jesus that he envisioned and intended to bring into being a visible community through whom he would continue his work by the Holy Spirit.[14] The *raison d'être* of the community was the kingdom of God, which was the good news Jesus proclaimed, demonstrated, and embodied. The community would constitute the new people of God in continuity with Israel. It would be a sign of God's kingdom in the world, a community that lives beneath the just and righteous reign of God by acknowledging, proclaiming, and demonstrating it. The community prays to the Father, "May your Kingdom come on earth as it is in heaven" (Mt 6:5-15) and looks forward to its final manifestation. As the Gospels record, Jesus taught his disciples what the victory of the reign of God looks like: freedom for the prisoners, recovery of sight for the blind, and liberation for the oppressed (Lk 4:18)—indeed, the triumph of justice (Mt 12:20).

The community was to derive its character not from its membership but from Jesus, the embodiment of God's reign—his life, death, resurrection, and ascension— who would continue to be with them, in them, and among them by the Holy Spirit. They were to be a people set apart for himself—his flock (Jn 10). The community would be distinct from the world as salt is from food and light from darkness (Mt 5:13-16). The impact of their witness to the world would not be achieved in withdrawal but rather through their presence preventing moral decay and in expelling the darkness of evil in the world by the proclamation and demonstration of the gospel of the kingdom. Just as love was the hallmark of God's action in Jesus, the community too would live by love—loving God and neighbor (Mt 22:39), one another (Jn 13:34), and even their enemies (Mt 5:44). Thus, during the three-and-a-half years of his ministry, Jesus was forming the nucleus of that community with the apostles as the core through whom he would gather all his other flock from all the corners of the earth (catholic-universal)—"one flock, one shepherd" (Jn 10:16). The climax would be in Jesus' death on the Roman cross, his resurrection and ascension, and the coming of the Holy Spirit! And, sanctified by him (set apart, holy),

---

[13]John Calvin, *The Institutes of the Christian Religion*, ed. John T. McNeill, trans. Ford Lewis Battles (Philadelphia: Westminster Press, 1960), 4.1.9, 1023. See also a shorter discussion of both Luther's and Calvin's positions in Jay, *Church*, 161-76.

[14]I concur with arguments that there is no evidence in the Gospels that Jesus was "founding the Church in the same way in which, for example, Baden Powell founded the Scout Movement . . . or indeed that he intended to 'found' a new religion" (Hanson, *Church, Sacraments and Ministry*, 3).

Jesus would then send his Spirit into the world, as the Father sent him into the world (Jn 17:6-19; 20:21-23) to bear witness to the reign of God.

Jesus charged his disciples that they should gather regularly (an *ekklēsia*) and eat together after his departure, invoking the memory of Jesus' life and death, dramatizing and celebrating their redemption and that of the whole world. It was also to act as a testimony to their belonging together and to the One who died ushering the reign of God into the world. Jesus gave his disciples another physical sign: baptism. This sign was for those who he would draw into the fold: "Make disciples of all nations, baptizing them in the name of the Father and of the Son and of the Holy Spirit" (Mt 28:19). It would be a mark distinguishing them from all others among whom they lived, signifying that they belong to another—the One who died on the Roman cross and rose, who now dwells in them and in whom they dwell by the Holy Spirit. Both eating together and water baptism were physical-material statements attesting to the historical fact of Jesus' life, death, and resurrection. Associating together as belonging to God in Christ anticipated the fullness of the kingdom of God when Jesus would return. In theological language, they were incarnational and eschatological: reflective of the nature of Jesus' community.

With the coming of the Holy Spirit at Pentecost, the new community of the kingdom of God was inaugurated and ushered into the world to embody the presence of Christ in the world by living by his Word and his Spirit. The universalization of the gospel of the kingdom of God was immediate upon the coming of the Holy Spirit, as Jesus' followers declared the wonders of God in the languages of "Parthians, Medes and Elamites; residents of Mesopotamia, Judea and Cappadocia, Pontus and Asia, Phrygia and Pamphylia, Egypt and the parts of Libya near Cyrene; visitors from Rome (both Jews and converts to Judaism); Cretans and Arabs" (Acts 2:9-11). The book of Acts tells the rest of the story of how Jesus, by the Holy Spirit and through the agency of the apostolic community, was gathering "the other flock": "all, whom the Lord our God will call" (Acts 2:39). It was all very real for those Spirit-filled followers in Jerusalem. Those added on the Day of Pentecost were baptized according to the charge of the risen Lord. And they began the special practice of eating together—"breaking bread in their homes . . . with glad and sincere hearts" (Acts 2:41) in remembrance of the death that had become their redemption and grounds of their apostolicity (sent-ness).

The account of the growth and spread of the nascent Jesus community, as recorded in the New Testament, is a story of community in and by the Holy Spirit in various contexts, beginning "in Jerusalem, and in all Judea and Samaria, and to the ends of the earth" (Acts 1:8). As the story unfolds, it is evident that the very tenets of being one, holy, catholic, and apostolic were manifested and asserted as being essential to the nature of the new community. In each context, what it meant was worked out in different ways in obedience to God's Word through the apostles and the leading of the Holy Spirit in response to the particular situation. In every context, however, those who were drawn into the fold were baptized, dramatizing the efficacy of the death and resurrection in bringing about the new birth into a new life, that is, from death to life (Rom 6:4). And in every place, they practiced eating together. This invoked the memory of the historical event of the death of Christ on the cross, but the same act also proclaimed the efficacy of that death (1 Cor 11:23-26). True to their Lord's charge, the sacraments were essential to their being a "community in Christ."

It is also the case that the tenets of being one, holy, catholic, and apostolic church were tested and contested. Whether with the tension and conflict between the Greek- and Aramaic-speaking Jews in Jerusalem and Judea (Acts 6), the personal misunderstanding and quarrels in the Philippian church (Phil 4:2-4), or the quarrels and divisions in the church in Corinth (1 Cor 1; 3), the apostles' response was that they should deal with conflicts and dissentions in the same way you deal with tensions and conflicts within a family: it is not a good reflection on the family to be divided, and therefore there must be a way to resolve the conflicts. Paul's message to the Ephesians urged them in this manner, and it was grounded in the indivisible unity of community-in-Christ:

> As a prisoner for the Lord, then, I urge you to live a life worthy of the calling you have received. Be completely humble and gentle; be patient, bearing with one another in love. Make every effort to keep the unity of the Spirit through the bond of peace. There is one body and one Spirit, just as you were called to one hope when you were called; one Lord, one faith, one baptism; one God and Father of all, who is over all and through all and in all. (Eph 4:1-6)

Paul is unequivocal: unity is a given because of the one Spirit, the Spirit of Christ in whom they dwell. The one catholic (universal) community, which transcends time, space, and culture, is made one by the Holy Spirit. It is the community for whom Jesus is the sovereign by faith and expressed through baptism, and it is a family for whom God is Father. It was therefore incumbent on the Christlike people to keep it; to do otherwise would not only be a contradiction but a denial of who they really are. The apostle Paul makes the point to the believers in Corinth in his response to their quarrels and divisions. First, he addresses them as members of the same family—brothers and sisters, in the name of the head of the family: "our Lord Jesus Christ!" And then he pleads with them to get on and do what a family does when there are conflicts: sort them out! (1 Cor 1:10-12). For the apostle, it is inconceivable that a community that is one because of the one Christ who has brought it into being should be divided. The apostle Paul was emphatic that there could be no justification for their partisanship (1 Cor 3:5-9). Hence the rhetorical questions to the Corinthian Christ-community: "Is Christ divided? Was Paul crucified for you? Were you baptized in the name of Paul?" Paul was making the point that divisions could not be substantial; the evidence that they were in Christ was their ability to transcend differences—and as a matter of fact make the differences work for the benefit of all. He drove his point home by expounding on the "body" metaphor, which illustrates unity in diversity (1 Cor 12:12-20). For "just as a body, though one has many parts, but all its many parts form one body, so it is with Christ. For we were all baptized by one Spirit so as to form one body—whether Jews or Gentiles, slave or free—and we were all given the one Spirit to drink. Even so the body is not made up of one part but of many" (1 Cor 12:12-14).

The two metaphors—family and body—explicate the outworking of the contours of the theology of the community in the Holy Spirit; indeed, the reality of the one, holy, catholic, and apostolic church. The community spans all time—past, present, and future—from the "great cloud of witnesses" in the past, who have completed their earthly journey, to those who would believe in Christ, "for only together with us would they be made perfect" (Heb 11:40). Christ is the one whom God "appointed heir of all things, and through whom he made the universe. [He is] the radiance of God's glory and the exact representation of his being, sustaining all things by his powerful word" (Heb 1:2-3). God purposed in Christ "to be put into effect when the times will have reached their fulfilment—*to bring all things in heaven and on earth together under one head*, even Christ" (Eph 1:9-10, italics mine). The community-in-Christ embodies this eschatological hope—a community of hope, by hope, in hope, and for hope.[15]

The community acts of baptism and "eating together"—later called sacraments—through which God acts as the name of the Father, Son, and Holy Spirit is invoked dramatize and embody that reality in a material and physical way—it is both incarnational and eschatological. Dulles has expounded:

---

[15]Niringiye, *Church*, 189-94.

A sacrament is, in the first place, a sign of grace. A sign could be a mere pointer to something that is absent, but a sacrament is a "full sign," a sign of something that is really present. Hence the Council of Trent could rightly describe a sacrament as "the visible form of an invisible grace." Beyond this, a sacrament is an efficacious sign; the sign itself produces or intensifies that of which it is a sign. Thanks to the sign, the reality signified achieves an existential depth; it emerges into solid, tangible existence. . . . Thus the Councils can say that the sacraments contain the grace they signify, and confer the grace they contain.[16]

The sacraments are a testimony and presence of the unity of the new community-in-Christ, now living between the times of the inauguration of the kingdom by Jesus and its final consummation. It continues to experience the redemptive reign of God through the Spirit in the world.

By implication, we should therefore go further and affirm that the church itself is a sacrament. As Anthony Hanson rightly asserts:

The Church is the means by which the life of Christ is mediated to the world. It is an "outward and visible sign of an inward and visible grace," to quote the Church Catechism. . . . It is a sign which effects something, not an indication of someone who is absent. The purpose of the Church is to enable mankind to enter into the life, death, and resurrection of Jesus Christ. But the two gospel sacraments do exactly this: they convey and express the life, death and resurrection of Jesus Christ.[17]

Being a sacrament in the world involves being the sign that manifests Christ and the reign of God, as well as being the agent of his reign. Authentic church is the presence of Christ in the world.

THE POLITICS OF THE SACRAMENTS: THE CHURCH OF UGANDA (ANGLICAN) AND THE ROMAN CATHOLIC CHURCH

Without entering into the debate on the political dimensions of the gospel (or even as to whether there is anything like a "political dimension to the gospel"), I associate myself with the long Christian tradition that has articulated the gospel in political terms—both in its content and implications.[18] *Political* here means "the distribution of [public] power, the means of wielding it, whether for

---

[16]Dulles, *Models of the Church*, 70.

[17]Hanson, *Church, Sacraments and Ministry*, 38.

[18]John Howard Yoder's book *The Politics of Jesus* (Grand Rapids: Eerdmans, 1994) captures some of this debate.

good, bad or an indifferent end."[19] At the heart of the message of the good news is that under the reign of God made present through the life, death, and resurrection of Jesus, to whom "all authority in heaven and on earth" is vested, the community in Christ is a community of justice, peace, and joy, where "there is neither Jew nor Gentile, neither slave nor free, nor is there male and female, for you are all one in Christ Jesus" (Gal 3:28). It is a community through whom he, the prince of peace and just one, works to bring peace and hope to those who are oppressed, blind, poor, marginalized, despised, and dehumanized—the "hungry or thirsty or a stranger or needing clothes or sick or in prison" (Mt 25:31-46). The point is that the presence of the community-in-Christ brings hope for the good of the others.

As the apostles taught, Jesus continues his work of bringing the reign of God "on earth, as it is in heaven"—working toward the triumph of righteousness and justice in and through the community-in-Christ. To the believers in Rome addressing the conflict over clean and unclean food, Paul reminds them to focus on what matters most for their community life: the kingdom of God. He then explains to them that "the kingdom of God is not a matter of eating and drinking, but of righteousness, peace and joy in the Holy Spirit" (Rom 14:17). Righteousness is a quality of being in right relationship with God, one's neighbor, and God's creation: a right relationship with a just God that is evident in just relationships. Peace is a quality of harmony and well-being of individuals and communities. Joy is a state caused by a full enjoyment of life as intended by God—a life of dignity in community and communion with others and God's creation. These three—righteousness (justice), peace, and joy—are the test of any community that makes a claim to the presence of Christ within it by the Holy Spirit. The community lives out its witness to Christ in the world both in its life and what it seeks to achieve beyond itself.

This is the politics of the good news of God's reign: justice, peace, and joy in the Holy Spirit. The sacraments are a political statement to the world. Irrespective of social-economic standing or ethnic-racial identity, there is only one baptism through the same waters and eating together from the one bread and drinking from one cup. Participating in the sacraments involves sharing in the politics of the kingdom of God—a commitment to being a community of justice and peace, and praying and being God's agency for his kingdom to come on earth as it is in heaven. The following words from the *Epistle to Diognetus*,

---

[19]Marcus G. Raskin, *The Common Good: Its Politics, Policies and Philosophy* (New York: Routledge & Kegan Paul, 1986), 19.

reckoned to date from the second century, capture the political character of the authentic community-in-Christ:

> For Christians are not distinguished from the rest of humanity by country, language or custom. For nowhere do they live in cities of their own, nor do they speak some unusual dialect, nor do they practice an eccentric life-style. . . . But while they live in both Greek and barbarian cities, as each one's lot was cast, and follow the local customs in dress and food and other aspects of life, at the same time they demonstrate a remarkable and admittedly unusual character of their own citizenship. They live in their own countries, but only as aliens; they participate in everything as citizens, and endure everything as foreigners. Every foreign country is their fatherland, and every fatherland is foreign.[20]

Thus authentic community-in-Christ, in its global and local visible presence in the world, is a political community embodying, demonstrating, and proclaiming the politics of the good news of the reign of God. This must not be confused with the notions of church establishment or a separate country or state for Christians. On the contrary, it is how the community-in-Christ lives and infects the rest of body politic in the world with the values of God's reign.

However, it is not always the case that communities that call themselves churches are signs of the reign of God, even when they share in the sacraments. Any community that claims to gather and scatter under the name of Christ should be judged on the basis of the standard of the kingdom of God. Andrew Walls, in his review of K. S. Latourette's work *A History of the Expansion of Christianity*, suggests that one of the contributions Latourette makes to understanding the expansion of Christianity is to subject the story of the church to what he calls "the kingdom test." He makes the point that although the presence of a community that claims to gather regularly in the name of Jesus may be a sign of the influence of Christ in society, the claim cannot be taken at face value.[21] Walls cautions that "the presence of the church . . . is no guarantee of the continuing influence of Christ. The church without the signs of the kingdom becomes a countersign of the kingdom, hiding Christ instead of revealing him to the world."[22] In the latter case, sacraments become a part of the system and mechanisms of divisions, rivalry, and injustice.

---

[20]*The Epistle to Diognetus*, in *The Apostolic Fathers*, ed. and trans. J. B. Lightfoot and J. R. Harmer (Leicester, UK: Inter-Varsity Press, 1990), 299.
[21]Andrew F. Walls, *The Cross-Cultural Process in Christian History* (Maryknoll, NY: Orbis, 2002), 14.
[22]Ibid., 15.

Alan Kreider's *The Change of Conversion and the Origin of Christendom* gives us some insights in understanding how churches and church life became fused with society in a way that the distinctiveness of "community-in-Christ" became marred—in other words, the emergence of Christendom.[23] Kreider also takes a cue from Latourette's work in reflecting on the distinctive features of Christendom wrought by the means of conversion that produced it. He shows how in the early period, the "conversion journey" into becoming a full member of the "one, holy, catholic and apostolic church" entailed a rigorous catechetical process ensuring change of belief and behavior and incorporation into the community through baptism. The significant shift was the emergence of Christendom in the period after the conversion of Emperor Constantine. According to Christendom, people who are within a particular territory should also share uniform beliefs and common standards of behavior. The process of conversion was reversed. Greater effort was put into belonging, because adherence to the emperor's religion came with some benefits, and belonging to the church became very attractive.

By the second half of the fourth century, a new era in church history had dawned. Christianity became the religion by royal appointment, and its numbers—and its place in society—were changing rapidly.[24] In Christendom, the meaning of conversion changed, and so did baptism, the act that was the culmination of the process of conversion. The church ceased to have a distinct identity. Moreover, church and state authority became reciprocal. In Christendom, there is a mutually reinforcing relationship between the church and the state. *Regnum* and *sacerdotium* are in a symbiotic relationship. The church provides the state with reliable religious legitimation; liturgically its services contribute to the unity of the civic body. The state in turn provides the church with protection and resources; it defends the church's monopoly and its place in the symbolic center of society. If necessary, the state may provide assistance in settling ecclesiastical disputes or in doing messy things such as executing heretics, who (in the language of sixteenth-century England) will be "delated to the secular arm."[25]

Pointing to the same Christendom phenomenon, Andrew Walls argues that it was the conversion of the barbarians in today's northern and western Europe that led to "a conception in which Christianity was essentially linked with territory and

---

[23]Alan Kreider, *The Change of Conversion and the Origin of Christendom* (Harrisburgh, PA: Trinity Press International, 1999). Peter Brown's work on Christendom, *The Rise of Western Christendom* (Oxford: Blackwell, 2003), is comprehensive.

[24]Kreider, *Change of Conversion*, 42.

[25]Ibid., 95.

the possession of territory,"[26] or the concept of a Christian nation. The process of indigenizing the Christian faith into the culture and thought patterns of these societies meant that religious belief could not be a matter of individual decision. It was essentially communal: "ancestral custom, acceptable modes of life within the community, and the sanctions governing both. It was therefore a matter of corporate discussion and consensual action."[27] Walls further observes:

> In earlier Christian history, in the Christianity of the old Roman Empire, conversion sealed by baptism, marked the person's entrance into a new community. In the experience of northern and western Europe, Christian conversion led rather to a symbolic reordering of the community already existing.[28]

Unlike the early centuries, in which extended catechism prepared converts to live Jesus' teachings, in Christendom, Christian behavior is simply a reflection of the common sense of the host societies. In Christendom, members of civil society and members of the church coincide precisely, and everyone is a Christian: a homogeneous society in which "people are Christians, not because of what they believe . . . nor because of how they behave . . . but rather because they belong—and their belonging is rooted in the primal realities of genes and geography."[29]

It is this Christendom that produced Christianity in Uganda. Andrew Walls has pointed out that the "Christendom idea has been extremely resilient. It survived the sixteenth century Reformation practically unscathed. The Protestant Reformation resulted in the division of Christendom, but not in the abandonment of the idea. The Protestant Reformers held to it as firmly as any Catholic."[30] The missionaries of these traditions carried Christendom with them wherever they went. The first Christian missionaries sent by the Anglican-leaning missionary society, the Church Missionary Society (CMS), arrived in Buganda in 1877 with the hope of transforming the kingdom of Buganda into a nation of Anglicans. The object of the Mission wherever its missionaries went was "that all nations should gradually adopt the Christian religion as their national profession of faith, and thus fill the universal church by the accession of national churches."[31] The kingdom of Buganda

---

[26]Walls, *Cross-Cultural Process*, 34.
[27]Ibid., 35.
[28]Ibid.
[29]Kreider, *Change of Conversion*, 94.
[30]Walls, *Cross-Cultural Process*, 36-37.
[31]Henry Venn, secretary of the Church Mission Society, quoted in Walls, *Missionary Movement*, 48.

had a centralized, hierarchical structure of government; at the top, and indeed the center, of the kingdom was the Kabaka (king of Buganda), the most powerful person, and "the symbol of social, political, economic and, to some extent, religious power."[32] The conversion of the king to their brand of Christianity would ensure territorial control of their mother church. The arrival of Roman Catholic missionaries (White Fathers) only two years later in 1879 was bound to ignite rivalry in the palace for the control of the king because the Roman Catholic missionaries, like their Anglican counterparts, hoped to establish a Roman Catholic kingdom over Buganda.[33] Mazrui has helpfully pointed to the sixteenth-century Christendom principle of *cuius regio eius religio*, "whosoever reigns shall determine the religion of his territory," in understanding religious establishment in the Ugandan context.[34] It was always the Kabaka's religion that constituted the official religion of the kingdom.

By the beginning of the 1880s Buganda had been divided into two parties—the "Bakatoliki" (Catholic) and the "Bapolostante" (Protestant), otherwise called "Bafalansa" (French) and "Bangeleza" (English), respectively, both referring to the Christian traditions and countries of origin of the two missions.[35] To complicate the matters further, the two foreign religions (for that is how they were perceived by the hosts) found Islam, already established in the kingdom (having been introduced in 1840 by Arabs from the east coast), setting the stage for a more vicious rivalry for control.[36] The defining moments in this contest were the religious wars of 1888–1892 as each of these groups sought to capture the soul and control of the kingdom of Buganda. First it was Muslims against the Christians. The Muslims were victorious and enthroned Muslim king Kalema, renowned today as the "only truly Muslim king" after making Islam the established religion for that period of time.[37] Then the Christians joined forces against the Muslims and deposed the Muslim king in late 1889. The next contest was among the Christians, which ended with the victory of the Protestants aided by the British colonial agent Captain

---

[32]Abdu B. K. Kasozi, *The Spread of Islam in Uganda* (Nairobi: Oxford University Press, 1986), 17.

[33]Aylward Shorter, *Cross and Flag in Africa: The "White Fathers" During the Colonial Scramble (1892–1914)* (Marknoll, NY: Orbis, 2006), 7.

[34]Ali Mazrui, "Religious Strangers in Uganda: From Emin Pasha to Amin Dada," *African Affairs* 76, no. 302 (1977): 21-26.

[35]F. B. Welbourn, *Religion and Politics in Uganda 1952–62* (Nairobi: East African Publishing House, 1965), 6.

[36]As Abdu B. Kasozi indicates, "Although Kabaka Mutesa I did not officially convert to Islam in the earlier period prior to the advent of Christian missionaries, the Islamic golden age of 1862-1875 was possible primarily because Mutesa I adopted Islam" (*Spread of Islam in Uganda*, 20-33).

[37]Ibid., 48. Kalema ruled for less than one year, spanning most of 1889.

Lugard over the majority Roman Catholics in 1892.[38] The victory of what had become a "Protestant party" (also known as the "English" Party) against the Catholics (also known as the "French" Party) in 1892 further entrenched its Protestant identity. It became the religion of the rulers of the kingdom, taking the place of traditional religion with Namirembe as the supreme *Kiggwa* (headquarters of a divinity) of Buganda.

This conflict and rivalry, particularly between the Roman Catholic and the Protestant churches, shaped colonial state building. In order to secure the privileged position they won, the CMS missionaries and their supporters in Britain led the campaign to persuade a reluctant British government to establish a protectorate over Buganda in 1894. They subsequently established a protectorate over the other territories, which were annexed to Buganda, to create Uganda.[39] Although the CMS believed that they were planting an Anglican church and christened it "the Native Anglican Church," in the consciousness of the indigenous people it was Protestant (a self-definition vis-à-vis the Roman Catholic Church). The installation of the Protestant king in 1897 and his coronation at an event at the headquarters of the Protestant Church not only sealed the political ascendancy of the Protestants but also confirmed the "established" position of the Protestant church.[40] Although the colonial government tried to preclude constitutional establishment by enforcing a policy of religious neutrality for the state, as Hansen notes, "religious divisions became the most important mechanism for allocative activity within the political system. . . . Religious factionalism was also political factionalism."[41] The Catholic Church attempted to claim establishment on the basis of its numerical majority but without success. The establishment of a colonial presence in Buganda and beyond was based on Protestant ascendency over rival religious factions, in particular the Roman Catholic Church.[42]

Once the Protestant Church won the contest for control and dominance of the colonial state establishment, the contest shifted to the population—the pursuit to create a Protestant or Roman Catholic society. Since the sacraments, and in

---

[38]Shorter, *Cross and Flag*, 9-10.

[39]Samwiri Karugire, *Roots of Instability in Uganda* (Kampala: Fountain Publishers, 1988), 14.

[40]The coronation took place at Namirembe Cathedral, in close proximity to Mengo, the administrative centre of the kingdom. As Aylward Shorter has observed in *Cross and Flag*, 35, this was further sealed by the Buganda Agreement of 1900, ensuring that the Buganda monarchy would be Protestant.

[41]Holger B. Hansen, *Mission, Church and State in a Colonial Setting: Uganda 1890–1925* (London: Heinemann, 1984), 18.

[42]Dan Mudoola, *Religion, Ethnicity and Politics in Uganda* (Kampala: Fountain Publishers, 1993), 11.

particular baptism, were the mark of "belonging" to the particular version of Christianity (church), and because belonging to a church had become a social imperative, baptism became the instrument of growing the numbers for each of the churches. This worked the numbers from two angles: the traditional culture and the Mission's involvement in social service delivery.[43] From the perspective of traditional culture, baptism was easily indigenized, thereby accelerating growth in numbers. For example, among the Baganda, baptism was the equivalent of the traditional ritual of incorporating the newly born into the clan. This is called *okwalula abaana,* which Anglican Bishop Wilson Mutebi explains "means to hatch the children just like a hen would hatch the chicks from the egg shells."[44] It is instructive that this ritual of *okwalula abaana* is a public clan-community event, superintended by select clan elders, involving the use of water and naming. The idea here is that the children are born physically into their families, but as far as the clan is concerned, they are still not yet born until the rite is performed. Mutebi explains:

> In a sense children before they are incorporated into the clan are really like chicks in the eggs for no one is sure where they belong and they are not known in the clan. Therefore strictly speaking at that stage they are not yet children as far as the clan is concerned. This rite in a way is seen and understood as a kind of giving another birth to the children. All the newly incorporated children in the clan are born again.[45]

The parallels between the traditional practice of *okwalula* and baptism are surprising and indicate why baptism was so easily incorporated into the traditional social culture of the Baganda.[46] Notable was the use of water, symbolizing cleansing,

---

[43]Catholic missionary theologian Adrian Hastings acknowledges that the rivalry over numbers and the mass conversions recorded by the two churches in the period 1890–1920 is unprecedented in all missionary history across Africa in *The Church in Africa 1450–1950* (Oxford: Clarendon, 1994), 464-78.

[44]Wilson B. Mutebi, *Towards an Indigenous Understanding and Practice of Baptism Amongst the Baganda* (Kampala: Wavah, 2002), 114.

[45]Ibid., 73.

[46]Wilson B. Mutebi describes what the ritual entailed in detail: "All mothers assemble seated on a barkcloth . . . or a mat. . . . They all sit in a line facing one direction with their children seated on each mother's lap. The fathers stand or sit opposite the mothers. The water is brought and placed in a basket which was made by the mothers. It is placed in the centre. The children to be incorporated are naked or half naked. . . . The paternal grandmother of the children takes the umbilical cords, smears them with ghee and then places them in the water. If they float, then all the people rejoice, saying Yi! yi! yi! yi! . . . and then the grandfathers proceed . . . to give names to each of the children, while welcoming them into the clan" (ibid., 72).

as part of the process of being born into the clan.[47] It therefore should not surprise us that baptism became a very popular ritual in traditional societies as a way of becoming part of the new social order. It was therefore the battle ground for rivalry between the two churches seeking to outnumber each other on numbers of adherents.

Introducing social services was used as part of increasing the number of adherents as well as forming Christian societies. Moreover, the colonial administration rented the delivery of services to the missionary groups. These rival groups were eager to run them, because through education they became part of the catechetical process leading to baptism.[48] As Asavia Wandira observes, "The pace of expansion of the Church and its quality became inextricably intertwined with the expansion and quality of education. To the outsider it looked as if there could be no education centre without the Church and equally there could be no Church centre without education."[49]

It was a social-political imperative to belong to a particular church. Schools became centers of Christian instruction, conversion, and the formation of character.[50] The Protestant and Catholic missions were seeking to outdo each other in monopolizing education as a way of propagating their "religions" and thereby ensuring dominance in society. In his research among the Bagisu, Sweeting observes,

> If anyone wanted a good post, he had to be a Christian. Anyone who wanted to marry a man with a good post had to be a Christian herself. In every case the first step was admission to the Church school. The catechumens and other readers were to be seen at Church worship, but not the baptised. Some immediately upon their baptism were found to have dropped all pretensions at Christian living according to the teaching of the Church. The tendency was to regard baptism as the be-all and end-all of Christian instruction.[51]

This led to a significantly large membership that had little or no understanding of Christianity. Reading as the primary means of "evangelization" had little to do with teaching the Christian faith and more to do increasing numbers.

---

[47]The water that is left in the basket is used to wash the mother's feet and the children, an act symbolizing that the mothers and the children are now clean in the eyes of the clan. Ibid., 115.

[48]Though development of health services was not to the same degree as the development of schools, they were also intended to serve the project by swelling the numbers.

[49]Asavia Wandira, "Missionary Education in Uganda Revisited," in *A Century of Christianity in Uganda 1877–1977*, ed. T. Tuma and P. Mutimwa (Nairobi: Uzima Press, 1978), 82.

[50]Hansen, *Mission, Church and State*, 249.

[51]Rachel Sweeting, "The Growth of the Church in Buwalasi—II," *The Bulletin of the Society of African Church History* 3 (1969–1970): 19.

The Protestant-Catholic rivalry was so ingrained in the psyche of the different ethnic communities and regions that it shaped the socio-political development of the country to the extent that on the eve of independence, political organizations were built along that divide. The two main parties, which contested the first general election in 1961—the Democratic Party (DP; formed in 1956) and the Uganda People's Congress (UPC; formed in 1960)—were aligned along religious lines. DP—also pejoratively also called Din ya Papa (meaning the religion of the Pope)—was overwhelmingly Catholic in membership and leadership; it was born out of the long-standing grievance against the Protestant church and its colonial allies for its control of the center. UPC (also pejoratively also called the "United Protestants of Canterbury") was overwhelmingly Protestant in its leadership and membership; it was born out of the interest to maintain control of the center.

It should be recalled that the Kabaka was Protestant and so was the majority of his administration. Thus when DP won the 1961 elections, it was not only a stunning shock to Kabaka's government but also considered an affront to Protestant hegemony. Moreover, Britain also did not relish the prospect of handing over the control of Uganda to a Catholic establishment. To counter the possibility of independent Uganda being governed by Catholics, Buganda mobilized around the Protestant identity and formed a movement of Kabaka's loyalists, Kabaka Yekka (KY; meaning "the King alone"), and allied with UPC to form the first government of an independent Uganda in 1962. Karugire observed that "the only explanation for this otherwise inexplicable partnership was the common denominator of the Protestant faith, so that beyond ousting the DP from office before granting independence the UPC and KY had nothing in common, the two parties being essentially antagonistic."[52] Anti-Catholic sentiments were instrumental in the momentous alliance on the eve of independence.

Attempts were made after independence to tamper the rivalry and find ways of mutual collaboration through the creation of an ecumenical platform: the Uganda Joint Christian Council (UJCC), constituting the Church of Uganda, the Roman Catholic Church, and the Orthodox Church, in 1963. The official narrative of the organization is that the platform was created out of recognition "for Christians to witness together and live in harmony" in Uganda. It is instructive how the founders thought of what it would take to achieve this objective.

---

[52]Karugire, *Roots of Instability*, 47.

UJCC was established with the purpose of: "working towards greater mutual understanding and unity; achieving cooperation by means of joint consultation and action in practical matters of common interest such as economic empowerment and development; and developing options for member Churches to pursue and enhance their capacity and responses to pertinent issues. UJCC was also established to make recommendations for actions to member Churches and other bodies; and working with member Churches to fulfil the great commission of Jesus Christ—Matthew 28:19-20."[53]

Thus although membership to the organization is conditional to upholding "the authentic teaching of the Bible and the Apostles' Creed and accepts baptism by water in the name of the Trinity," it was not until after about forty years that a common position was reached to remove the requirement for re-baptism for a Christian who chose to change "belonging" from one of the member churches to the other. This, I argue, was possible because the churches had worked together on what they called "pertinent issues" relating to public goods and services in Uganda, which enabled them to develop "greater mutual understanding" and coexistence. Ominously, there is no mention of unity around Holy Communion in any of the official statements, an indication that accepting each other's baptism was not about coming to theological agreement but rather a statement of mutual respect.

It is also foolhardy to imagine that the goal to "witness together" is a statement of aspiration of belonging together as "one family" and "one body," since they are not able to share in Holy Communion, the sacrament that gives full testimony and effect to this as sharing together in the death and resurrection of Jesus Christ. Clearly, UJCC could not witness to the idea of being together as "one, holy, catholic, apostolic Church." I submit "witness together" in UJCC needs to be understood more in terms of "achieving cooperation by means of joint consultation and action in practical matters of common interest such as economic empowerment and development, and developing options for member churches to pursue and enhance their capacity and responses to pertinent issues"—in other words, cooperation for the common good of their members, who share the same territorial boundaries and are under the same state authority, in order to "live in harmony." It is not a witness to being "one, holy, catholic and apostolic church" but rather to being disparate communities that need to coexist harmoniously in the same country. It is "witness together" to being bodies whose members belong not only to them separately but also to the same country. The kind of work in which the member churches have cooperated gives credence to this view.

---

[53]Uganda Joint Christian Council, "Background," 2017, http://ujcc.co.ug/?page_id=10.

The two historical rivals under the UJCC umbrella have succeeded in working together on a common Christian religious education curriculum; a shared agenda and action around civic education on political governance issues, such as the process of the making and promulgation of the 1995 constitution and the various election cycles since then; addressing national crises, such as the HIV/AIDS epidemic and the prolonged war in Northern Uganda; and the formation of another platform that brings other faith groups on board (notably the Muslim community), the Inter-Religious Council (IRCU), to mention but a few.[54] Thus, the two churches in Uganda, while unable to agree on sacramental unity, have been able to find a path toward "harmonious co-existence," meaning "to promote consensus among men, women, youth and children in member churches to uphold Christian values and address issues of economic and social justice through representatives at various levels." Stated differently, this is a witness for the common good.

RETHINKING "UNITY OF THE CHURCH"

The story of the two churches in Uganda can be repeated elsewhere. Needless to say, the details will be different, but the same issues may be reflected in varying degrees and proportions. It is a story of communities that claim to gather and scatter in the name of Christ failing to share together in the very symbols that ought to be marks of their shared identity as the "one, holy, catholic and apostolic church." Attempts towards sacramental unity through the agency of the UJCC did not succeed because the real challenge is that the two churches' self-definition can't allow for such unity. The failure to have meaningful discourse and find common ground to sacramental unity is not only a reflection of the political struggle between the two churches but also a different self-definition of "being church." There is hardly any sense of a common identity, of "belonging together" in Christ, precisely because identity is constituted by experiences and relationships, that is, to whom we belong and who we feel belongs to us.

---

[54]IRCU was founded in 2001 with the help and support of Religions for Peace, an international multi-faith organization working for global peace and peaceful interfaith coexistence. The immediate cause for its founding was to create a mechanism through which international development support to interfaith-based HIV and AIDS programs could be channeled. Of particular interest to the donor community was the need to have a faith-based mechanism that would include Muslims. As the organization's credibility and capacity grew, more programs were added, among them a Peace and Conflict Resolution program, which was established in 2006. It was a precursor to the more intentional, programmatic focus on national political governance issues, which began with the first National Conference on National Reconciliation, Justice and Peace held in September 2009.

What Latourette called the "the kingdom test," which was echoed by Walls, is in fact a sacramental test: that the continued failure of the two churches to find a path toward sacramental unity and their use of the sacraments are instruments of scoring against each other suggests that they are witnesses to Anglican and Roman Catholic "kingdoms" rather than to the reign of the crucified, risen, and ascended Christ. In spite of their individual claims to be regularly gathering and scattering in the name of Jesus, they have failed the sacramental test; they are not together a sign of the influence of Christ in Ugandan society. The evidence is overwhelming in the story of Uganda: their active participation in fueling politics of division, which consequently created narratives of rivalry, violent conflict, and injustice.

As this account has shown, although each of the two churches in Uganda—the Church of Uganda (Anglican) and the Roman Catholic Church—confesses to belong to the "one, holy, catholic, and apostolic church," failure to share together in the sacraments is evidence that they do not consider each other as belonging to the same "one, holy, catholic, and apostolic church." The fundamental question is whether they are "united in Christ"; this answer is clear when the sacramental test is administered. The rivalry and conflict between the Church Mission Society and the White Fathers, and the two churches, the Church of Uganda and the Roman Catholic Church, is one of two feuding families rather than a case of two feuding members of the same family. I submit that we make a mistake to bemoan the lack of unity and division in the Church in Uganda because this presupposes that the churches in Uganda consider each other as being of the same family and body.

The creation of the UJCC platform and the way it has worked over the last five decades is instructive. As I have suggested, it is clearly not a platform for the "unity of the church" but rather cooperation by churches for "joint consultation and action in practical matters of common interest." This is especially significant given that the two leading churches have been part of the narrative of violence in Uganda. It is good that the search for the common good led them to seek cooperation with the Muslim community under the umbrella of IRCU. This discovery and commitment to work for the common good is one to commend to other churches. "Unity of the church" in this sense means "cooperation for the common good."

3

IN PERSONA CHRISTI

The Catholic Understanding
of the Ordained Priesthood
in Relation to the Eucharist

THOMAS G. WEINANDY, OFM, CAP.

I AM PLEASED AND HONORED to have been invited to this ecumenical conference commemorating the five-hundredth anniversary of the Protestant Reformation. The stated theme of our conference is well chosen: "Come, Let Us Eat Together! Sacraments and the Unity of the Church." For the sacraments, by their very nature, establish and foster the community of faith. For example, through faith and the sacrament of baptism, we become living, Spirit-filled members of the one body of Christ, and, having been conformed into the likeness of Jesus through the Spirit of sonship, we become children of our one Father. The Eucharist continues to express and nurture our union with Christ through the Holy Spirit and continuously deepens our relationship with the one God and Father of our Lord Jesus Christ. Unfortunately, for five hundred years, not all Christians have been able to share all of the sacraments as the one body of Christ, and so we have been unable to reap the fullness of their blessings together. This inability is nowhere more evident than in the sacrament of the Eucharist—we have not been able to come together to eat the bread of life and to drink the cup of salvation that is the body and blood of the risen Lord Jesus Christ.

In the light of this disunity, I have chosen to examine what I consider to be one of the greatest ecumenical issues of our time, stemming from the Reformation itself, namely, the nature of priesthood and its relationship to the Eucharist. I cannot address the way in which various denominations understand

the priesthood of Christ and the manner in which Christians share in that priesthood. To do so would require a major study beyond the scope of my competence and beyond the time and space permitted for our purposes here.[1] Rather, I will address, however briefly, how the Catholic Church understands the nature of the ordained priesthood and its relationship primarily to the sacrament of the Eucharist.

THE CATHOLIC UNDERSTANDING OF SACRAMENT

In the Spirit of holiness, Jesus, the great high priest, offered himself out of love for us and in love to the Father as a redeeming and atoning sacrifice so that we might be reconciled to the Father and be made righteous in his sight. This once-for-all sacrifice is efficacious for all time, allowing all to find salvation in him alone. Moreover, in order to partake of Jesus' redemptive acts, that is, his passion, death, and resurrection, the human person must be taken up into those saving mysteries so as to reap their saving fruit. Herein lies the importance of faith and, in particular, the significance of the sacraments: they effect this being taken up into the saving mysteries. In order to comprehend the Catholic understanding of the relationship of the ordained priesthood to the Eucharist, we must first address the nature of sacraments as a whole.

As is well known, the Catholic Church believes that Jesus Christ instituted seven sacraments. All of these sacraments find their origin within the life, death, and resurrection of Jesus. While Jesus enacted these saving mysteries once for all at a specific time and place in history, these mysteries are to benefit all people for all ages. Jesus instituted the sacraments so as to make present his saving mysteries and the benefits that accrue within them, that is, he so acts within the sacraments that his saving mysteries would be always present to those who believe. By instituting the sacraments, Jesus established the means by which all of humankind is able to be joined to him and to his redemptive work, and thus to appropriate the fullness of his salvation. As the *Catechism of the Catholic Church* states: "He [the risen Jesus] acts through the sacraments in what the common Tradition of the East and West call 'the sacramental economy'; this is the communication (or 'dispensation') of the fruits of Christ's Paschal mystery in the celebration of the Church's 'sacramental'

---

[1] For an excellent short account of Martin Luther's and John Calvin's understanding of the priesthood, see P. Gerard Damsteegt, "The Magisterial Reformers and Ordination," Seventh-Day Adventist Theological Seminary, Andrews University. It can be found at www.adventistarchives.org/magisterial -reformers-and-ordination.pdf.

liturgy."[2] Thus, Jesus himself, as the risen Lord and Savior, is the principal actor within the sacraments, and he acts through them so as to allow the faithful, in various ways, to be in communion with him and so partake of his saving mysteries.

Moreover, and again as is well known, the Catholic Church holds that "the sacraments are perceptible signs (words and actions) accessible to our human nature. By the action of Christ and the power of the Holy Spirit they make present efficaciously the graces that they signify."[3] This means that what the sacraments visibly signify they actually effect or accomplish. The signifying action is itself the cause of the effect signified. For example, within baptism, the initial sacrament of faith, the minister's actions of pouring the water and pronouncing the baptismal formula effect the cleansing of sin and, through the outpouring of the Spirit, make the person holy—a child of the Father in communion with Jesus his Son. The baptized is actually taken up into the very life of the Trinity the baptismal formula declares. Precisely because Christ himself is acting through the sacramental actions of the minister, the sacraments are always efficacious in that they always accomplish their end. This is why the Catholic Church holds that the sacraments "act *ex opere operato* (literally 'by the very fact of the action's being performed'), i.e., by virtue of the saving work of Christ, accomplished once for all."[4] Nonetheless, the Church realizes that, while Christ always acts within the sacraments, "the fruits of the sacraments also depend on the disposition of the one who receives them."[5] Only to the extent that a person participates in the sacraments in faith, hope, and love does the person acquire the saving benefits offered.

Now the Catholic Church believes, and here we enter into the subject of priesthood, that all baptized Christians share in the one priesthood of Christ. While Christ is the "one mediator between God and men" (1 Tim 2:5), the Church also professes, in accord with 1 Peter 2:9, "The baptized, by regeneration and the anointing of the Holy Spirit, are consecrated as a spiritual house and a holy priesthood."[6] Within the sacrament of baptism the Holy Spirit permanently

---

[2] *Catechism of the Catholic Church* (Washington, DC: USCCB, 1995), 1076; see also 1084. Hereafter *CCC*.

[3] *CCC*, 1084.

[4] *CCC*, 1128. It should also be noted that "since it is ultimately Christ who acts and effects salvation through the ordained minister, the unworthiness of the latter does not prevent Christ from acting" (*CCC*, 1584).

[5] *CCC*, 1128.

[6] Second Vatican Council, Dogmatic Constitution *Lumen Gentium*, 10. Hereafter *LG*. Quotations from the Second Vatican Council are taken from *Vatican Council II: The Conciliar and Post-Conciliar Documents*, ed. A. Flannery (Northport, NY: Costello, 1975).

conforms or seals the Christian into the likeness of Jesus Christ, the high priest. This indelible conformity is called, within the Catholic Church's tradition, the "sacramental character." Being so conformed into the likeness of Jesus, the high priest, the baptized are empowered "for the worship of the Christian religion."[7] Baptism, with its consecratory character, enables Christians, through the power of the Holy Spirit, to worship the Father in communion with Jesus, the one priest and mediator, and in so doing is "the gateway to life in the Spirit, and the door which gives access to the other sacraments."[8] This privilege and right to participate in true worship of God finds its completion within the sacrament of the Eucharist, which is "the source and summit of the Christian life."[9] "The other sacraments, and indeed all ecclesiastical ministries and works of the apostolate, are bound up with the Eucharist and are oriented toward it. For in the most blessed Eucharist is contained the whole spiritual good of the Church, namely Christ himself our Pasch."[10]

While all baptized Christians participate in what the Church calls "the common priesthood of the faithful," those who are ordained share more fully in the priesthood of Christ, and they do so in a manner that differs not only in degree but in kind.[11]

THE SACRAMENT OF ORDINATION

All Christians believe that Jesus established his church, and within his church he commissioned his twelve apostles to continue his saving mission, that is, to continue his threefold kingly, prophetic, and sanctifying salvific work. The apostles were called to shepherd God's people, proclaim the fullness of the gospel, sanctify

---

[7]*LG*, 11. See also *CCC*, 1272-74.

[8]*CCC*, 1213. The Catholic Church also holds that the sacrament of confirmation, as a sacrament of initiation, confers a sacred character. "Like Baptism which it completes, Confirmation is given only once, for it too imprints on the soul an *indelible spiritual mark*, the 'character,' which is the sign that Jesus Christ has marked a Christian with the seal of the Holy Spirit by clothing him with power from on high so that he may be a witness." Thus, "this 'character' perfects the common priesthood of the faithful, received in Baptism, and 'the confirmed person receives the power to profess faith in Christ publically and as it were officially (*quasi ex officio*)'" (*CCC*, 1304-5). The quotation is from Thomas Aquinas, *Summa Theologica* III.72.5, ad. 2.

[9]*LG*, 11. See also Second Vatican Council, The Constitution on the Divine Liturgy *Sacrosanctum Concilium*, 10. Hereafter *SC*.

[10]Second Vatican Council, Decree on the Ministry and Life of Priests, *Presbyteroum Ordinis*, 5. Hereafter *PO*.

[11]*LG*, 10 states, "Though they differ essentially and not only in degree, the common priesthood of the faithful and the ministerial or hierarchical priesthood are nonetheless ordered one to another; each in its own proper ways share in the one priesthood of Christ." See also *CCC*, 1546-47.

all the faithful, and to do so particularly through the liturgical acts of baptism and the Eucharist. Herein lies the apostolic foundation of the priesthood. The Catholic Church believes that "Holy Orders is the sacrament through which the mission entrusted by Christ to his apostles continues to be exercised in the Church until the end of time: thus it is the sacrament of apostolic ministry."[12] As Jesus, the founder of the Church and the head of his body, personally commissioned and consecrated his apostles, so this sacred commission continues in the ordained ministry within the Church today. "The apostles were endowed by Christ with a special outpouring of the Holy Spirit coming upon them (cf. Acts 1:8; 2:4; Jn 20:22-23), and, by the imposition of hands (cf. 1 Tim 4:14; 2 Tim 1:6-7), they passed on to their auxiliaries the gift of the Spirit, which is transmitted down to our day through episcopal consecration."[13] This "passing on" of the apostolic mandate, which was initiated by Christ himself, continues to the present. It is known as "apostolic succession"—the unbroken sequence of the consecratory laying on of hands from one episcopal generation to the next.[14] The bishops, in turn, share this apostolic ministry and mandate with those whom they sacramentally ordain as priests.[15]

While those to be ordained are taken from within the Christian community, the grace of ordination does not arise from within the community but is given by Christ himself. He alone, as the head of his body, has the authority and power to enact such an apostolic ministry.[16] "From him [Jesus], they [the ordained] receive the mission and faculty ('the sacred power') to act *in persona Christi Capitis*."[17] Those who have been sacramentally ordained are empowered to act "in the person of Christ," who is the head of his body. Through those who have been sacramentally ordained "it is Christ himself who is present to his Church as Head of his Body, Shepherd of his flock, high priest of the redemptive sacrifice, Teacher of Truth. This is what the Church means by saying that the priest, by virtue of the sacrament of

---

[12]*CCC*, 1536.

[13]*LG*, 21. See also Second Vatican Council, Decree on the Pastoral Office of Bishops in the Church, *Christus Dominus*, 2. Hereafter *CD*.

[14]See Second Vatican Council, Dogmatic Constitution on Divine Revelation, *Dei Verbum*, 7; *LG*, 20; and *CCC*, 77, 861. For an excellent biblical and theological exposition of the Catholic understanding of apostolic succession, see J. Ratzinger (Pope Benedict XVI), *Principles of Catholic Theology: Building Stones for a Fundamental Theology* (San Francisco: Ignatius, 1987), 239-84.

[15]See *LG*, 21; *PO*, 2; and *CCC*, 1562, 1576.

[16]See *CCC*, 1538. It states that the sacrament of ordination "goes beyond a simple *election, designation, delegation,* or *institution* by the community, for it confers a gift of the Holy Spirit that permits the exercise of a 'sacred power.'"

[17]*CCC*, 875.

Holy Orders, acts *in persona Christi Capitis*."[18] That bishops and priests act *in the person of Christ* is the primary concern of this essay. What does this designation fully mean, and what is its foundation?

IN PERSONA CHRISTI

As the baptismal character conforms the baptized into the priestly likeness of Christ, the high priest, and so empowers them to participate in Christian worship, especially in the Eucharistic liturgy, so the sacrament of holy orders "configures the recipient by a special grace of the Holy Spirit, so that he may serve as Christ's instrument for his Church. By ordination one is enabled to act as a representative of Christ, Head of the Church, in the triple office of priest, prophet, and king."[19] Thus, "the sacrament of Holy Orders . . . confers an *indelible spiritual character*."[20]

As intimated above, the ordained priest, founded upon the indelible character he received upon his ordination and so being conformed into the priestly likeness of Christ, acts *in persona Christi* in various manners and degrees. Throughout this essay we must always remember that to speak of the priest as acting *in persona Christi* means that the person of Christ is acting in, with, and through the priest, and that is precisely why the priest is acting *in persona Christi*. The singular primacy of Christ's priesthood is always present.

First, his very ordination establishes the priest as one within the Christian community who is marked and empowered as Christ's representative to act on behalf of Christ. The priest, then, is an official, ordained, ecclesial minister of the Church. "Hence the priesthood of priests, while presupposing the sacraments of initiation, is nevertheless conferred by its own sacrament. Through that sacrament

---

[18]*CCC*, 1548.

[19]*CCC*, 1581. The *Catechism* also states, "The grace of the Holy Spirit proper to this sacrament is con-figuration to Christ as Priest, Teacher, and Pastor, of who the ordained is made a minister" (1585). The laity, through baptism, act *in persona Christi* in that they, as members of his body, are empow-ered in the Holy Spirit to live holy lives and so offer themselves to others in sacrificial charity. They too proclaim the gospel and above all give praise and worship to the Father in union with Jesus, especially in the Eucharistic liturgy.

[20]*CCC*, 1582. The "indelible spiritual character," while it conforms the person in some manner to the priestly likeness of Jesus and empowers the person to exercise a priestly ministry—whether in the priesthood of the faithful or in the ordained ministry—is not that sanctifying grace that pertains to one's sanctity, one's spiritual likeness to Christ or holiness. This sanctifying grace is the indwelling of the Holy Spirit, first received through faith and baptism, which conforms one into a righteous and holy child of the Father. The "character" pertains only to the empowering of the person to act *in persona Christi* in his priestly capacity. This is why an ordained minister may be living a seriously sinful life and still be able to act *in persona Christi* in efficaciously celebrating the sacraments.

priests by the anointing of the Holy Spirit are signed with a special character and so are configured to Christ the priest in such a way that they are able to act in the person of Christ the head."[21] Second, the sacerdotal acts that the priest performs in conformity with Christ's own ministry entail his pastoral care of those under his guardianship and his proclaiming of the gospel both to his own flock and to those who have yet to hear the gospel. Moreover, as the shepherd of his flock, he is to govern his sheep so that together they give expression to the reality that they ultimately constitute, namely, the vibrant and ever-maturing body of Christ.[22] In these sacerdotal acts, that is, proclaiming the gospel and shepherding his flock, while the priest does act *in persona Christi*, he can be more or less successful. His witness to a priestly gospel way of life may be wanting. He may not be the best confidant and counselor. His proclamation and teaching of the gospel may be ill-informed in thought or muddled in expression. He may be irresponsible in his pastoral duties and disorganized in the administration of his parish. Thus, the priest may be acting *in persona Christi*, but, being a sinful person himself with limited talents, he may not always be acting as the perfect reflection of Christ.[23]

Thirdly, however, within the context of the sacraments, the ordained priest, no matter what his moral standing, intellectual gifts, or personal talents may be, always acts *in persona Christi*; what these sacramental actions symbolize, they truly achieve. Here, in the sacramental acts, we find the ordained priest acting *in persona Christi* in a manner that is unconditionally efficacious, and, being conformed into the likeness of Christ, the power that flows from his sacramental actions always achieves its sacramental end. When, for example, the priest absolves someone of their sins within the sacrament of penance, he is acting by the power of Christ, and the sinner is assured of Christ's forgiveness. This assured absolution of sin is founded upon the priestly character the priest received upon his ordination, that is, the assurance that he is acting efficaciously *in persona Christi*. To hear the voice of the priest saying, "I absolve you from your sins in the name of the Father, the Son and Holy Spirit" is to hear the voice of Jesus himself; these sacramental words of the priest provide, with certainty, the actual forgiveness of sins. Here we see why the Catholic Church holds that the ordained priesthood differs in kind and not simply in degree from the priesthood of the faithful. The ordained priest is so conformed into the likeness of Jesus, the high priest, that in Jesus' name and by his power, he can forgive sins.

---

[21]*OP*, 2. See also *LG*, 21.
[22]See *OP*, 3-4, 6.
[23]*CCC*, 1550.

To summarize thus far, through the sacrament of priestly ordination, the priest acts *in persona Christi*, and he does so in a variety of ways and degrees. Priests, "in virtue of the sacrament of Orders, after the image of Christ, the supreme and eternal priest (Heb 5:1-10; 7:24; 9:11-28) are consecrated in order to preach the Gospel and shepherd the faithful as well as to celebrate divine worship as true priests of the New Testament."[24] Thus, as an officially ordained minister of the Church, a priest manifests Christ's priestly presence within the Church and within the world in his very person. In this sense, his very ordination marks him as one who is *in persona Christi*—the sacramental sign of Christ's presence to the end of the ages. Moreover, through his proclamation of the gospel, pastoral care, and ecclesial governance, he also acts *in persona Christi*. Further, as the minister of the sacraments, the priest acts *in persona Christi* in a manner that exceeds his proclamation of the Word and his pastoral care; his sacramental acts, by their very nature, unfailingly enact and make present the saving works of Christ they signify. With this in mind, it is necessary to make another extremely important distinction in regard to the priest sacramentally acting *in persona Christi*.

The sacrament of the Eucharist, it must be understood, is a different kind of sacrament. Within the sacraments, such as baptism, confirmation, penance, and the anointing of the sick, Christ acts through his priestly power. The priest, as the representative of Jesus, acts in the name of Christ and by his power, and in this sense he is acting *in persona Christi*. Within the sacrament of the Eucharist, Christ is not only present simply through his power, but he is also present in the fullness of who he actually is as the risen Savior and Lord, that is, both in the offering of himself as the one saving sacrifice and in his truly being present under the sacramental signs of bread and wine. Thus, within the Eucharistic liturgy, the priest not only employs the saving power of Jesus when he acts *in persona Christi*, but he himself also sacramentally signifies, in his very person, the person of Christ himself in the wholeness of who Christ is. As Christ is present and active in the Eucharist in a different kind of way from that of his presence and activity in the other sacraments, so the priest images Christ and acts *in persona Christi* in a different kind of way than he does within the other sacraments.[25] This Eucharistic understanding of the manner of Christ's presence and action and the manner of the priest acting *in persona Christi* demands a more careful and extended theological explanation.

---

[24]*LG*, 28.
[25]See *ST* III.65.3.

THE EUCHARISTIC LITURGY: THE MAKING PRESENT OF
THE ONE SACRIFICIAL OFFERING OF CHRIST

The Catholic Eucharistic celebration is divided into two parts: the liturgy of the Word and the liturgy of the Eucharist. Within the liturgy of the Word, the Scriptures are proclaimed, and the priest expounds upon God's Word in order to build up the faith of the people and renew their commitment to living their life in Christ faithfully. He is simultaneously preparing them to participate worthily in the liturgy of the Eucharist, that is, that they might participate with a deeper faith in and more ardent love for Jesus. This twofold structure follows the example of the risen Jesus himself when he appeared to the men on the road to Emmaus. He first "interpreted to them in the scriptures the things concerning himself." In explaining to these men God's prophetic Word, Jesus prepared them to recognize him "in the breaking of the bread" (Lk 24:13-35). The spoken and written Word of God ultimately finds its end in coming into communion with the embodied Word of God—the living Jesus himself. The fullest expression of this bodily communion with Jesus is found in the liturgy of the Eucharist, as exemplified in the Emmaus story. With this in mind, we can proceed to examining the liturgy of the Eucharist.

Within the sacramental Eucharistic liturgy, the priest uniquely acts *in persona Christi* in a twofold, interrelated manner.[26] The first is that the priest, in communion with Christ, makes present the once-for-all sacrifice offered on the cross. The second is that the priest, acting in the person of Christ and by the power of the Holy Spirit, efficaciously changes the bread and wine into the body and blood of the risen Lord Jesus. I will examine each aspect separately and then conjoin them, for they are fundamentally one sacramental, liturgical action.

First, the Catholic Church believes that within the Eucharistic liturgy, Christ makes present and represents, through the sacramental actions of the priest, his once-for-all sacrifice. The *Catechism of the Catholic Church* states, quoting the Council of Trent:

> The sacrifice of Christ and the sacrifice of the Eucharist are *one single sacrifice*: "The victim is one and the same: the same now offers through the ministry of priests, who then offered himself on the cross; only the manner of offering is different." "In this

---

[26]Within the Eucharistic liturgy, the priest acts *in persona Christi* when proclaiming the gospel during the liturgy of the Word and within the liturgy of the Eucharist. Since I have already spoken of the priest within in the context of his preaching and teaching ministry, I will not do so here.

divine sacrifice which is celebrated in the Mass, the same Christ who offered himself once in a bloody manner on the altar of the cross is contained and is offered in an unbloody manner."[27]

Because the same sacrifice of Christ is made present within the Eucharistic liturgy, the Second Vatican Council highlights that it is within this liturgy that the priest most fully acts in the person of Christ.

> It is in the Eucharistic cult or in the Eucharistic assembly of the faithful (*synaxis*) that they [the priests] exercise in a supreme degree their sacred functions; there, acting in the person of Christ (*in persona Christi*) and proclaiming the mystery, they unite the votive offerings of the faithful to the sacrifice of Christ their head, and in the sacrifice of the Mass they make present again and apply, until the coming of the Lord (cf. 1 Cor. 11:26), the unique sacrifice of the New Testament, that namely of Christ offering himself once for all a spotless victim to the Father (cf. Heb. 9:11-28).[28]

Of utmost importance for the Catholic Church is the belief that within the Eucharist, Christ is fully present and active not simply by means of his power but in his very person. As the supreme priest, he fully offers himself as victim, the one holy and perfect sacrifice of himself. As Christ fully offered himself to his Father on the cross as an atoning sacrifice, so now within the Eucharist, Christ, in the fullness of who he is, offers himself fully to his Father. Christ the priest and Christ the victim are fully one and the same. The Church holds, then, that since Christ is both priest and victim, he must fully be present as priest in order to make present the full sacrifice of himself. Because Christ is fully present as the acting priest offering himself as the all-holy victim through the sacramental ministry of the ordained priest, the priest must then sacramentally image Christ himself fully as Christ's priesthood so that he can properly act in the person of Christ, offering the one sacrificial offering of Christ himself to the Father. The priest, therefore, having been conformed into the likeness of Christ by means of the priestly character conferred upon him by the Holy Spirit at his ordination, is the efficacious sign of Christ himself by which Christ is making present—or representing within the liturgy—his one loving sacrifice to his Father.[29]

---

[27] *CCC*, 1367. See also the Council of Trent, Doctrines and Canons on the Sacrifice of the Mass, DS, 1743. See also the Council of Trent, DS, 1740.

[28] *LG*, 28. The *Catechism of the Catholic Church* states, "The redemptive sacrifice of Christ is unique, accomplished once for all; yet it is made present in the Eucharistic sacrifice of the Church. The same is true of the one priesthood of Christ; it is made present through the ministerial priesthood without diminishing the uniqueness of Christ's priesthood" (1545).

[29] See *CCC*, 1362-66.

For the priest to be this efficacious sign of Christ offering himself to his Father, he must be acting completely *in persona Christi*. He must himself *be* the person of Christ so that he can efficaciously signify Christ. He is not simply acting *in persona Christi* in order to exercise the power of Christ and act in his name, as in the other sacraments, but he is fully acting *in persona Christi* in order to signify and make present the actual person of Christ as Christ is in himself. Precisely because the priest, in his very sacerdotal person, signifies the very person Jesus, the high priest, he and the faithful participating with him in the Eucharistic liturgy are actually conjoined to the one sacrifice of Christ and his offering of himself to the Father. They reap the salvific blessings that accrue from that once-for-all sacrifice. If the priest were not acting in the person of Christ in this singular manner within the Eucharistic liturgy, the Eucharistic liturgy would not be the genuine and full sacramental expression of Christ's one, sacrificial offering of himself to his Father. Rather, the Eucharistic liturgy would be some lesser, merely figurative, commemorative expression, a recollection or reminiscence of a historical past event of Christ's one sacrifice of himself. The faithful would not procure the fullness of its heavenly benefits. Yet, it is precisely by being taken up into the one sacrifice of Christ, by being conjoined to the whole Christ, the high priest, through the sacramental prayers and actions of the ordained priest, that Christians are able to share fully in the graces of Christ's once-for-all sacrifice. They are able to share a full reconciliation with the Father that results in complete, Spirit-filled communion with the Father in Christ Jesus, their Savior.

Moreover, Jesus' sacrificial offering of himself on the cross is the consummate act of worship: he, as the Father's Son, is the all-holy priest who offers the most holy sacrifice, that of his own Spirit-filled humanity. Consequently, the Eucharistic liturgy is also the Church's supreme act of worship, for she, in union with Christ her head, offers this same saving act of worship to the Father, that of Christ himself. Therefore, since the priest and the faithful present at the Eucharistic liturgy offer Christ's one saving sacrifice in union with Christ, he offers it on behalf of and in communion with the faithful. Again, precisely because the priest, in his very sacerdotal person, sacramentally signifies the very person Jesus, the high priest, he and the faithful participating with him in the Eucharistic liturgy, having been conjoined to the one sacrifice of Christ, offer to the Father the consummate act of worship: the offering of Christ himself and the full offering of themselves in communion with Christ.

The Church which is the Body of Christ participates in the offering of her Head. With him, she herself is offered whole and entire. She unites herself to his intercession with the Father for all men. In the Eucharist the sacrifice of Christ becomes also the sacrifice of the members of his Body. The lives of the faithful, their praise, sufferings, prayer, and work, are united with those of Christ and with his total offering, and so acquire a new value. Christ's sacrifice present on the altar makes it possible for all generations of Christians to be united with his offering.[30]

Thus, within the Eucharistic liturgy, the priest not only sacramentally acts *in persona Christi* in so far as he makes present the one sacrifice of Christ, but he also sacramentally acts *in persona Christi* in the name of the Church (*in nomine ecclesiae*). On behalf of the Church, he simultaneously offers the one sacrifice of Christ to the Father. We find here two conjoined actions. The sacramental action of the priest makes present both the one sacrifice of Christ and the Church's holy offering to the Father for the sanctification of the Church. He does both because he is acting *in persona Christi capitis*, that is, in the person of Christ, who is the head of his body. Through the sacramental actions of the priest, Christ himself offers his body, the Church, to his Father so that his body can partake of the salvific benefits of his once-for-all sacrifice.[31]

THE EUCHARISTIC LITURGY: JESUS' EUCHARISTIC DECLARATION

Within the Eucharistic liturgy, I have been emphasizing that Christ, the one priest, acts through the ordained minister and thus the way in which the priest, in the person of Christ, makes present Christ's one, salvific, sacrificial act. This sacramental action finds its culmination in the priest performing the same liturgical actions and pronouncing the same declarative words that Jesus himself liturgically performed and uttered at the Last Supper. Here we come to the second manner in which the priest acts *in persona Christi* within the Eucharistic liturgy.

Jesus, at the Last Supper, commanded his apostles to do what he himself had just done: "Do this in remembrance of me" (Lk 22:19; see also 1 Cor 11:24-25). What did Jesus do? Since the Gospel narratives and Paul have slightly differing accounts

---

[30]*CCC*, 1368. See also 1552-53. *LG*, 10, states that the priest "effects the Eucharistic sacrifice and offers it to God in the name of all of the people. The faithful indeed, by virtue of their royal priesthood, participate in the offer of the Eucharist."

[31]Because the Eucharist is Christ conjoining his body, the church, to his one, Spirit-filled, perfect, sacrificial act of worship of his Father, it makes present, reflects, and anticipates the heavenly Eucharistic banquet. See *CCC*, 1326, 1402-5.

of what Jesus did and said, I will use here the Catholic liturgical formula of what Jesus did and said, since it is a blend of all the various biblical accounts; specifically, I will use the form from Eucharistic Prayer III.

The priest, having invoked the Father to send forth the Holy Spirit to make holy the gifts of bread and wine, prays "that they may become the Body and Blood of your Son our Lord Jesus Christ, at whose command we celebrate these mysteries." He continues:

> For on the night he was betrayed he himself took bread, and, giving thanks, he said the blessing, broke the bread and gave it to his disciples, saying: Take this, all of you, and eat of it, for this is my body, which will be given up for you.
>
> In a similar way, when supper was ended, he took the chalice, and, giving you thanks, he said the blessing, and gave the chalice to his disciples, saying: Take this, all of you, and drink from it, for this is the chalice of my blood, the blood of the new and eternal covenant, which will be poured out for you and for many for the forgiveness of sins.
>
> Do this in memory of me.

Jesus wants his disciples to do what he just did; he commissions them to perform his same liturgical actions and to pronounce his same declarative words.[32] Recall that within the Eucharistic liturgy, Christ is acting through the priest, and thus the priest is never acting apart from Christ, as if some miraculous power was bestowed upon him other than Christ. The priest does not, nonetheless, simply act *in persona Christi* by invoking the power of Jesus and acting in his name; he acts *in persona Christi* in that he truly acts *as* the person of Christ himself. This now finds its cumulative termination within the consecratory actions the priest performs and the words he declares.

The priest is not simply mimicking or repeating what Jesus did and said as in a play, where an actor recites verbatim the words of a historical person. Rather, having been conformed into the likeness of Jesus the High Priest through the sacramental character conferred upon him, the ordained priest so acts that it is the risen person of Jesus himself who acts in and through and with the priest. Thus, when the priest takes the blessed bread and says, "This is my body, which is given up for you," he does so in the person of Christ. What was once bread becomes the body of Jesus Christ. As Jesus declared that what was in his hand (the "this") was not bread but his body, so the priest declares that what is in his hand (the "this") is not bread but Jesus' body. There is a change of "whatness." What was being held in

---

[32]Within the Catholic doctrinal tradition, Jesus' commissioning of the apostles to enact his own Eucharistic liturgy is the occasion of his ordaining them priests. See *CCC*, 611, 1337.

the hands of Jesus and now is being held in the hands of the priest was once bread, but *what* "this" is now is Jesus' body. A similar analysis can be made with regards to the actions and words pronounced over the cup. What was once the cup of wine now becomes the cup of Jesus' blood, the blood that was poured out for many: the blood of the new covenant. For the priest to be speaking the literal truth—"This is my body"—demands that he must be fully conformed in a priestly manner to the person of Christ as Christ is in himself as the supreme high priest. Only if he is so conformed and so acting in the full reality of being *in persona Christi* could that declaration be literally true. Here Christ and the priest are acting and speaking as one: Christ, the principal actor, acts through and in the actions of the priest, for the priest is the sacramental embodiment, the efficacious visible sign, of Christ himself and through whom Christ acts and speaks.[33] What the priest does and says,

---

[33]To my knowledge the Catholic Church has never officially stated, doctrinally, the manner in which Christ and the ordained minister act as one within the Eucharistic liturgy or specified the causal relationship between Christ and the priest when the priest, *in persona Christi*, pronounces the declarative words of consecration over the bread and wine—"This is my body" and "This is my blood." The Church does recognize that there is a "oneness" between Christ and the priest and that there is a causal relationship between the two, but it has never precisely stated the manner of that causal relationship by which Christ and the priest act causally as one.

Traditionally, the most common theological view is that proposed by Thomas Aquinas. He argues, in keeping with the Church's doctrine, that Christ, being the principal actor or agent within the Eucharist, is the primary cause in that he, through the power of the Holy Spirit, is the ultimate cause of the bread and wine becoming his body and blood. He then argues that the priest is the secondary instrumental cause, because of his sacramental character, through whom Christ acts (see *ST* III.62.4; 63.1-5; 64.1-5; 82.1). One analogous example that Aquinas uses is that of a soldier being physically marked with their military leader's sign (see *ST* III.63.3).

Because Aquinas speaks of the priest being a secondary instrumental cause employed by Christ, it could be thought that the priest is like a hammer in the hand of the carpenter or a pen in the hand of a writer. As the carpenter employs the hammer to make a bench and the writer uses a pen in composing a letter, so Christ employs the priest to consecrate the Eucharist. The causal relationship between Christ and the priest, even if the priest is in some sense a secondary instrumental cause, has to be more intimate and more immediate than that of the carpenter employing his hammer and a writer using his pen. Nor does the soldier analogy work adequately. The soldier may possess the sign of his leader and so act at his leader's command, but the soldier does not act as one with his leader in that they do not simultaneously act together in the performance of the same act. More thought and clarity, I think, needs to be brought to this issue, even from within Aquinas's understanding.

I would propose, as does Aquinas, that the foundation of this more immediate causal relationship resides in the priest being, as is the case with all Christians, a member of the one body of Christ in that they are one entity; they are one living reality in and with Christ through the one life-giving principal of the Holy Spirit. Thus, we have a foundational relationship that has no parallel in the natural order of things. Therefore, the causal relationships between Christ and his body must be unique in order to correspond to the singular new kind of relationship Christ has in relationship to his body. Moreover, then, when the ordained priest is empowered to act uniquely *in persona Christi Capitis* through his priestly "character" as a member of Christ's body, a causal relationship is established between Christ and the priest that has no equal in the natural order of things. The priest, therefore, not only lives in and with Christ, but he also now acts in personal communion with

therefore, effects what it symbolizes—the bread ceases to be bread and becomes the body of Christ. At this juncture, we bring together the two aspects of this twofold manner of the priest acting *in persona Christi* within the Eucharistic liturgy.

I have attempted to demonstrate that within the Eucharistic liturgy, the Catholic Church perceives the priest acting *in persona Christi* in a unique manner. He sacramentally makes Jesus Christ present in the fullness of who Christ is. The fullness of his salvific sacrifice is made present, and the fullness of his risen presence is made real in his Eucharistic body and blood. Now, it is precisely because the priest sacramentally images the fullness of Christ, the high priest, that he, in the person of the risen Christ, is able to make present the whole reality of the risen Jesus through his consecratory declaration that "This is my Body given up for you" and "This is my blood poured out for you." Christ's once-for-all sacrifice is actually present through the priest sacramentally acting in the person of Christ because the body that was once "given up for you" and the blood that was once "poured out for

---

Christ; or rather Christ now acts in, with, and *through* the priest. They become one acting subject because the priest actually shares, in union with Christ, the fullness of Christ's priestly office. Thus he acts in the fullness of Christ's priestly power. This new type of "secondary" causality between Christ and the priest might be termed a *mystical causality* in keeping with mystical body of Christ being in communion with Christ, its head. There is, then, a mutual "ontological," personal, intertwining founded upon their being one in the Holy Spirit. A personal, sacerdotal identity between Christ and the priest founded upon the priestly character, and so priestly power, inheres within the priest. This identity, again, is founded upon the Holy Spirit, who conforms the priest into the personal likeness of Jesus, the priest, so that the priest shares fully in his priestly likeness and personal priestly power.

I would like to suggest, further, an analogy taken from Trinitarian theology. Within traditional Trinitarian theology, theologians speak of the *perichoresis* of the persons of the Trinity, that is, that the Father, the Son, and the Holy Spirit mutually co-inhere. This mutual co-inherence ontologically establishes their identity as distinct persons as well as their unity as the one God. While Christ and the priest are not in a *perichoretic* relationship in that it ontologically establishes who they are as existing beings, they are in a mystical relationship such that, sacramentally, they ontologically act as one. When the priest says, "This is my body," that "my" of the priest is literally the "my" of Christ—there is a mystical *perichoretic* "my": that of Christ and the priest. Because of the priest's sacerdotal character, his ability to act *in persona Christi*, he and Christ share the same priestly "I"— they speak as one person under the auspices of their mutually co-inhering "my's." The priest, then, may be a secondary instrumental cause in a unique mystical manner that differs in kind from any other known secondary instrumental cause. A causality that is unique to it is enacted within the living relationship between Christ and his mystical body.

I am obviously struggling to express the unique causal relationship between Christ and the priest when the priest acts *in persona Christi* within the Eucharistic liturgy. I hope that I have brought some clarity to the question even if I have not provided an entirely satisfactory answer. I have previously attempted to address this issue in my article "The Human Acts of Christ and the Acts That Are the Sacraments," in *Ressourcement Thomism: Sacred Doctrine, the Sacraments, and the Moral Life*, ed. R. Hütter and M. Levering (Washington DC: Catholic University of America Press, 2010), 150-68. This article has been reprinted in T. G. Weinandy, *Jesus: Essays in Christology* (Ave Maria, FL: Sapientia, 2014), 190-209.

you" are now actually present. The risen Jesus, who once for all offered himself to the Father for the forgiveness of sins and for the establishing of the new covenant, is himself really and truly present in the manner in which he now actually exists as risen Lord and Savior. The whole point of Jesus declaring that "This is my body given up for you" and "This is my blood poured out for you" is to accentuate the sacrificial nature of this liturgical action—on the cross he offered up his human life and poured out his human blood, the totality of himself, for the forgiveness of sins and the making of the new covenant. Now, as the risen Lord Jesus, his once-for-all saving act is ever present before the Father because he, the crucified and risen Lord, is ever before the Father interceding on our behalf (see Heb 7:23-25). He makes present his saving sacrifice, and he does so by becoming fully present within the Eucharist itself. Those who partake of the once-sacrificed body and blood of the now-risen Lord Jesus are personally united to him as he is, and they are in communion with his one everlasting sacrifice. They thus share in its everlasting salvific benefits—being made righteous before the Father through dwelling in communion with his risen, Spirit-filled Son. They are literally in communion with the risen Lord Jesus, one with him, and this communion is itself the principal fruit of his saving death and glorious resurrection. As Jesus proclaims, "He who eats my flesh and drinks my blood abides in me, and I in him" (Jn 6:56). Being a member of Christ's body finds its fullest expression and reality in being in communion with him through partaking of his risen and live-giving Eucharistic sacramental presence—eating his flesh and drinking his blood (see Jn 6:52-59). As the *Catechism of the Catholic Church* states, "The principal fruit of receiving the Eucharist in Holy Communion is an intimate union with Christ Jesus."[34]

Now, again, all of the above is possible only because, within the Eucharistic liturgy, Christ and the priest act sacramentally together as one—Christ fully acting through, with, and in the priest. They act as one because the priest, through the priestly character that he received upon his ordination, is able to sacramentally image Christ, the high priest. He makes Jesus himself sacramentally present so that he and all the faithful might become one in Christ, and in Christ one with the Father in the unity of the Holy Spirit.

What may not be immediately evident, but which lies at the heart of all that has been said, is that Jesus' saving death and resurrection finds its end, its goal and purpose, in the sacraments. Yes, Jesus did die for the forgiveness of our sins

---

[34]*CCC*, 1391.

and to reconcile us to his Father. Yes, Jesus did rise from the dead to conquer death and, as the risen Lord, to pour out his Holy Spirit upon those who believe. Yet one must nonetheless be united through faith to these saving events if one is to be saved. Only in the sacraments—initially in baptism, the sacrament of faith, and most fully in the Eucharistic liturgy, the sacrament of Christ's body and blood—do the faithful come to share in these saving events and come into full communion with Jesus himself as their Savior and Lord.[35] Without the sacraments, humankind would not be able to be united to Jesus' death and resurrection and share in their saving graces. They would not share in his once-for-all saving death and resurrection. Ultimately, then, Jesus established the sacrament of the ordained priesthood so that the priest could sacramentally act *in persona Christi*, thus making, above all, the Eucharist possible with all of its saving blessings.

CONCLUSION

I have attempted to articulate correctly and clearly the Catholic Church's understanding of the ordained priesthood as acting *in persona Christi* in relation to the Eucharist. I have done so in the hope that it will foster an informed ecumenical discussion, nurture our mutual understanding, and further our growth in Christian unity.

Because the Catholic Church's belief in the nature of the ordained ministry and the Eucharist is radically different from the belief held by the Protestant tradition, I do not see how presently we Catholics and Protestants can eat together at the same table or altar of the Lord. For our Protestant brothers and sisters to do so would mean that they accept the Catholic teaching and understanding. At the end of the Eucharistic prayer, the priest elevates the consecrated bread and wine, the body and blood of Jesus, and offers it to the Father, saying, "Through him, and with him, and in him, O God, almighty Father, in the unity of the Holy Spirit, all glory and honor is yours, for ever and ever." The priest and faithful together then declare "Amen." That "Amen" is an affirmation of faith that the whole Eucharistic assembly believes all that has been enacted within the Eucharistic sacrifice as well as all that the

---

[35]The Catholic Church holds that "for believers the sacraments of the New Covenant are *necessary for salvation*" (*CCC*, 1129). See also *LG*, 14. This is true for those who have come to faith and acknowledge that, because of their faith, they need to be baptized, for baptism is the sacrament of faith. However, "those who, through no fault of their own, do not know the Gospel of Christ or his Church, but who nevertheless seek God with a sincere heart, and, moved by grace, try in their actions to do his will as they know it through the dictates of their consciences—these too may achieve salvation" (*LG*, 16).

Catholic Church teaches implicitly and explicitly. The Eucharistic liturgy conveys and comprises the fullness of the gospel as professed by the Catholic Church. I would imagine that most Protestants, in good conscience, could not proclaim that "Amen." Moreover, when the faithful receive the sacred body and blood of Christ, the priest declares, "The body of Christ" and "The blood of Christ." The faithful again respond, "Amen." Once more, I would imagine that most Protestants, in good conscience, could not proclaim "Amen" to this proclamation, for they would not hold, in accordance with their tradition, what Catholics hold: that the bread and wine have been substantially changed into the risen Jesus—his risen body and his risen blood. Because of the faith demands that these Catholic "Amens" make, I would imagine, from a Protestant perspective, that most faithful Protestants would feel awkward, because of their faith, to say "Amen."

Catholics, for their part, because they do not believe what the Protestant tradition holds with regards to the priesthood and the memorial of the Lord's Supper, would feel that they cannot truthfully and rightly say "Amen" to the Protestant Eucharistic assembly. Moreover, the Catholic Church, precisely because it believes that the Eucharistic liturgy is the full expression and supreme enactment of the Catholic faith and its Catholic unity, feels obliged to disallow the Eucharist to those who do not share in its unity of faith. To do so would not be an authentic manifestation of the faith or a genuine expression of the unity that inheres within the faith. Thus, we must pray together in love that through the light and truth of the Holy Spirit we might obtain unity of faith in order that together we might eat of the Lord Jesus Christ to the glory of God the Father.

4

A WAY FORWARD

A Catholic-Anabaptist Ecclesiology

D. STEPHEN LONG

I WAS BAPTIZED AT THE AGE of eleven in the Church of the Brethren by a farmer preacher, a big man with rough hands, or so it seemed at the time. He submerged me three times in a baptismal pool, and each time he held me under longer than the time before. By the third submersion I was praying for resurrection because I was certain I was going to die. My baptism occurred under unusual circumstances. My family were not Anabaptists; we were Methodists, but we had moved into a rural area north of Goshen, Indiana, in 1970, and the Church of the Brethren was the closest church to our home. The two years we lived there, we attended that church, a place I can remember when I remember my baptism.

How should I remember it? Into what was I baptized? A preliminary answer to that question is straightforward. I was baptized into the church, the body of Christ, and in so doing received the Holy Spirit. Baptism makes no sense apart from ecclesiology and pneumatology. The liturgy and/or doctrine of nearly every church acknowledges as much; this is unsurprising because those liturgies and doctrines emerge from passages in Scripture such as 1 Corinthians 12:13: "For in the one Spirit we were all baptized into one body, Jews or Greeks, slaves or free—and we were all made to drink of one Spirit." Every baptism is a baptism into the universal or catholic church, a church all Christians should confess faith in. It is good, I would suggest, that we confess faith in it because no one has seen it. I mean that literally—no one can see at one time the fullness of the catholic church scattered throughout every nation and people in every time. We are baptized into the catholic church, an object of faith, but that baptism only occurs through the mediation of a local church. These two, the local and catholic, are

one. To remember well any baptism requires remembering both the local traditions and the catholic unity into which we were baptized. But no one can remember catholic unity per se; any remembering of it must begin at the local level. Relating local memory to catholic unity is where matters become difficult and divisive.

Before entering the difficult and divisive, let me begin with the local; for only in remembering the conditions that made my own baptism possible will my controversial account of the relation between the local and catholic unity make sense.

BEGINNING WITH THE LOCAL

Into what was I baptized? I was baptized into a local church, the Jefferson Brethren Church just north of Goshen, Indiana. Because of my family's brief presence in that church, I had no ongoing connection. I primarily remember two things about it: I was baptized, and they often discussed nonviolence. I remember the latter more because of the conversations my parents had after church. My father had served in the military, and although he is an admirably nonviolent human being, he did not find Christian discipleship and the practice of war contradictory. The Vietnam War was in full force during my baptism, and while my father affirmed the right of conscientious objection by the Mennonites (we had a Goshen College student stay with us for a brief time), he was unconvinced by their pacifist witness. The war ended after I turned fifteen. By then we had moved again and returned to the Methodists. By receiving my baptism, the United Methodist Church in Knox, Indiana, affirmed, in part, the local community that baptized me in the first place. I was not asked to repudiate it. I was not asked to be re-baptized. My reception brought some aspect of the Jefferson Brethren Church into the United Methodist Church, at least in practice if not in theory. The history of the church is itself a complicated practice that often proceeds without a theory. Take as an example the history of the United Methodist Church. Like all practical histories of the church, it is an unstable blend of diverse traditions, mired in conflict amidst its continuities. We could extend this history to the conflicts within the Anglican tradition that gave rise to the Methodists, and we could extend the Anglican history to the contested histories that make up the Roman Catholic Church and gave rise to the Anglicans. No historical practice of any church has preserved some pure tradition immune to conflicts. Space does not permit a detailed account of those conflicts, so I will focus on one small part, the particular narrative of the United Methodist Church that made it possible for Knox United Methodist Church to receive my baptism from Jefferson Brethren Church.

The United Methodist Church came into existence through a merger of the Evangelical United Brethren and the Methodist Episcopal Church, which brought together Reformed, Mennonite, Lutheran, and Anglican strands of the Christian tradition. The Anglican strand came from John Wesley, who started the Methodist movement, ordained its clergy, and died in good standing with the Anglican Church. The Lutheran strand came from the Evangelical Association, which originated from Jacob Albright, who was baptized in the Lutheran Church but converted to Methodism in 1790 and was then licensed as a Methodist preacher. However, the English Methodists would not allow him to preach in German. In turn, he established a German-speaking association that came to be known in 1816 as *Evangelische Gemeinschaft*, or "Evangelical Association." The Reformed and Mennonite strands came from the United Brethren Church; it arose from the Methodist work of two other persons of German heritage: Philip William Otterbein, who had been ordained in the Reformed Church and was well educated in theology—he read Hebrew and Greek—and Martin Boehm, a Mennonite farmer who had no formal theological education. In 1766 the educated Otterbein heard the Mennonite Boehm preach and was so moved that he responded to him with the words *Wir sind Brüder* ("We are brothers"). Hence the name "United Brethren." Boehm had been elected as bishop to the Mennonites in 1761, but his work among the Methodists was not well received by the Mennonites. In 1800 he was excommunicated, which was lifted by the Mennonite Church on June 27, 2016, and celebrated by both Methodists and Mennonites at Boehm's Chapel near Lancaster, Pennsylvania.

These diverse strands flow into the United Methodist Church, which may have a very brief history of its own as it is quickly unraveling today over questions of sexuality. The practical messiness of this history defies any simple, systematic ecclesiology. How is it possible to take all these strands with their incoherencies, confusions, and contests and iron them out into a comprehensive ecclesiological vision? And yet—for me to remember my baptism is to remember this history. Its unity may not be found in a comprehensive ecclesiological theory, but it is found in me. The story of my baptism, like that of so many, is not a story of a baptism into some lucidly coherent tradition or into a church that has maintained its purity since Jesus gave the keys to the kingdom to Peter. I did not know at the age of eleven that I had been baptized into a radical tradition of re-baptizers, a people who had been perceived as such a threat to the political order that they were hunted down and killed by other Christians several centuries earlier. I did not know my baptism was received by a sect that emerged within Anglicanism, which was a Gallican form of Catholicism that refused to grant papal jurisdiction over General Councils.[1] Like all the local traditions into which we have been baptized, it is a story of division and conflict, but I would suggest there is continuity within it.

THE LOCAL IS THE CATHOLIC

Although we do not have, and need not seek, a comprehensive ecclesiology that could somehow smooth out the rough places of our ecclesial histories, naming the continuity between local baptism and catholicity is an important theological task, albeit not an easy one. Rowan Williams, former Archbishop of Canterbury, gives us a basic principle to observe. He states, "The entire Church is present in every local church assembled around the Lord's Table. Yet the local church is never the entire Church."[2] If you find wisdom in this principle as I do, then it brings with it theological encumbrances that should be observed in relating the local and the catholic. First, any church that denies a connection between its local assembly and the universal church misunderstands what it means to be a church. If the entire church is present in the local church, then every local church has a theological responsibility to explain that connection to the church. Answers will differ as to how a local church narrates the way in which the entire church is present in it, but each church is theologically obligated to offer such an account. Several means are available to narrate the communion between the local and the catholic church: the episcopacy, ecumenical councils, Scripture, the communion of saints, the Holy Spirit, eschatology, and Christology. These means are not mutually exclusive, but local churches should have a theological obligation to explain how they relate to the catholic church. I will call this first encumbrance "the local church's fit with the catholic church." Second, no local church should equate its existence with the entirety of the church. While the catholic church is present in the local gathering, no single gathering place is the fullness of the catholic church. In practice, then, no local

---

[1]See Bruce N. Kaye's *Conflict and the Practice of Christian Faith: The Anglican Experiment* (Eugene, OR: Cascade, 2009), 35. He states, "So-called Episcopal Gallicanism held not only that kings were independent of the Pope, but that, in matters spiritual, supreme authority belonged to General Councils, and popes should obey their canons. This was decisively claimed by the council of Constance 1414-1418 when the Papacy was divided and the Avignon Papacy was clearly subject to the influence of the French King. While this Gallican tradition held sway late into the eighteenth century, it virtually disappeared as a political force under Napoleon."
[2]Ibid., 169.

church can claim to be self-sufficient. If it is to claim the validity of its baptisms, then it should be able to offer a theological rationale to its own members as to how the catholic church is visibly present in its gathering without that gathering hubristically claiming to be the fullness of catholic unity. I will call this second encumbrance "the catholic church's presence in the local church." Third, each church should be open to discernment on the adequacy of its answers to those who narrate that communion differently. This third encumbrance is "openness to ecumenical admonition."

I will now recall my baptism into a Brethren Church as it was received into Knox United Methodist Church as a memory of the one, holy, catholic, and apostolic church by attending to these three encumbrances:

1. The local church's fit with the catholic church

2. The catholic church's presence in the local church

3. Openness to ecumenical admonition

FREE, VOLUNTARY CHURCH

First, I will begin with an ecclesiology that makes sense of my local baptism by drawing upon "baptist" theologian James William McClendon, who was a member of the Pasadena Church of the Brethren. McClendon's ecclesial situatedness was as confused as mine. He was raised Southern Baptist but became discouraged by the racism he found in the church. He was one of the first Protestant theologians to be invited to teach in a Jesuit school but was asked to resign, which he did, because of his opposition to the Vietnam War. In 1982 McClendon wrote an essay titled "What Is a 'Baptist' Theology?" in which he outlined the basics of a Baptist ecclesiology. Nearly two decades later in 1998, two years prior to his death, he published an essay titled "The Voluntary Church in the Twenty-First Century" that advanced similar themes to his 1982 essay. Both essays looked to Acts 2:16, Peter's address to his fellow Jews at Pentecost, as the biblical basis for a Baptist ecclesiology. In explaining that the disciples were not drunk, since it was only nine o'clock in the morning, Peter said, "No, this is what was spoken through the prophet Joel." McClendon takes the structure of Peter's claim "this is that" as the basis for the "baptist vision." Peter points to a present reality—Pentecost—and interprets it in terms of something prior, to a "that." McClendon moves from the specific instance of "this is that" in Acts 2 to a general ecclesiological claim. What occurs in the local gathering is nothing less than an instance of both the primitive and eschatological community coming together at this particular space and time—the only space and time we can inhabit. McClendon writes, "The baptist vision is none other than the shared awareness of the present Christian community as the primitive community and the eschatological community."[3] In its present gathering, it is connected to the past and the future, making it more than it would otherwise be. The primitive connection is Jewish; "this is that" is a reminder of the Passover. On another occasion when he explains the "this is that" ecclesial logic, McClendon points to Deuteronomy 6:20-21: "When your children ask you in time to come, 'What is the meaning of the decrees and the statutes and the ordinances that the Lord our God has commanded you?' then you shall say to your children, 'We were Pharaoh's slaves in Egypt, but the LORD brought us out of Egypt with a mighty hand.'"[4] The present community was already contained in the primitive people of God, so the present community can point to it and say, "This is that." McClendon also cites the Roman Catholic theology of the Eucharist to explain the logic of "this is that."[5]

McClendon's use of "this is that" contributes to his "voluntary" ecclesiology, but the church is not a "liberal" voluntary society created by free, autonomous individuals who come together. The church is "gathered." He cites the Methodist theologian Harris Franklin Rall, connecting his "baptist" ecclesiology to Methodism. Rall distinguished between the "given" church, which was the "existing, institutional Church of England spread in its parishes across the land" with the "gathered" church. It depended less on parish boundaries, was free from establishment, and identified the church by the material, gathering of persons. The given church existed independently of gathered persons. The gathered church only exists in its local, particular visibility. McClendon admits that these terms are fluid; the given becomes the gathered, the gathered the given. He also identifies the "gathered" church as a condition for witness: "I do believe the term 'gathered church' bears an ongoing witness—its passive verb form declares that it is not we who gather but God who gathers us: the church is called out before it can call others; it is gathered before it witnesses to God on earth."[6] For McClendon the church is first and foremost a freely gathered local body. It is voluntary in the minimal sense that it is not a function of the government; it is not established, and does not receive tax

---

[3]McClendon, "What Is a 'Baptist' Theology?," in *Collected Works*, vol. 1, ed. Ryan Andrew Newson and Andrew C. Wright (Waco, TX: Baylor University Press, 2014), 103.
[4]McClendon, "Concept of Authority," in *Collected Works*, 1:123.
[5]McClendon, "What Is a 'Baptist' Theology?," 104.
[6]McClendon, "The Voluntary Church in the Twenty-First Century," in *Collected Works*, 1:153-55.

support. It does not seek to impose its way of life through state power.[7] But McClendon rejects a voluntarism in which each local church is free to make autonomous decisions.[8]

The Free Church takes the "call to shared discipleship" on all its members as a distinctive feature. No two-tiered ethic exists—one for the religious called to counsels of perfection and another for those called to the precepts of ordinary life. All are called to "gospel witness as the call to shared discipleship." The basis for discerning Scripture in a life of shared discipleship is found in the form that the local church takes: "A free common life in Christ, in gathered reforming communities." The Free Church affirms liberty, but it is not a negative liberty; it is a liberty born out of the call to discipleship directed to the full maturity of Christ.[9]

McClendon emphasizes the local, voluntary church. By no means does he reject a visible presentation of the catholic in the local, but it is not identified by bishops, councils, or a deposit of faith passed down and received in each generation without rupture. Catholicity is identified by faithful discipleship made possible through the Holy Spirit, producing a communion that is at one with the primitive and eschatological community. McClendon poses a question that acknowledges the problem that his emphasis on a local, gathered church faces: What keeps it from falling into "heresy and schism"? His answer is found in what was already alluded to—maturity in Christ, recognized by the presence of the gifts Christ gives to the church in Ephesians 4:1-16: "The gifts he gave were some would be apostles, some prophets, some evangelists, some pastors and teachers, to equip the saints for the work of ministry, for building up the body of Christ, until all of us come to the unity of faith and of the knowledge of the Son of God, to maturity, to the measure of the full stature of Christ."[10] Only as the church moves toward this full stature can it be said to be avoiding heresy and schism.

---

[7]The church offers, McClendon writes, "liberty without coercion as a distinct people under God rather than relying on political theories, principalities or powers" (McClendon, "Voluntary Church," 163).

[8]In 1982, McClendon's "baptist vision" identified five characteristics of the church: biblicism, mission, liberty, discipleship, and community. In 1998 he "re-envisioned" the voluntary church, drawing on similar themes and identifying four marks that characterize the free or voluntary church: (1) reading Scripture in community; (2) "gospel witness as shared discipleship"; (3) "a free common life in Christ in gathered reforming communities"; (4) liberty. In these revised marks, biblicism and community came together. To say that the "free" church is biblicist is insufficient if that assumes an individualist orientation, each person reading the Bible for her- or himself. The Bible should be studied and discerned in "reading communities." Mission and discipleship are also brought together (ibid., 163).

[9]Ibid.

[10]Ibid., 165.

ECCLESIAL OFFICE

McClendon offers a compelling theology of the local, gathered church. He helps me remember well what happened during my baptism at Jefferson Brethren Church. His work is faithful to the first theological encumbrance noted above. He connects the local, voluntary church to the catholic church through eschatology and Christology. The local church, he acknowledges, should avoid heresy and schism; it does so by seeing the catholic in the local gathering by using the gifts Christ gives to move the faithful "to the measure of the full stature of Christ."[11] The unity of local and catholic is found in Christ. No faithful Christian could disagree with that claim; who is against the need for the church to measure itself against the "full stature of Christ"? But is this adequate as a *visible* presentation of catholic unity in the locally gathered church? The Ephesian passage points to the importance of ecclesial offices—apostles, prophets, evangelists, pastors, and teachers—but McClendon left the role of office unexplored. He had little to no theological compunction to set forth a role for an ecclesial office that would visibly represent the unity of the catholic church in the local church. He did not provide much of a theological rationale as to how the catholic church is present in the local church. Is there a way forward that can affirm the central place of the free, gathered ecclesiology of the Anabaptists and offer something more, something concrete, as to how the unity of the catholic church is present in the local, gathered church? If we only had a "high church Mennonite" approach to ecclesiology, we could affirm both McClendon's baptist ecclesiology and satisfy more fully the second encumbrance noted above—materially representing the catholic church's presence in the local church.[12]

---

[11] Kevin Hector's *Theology Without Metaphysics: God, Language and the Spirit of Recognition* (Cambridge: Cambridge University Press, 2011) could help strengthen McClendon's ecclesiology with his understanding of how concepts are pneumatologically used. He states, "On the model defended here, then, to use a concept is to intend for one's use to be recognizable as such by those whom one recognizes as users of the concept, and one intends this by trying to go on in the same way as precedent uses which one recognizes as correct" (64). The Spirit guides the church by informing present users of concepts to recognize previous uses based on "performers and performances as precedential." Hector notes that this understanding is "a trajectory internal to Christian (especially Protestant) thought" (73). Hector's pneumatology gives theological substance to McClendon's "this is that" ecclesiology.

[12] McClendon was well known for his early espousal of narrative theology; it was not a theory-laden method but an insistence on the place of local histories. He wrote, "It is only as the story of our lives meets the great ongoing story of Jesus, called the Christ, that we are by any means prepared to make sense of our individual stories." Theology as biography seeks to render our individual stories intelligible by placing them within the plot line of the "ongoing story of Jesus." There are, as McClendon noted, drives "to truth and self-deception" in such narration, especially when it is autobiography; I

Peter Dula, a Mennonite theologian, met Stanley Hauerwas as a prospective student in 1997 and recounts the encounter: "We had barely introduced ourselves when he said gruffly, 'When are you Mennonites going to give up and admit that you need a magisterium?'"[13] Hauerwas is well known for his claim to be a "high church Mennonite." As Dula notes, few Mennonites take this claim seriously. Dula refers to it as an "internal conflict" and not a "coherent position." Few Catholics or Orthodox take it seriously either, although Anglicans have, in particular Hauerwas's coauthor Samuel Wells. Gerald Schlabach, a Mennonite turned Catholic, offers a succinct interpretation of Hauerwas's claim. He writes, "Hauerwas's project is to call Catholics and Protestants to be more Anabaptist, and to call Anabaptists and Protestants to be more Catholic."[14] Dula is not unsympathetic to Hauerwas's ecclesiology; he calls upon Anabaptists to be "for and against Hauerwas" as he is "against Mennonites." Although he finds "high church Mennonite" incoherent, he also acknowledges it expresses a tension that should not be resolved. He notes, however, that Hauerwas has been "invulnerable to [Anabaptist] ecclesiology."[15] By beginning with McClendon's ecclesiology, I have attempted to affirm an Anabaptist ecclesiology, but I also think Dula has been inattentive to Hauerwas's "Methodist" context. Michael Cartwright, a Methodist theologian, offers a better interpretation of Hauerwas's claim to be a "high church Mennonite"; his statement requires attention to his Wesleyan-Methodist heritage if we are to make sense of it.[16] On the one hand, a Wesleyan ecclesiology shares with the Anabaptists that the church is free, disestablished, and identified by discipleship and the pursuit of holiness. McClendon saw the consanguinity between them in Ralls. On the other, it is an episcopal ecclesiology in which the church's being is received and mediated to it through the office of the bishop and priest presiding at the sacrament. In its emphasis on freedom and disestablishment, emphasizing the gathering of the local congregation, it approaches the Anabaptists. In its emphasis on the place of the bishop as a mark of the church's catholicity, it is "high church."[17]

---

confess that both are present in the story I am telling by seeking to remember my baptism. McClendon, "Story, Sainthood and Truth: 'Biography as Theology' Revisited," in McClendon, *Collected Works*, vol. 2, ed. Ryan Andrew Newson and Andrew C. Wright (Waco, TX: Baylor University Press, 2014), 216.

[13]Peter Dula, "For and Against Hauerwas Against Mennonites," *Mennonite Quarterly Review* 84 (2010): 375.

[14]Michael G. Cartwright, "Afterword: Stanley Hauerwas's Essays in Theological Ethics: A Reader's Guide," in *The Hauerwas Reader*, ed. John Berkman and Michael Cartwright (Durham, NC: Duke University Press, 2001), 665, 668.

[15]Dula, "For and Against Hauerwas," 377.

[16]Cartwright, "Afterword," 667.

[17]These two emphases are how Albert Outler identifies Wesleyan ecclesiology.

The United Methodist Church places the mission of catholicity within the episcopacy. Its *Book of Discipline* states, "The role of the bishop is to be the shepherd of the whole flock and thereby provide leadership toward the goal of understanding, reconciliation and unity within the Church—the United Methodist Church and the church universal." To do this, "bishops are authorized to guard the faith, order, liturgy, doctrine, and discipline of the Church."[18] At the same time, it subordinates the bishop to the Conference, which is best understood as a conciliar form of lay and clerical authority emerging from the local church. The bishop, even the council of bishops, is not a monarch or authoritative ruler who acts independently from the local gathering. Ecclesial authority is complex, messy, and mired in conflict. No single authority—local church, conference, or bishop—can impose his, her, or their will on everyone else. The gathered church, as McClendon suggested, receives its being from God. The reception occurs, which McClendon did not suggest, through ecclesial office when clergy "take authority" from the bishop to order the church through Word and sacrament. The church is ordered to holiness, and it is never a secure possession that can be produced simply by right order. The holiness of the local church should take precedence over ecclesial office, challenging it when it inhibits holiness as it did when it excluded women from office. Office unites local churches by "guarding" faith and practice by ensuring the local church does not claim for itself the entirety of the church. It only does this as it is attentive to the conditions that make for holiness within the particularity of the local gathering.

I am not arguing that Methodist ecclesiology is the true church, that it alone possesses the fullness of faith, or that the truth of all other local gatherings is validated by the fact that they "subsist" in this putative true church. The church is an object of faith. Seeking "the only true church" is a theological mistake. Hauerwas and Wells are explicit in rejecting such a search. After laying out "criteria" for what constitutes the church, they ask, "Which church is the Church?" Their answer should not be forgotten:

> It is an understandable question, but not a helpful one. It is unhelpful because it encourages a sense of finality that diminishes, rather than builds up, the Church. This is a finality that suggests it is possible to "arrive" as a "right" church. Such a church would be almost bound to foster pride rather than honesty, complacency rather than confidence. It would resemble a too-tidy dogmatics, in that it would provide such a

---

[18]*United Methodist Book of Discipline* (Nashville: Abingdon, 2016), §403.

conclusive guarantee of God that witness would seem unnecessary and service would be neglected. It would misunderstand every aspect of worship.[19]

What we should avoid is the search for the "right" church.

ECUMENICAL ENCUMBRANCE

Hauerwas and Wells's nonsystematic ecclesiology should not cause us to neglect discussion of the third encumbrance: openness to ecumenical admonition. Their ecclesiology is not a neutral arbiter that hovers above the fray of ecclesiological conflict; it reflects the Gallican Catholicity affirmed (perhaps) by de Lubac and Congar and present in the Anglican communion: an ecclesiology that has a place for but limits the authority of the bishop of Rome. Opposition arises from opposite critiques: first from a low ecclesiology present in nondenominational evangelical and Anabaptist churches that suggest that the only thing that matters is the local church; it is *adiaphora* to ask how the local church communicates catholic unity. Even providing a place for the bishop of Rome, or any bishop as the office of unity, goes too far. The second comes from Roman Catholicism. Many Catholics recall that the consistent teaching of the Roman Catholic Church is that it alone represents the true church. Those outside it are no longer heretics, but we lack the "fullness of faith" because we are not in communion with the "one Church of Christ." The change in Vatican II that no longer anathematized us did not fundamentally alter that claim. The document *Lumen Gentium* maintained that the church is a "single reality," and as such it "subsists in the Catholic Church which is governed by the successor of Peter and by the Bishops in communion with him, although many elements of sanctification and of truth are found outside of its visible structure. These elements, as gifts belonging to the Church of Christ, are forces impelling toward catholic unity." Someone as sympathetic to Hauerwas's "high church Mennonite" ecclesiology and open to ecumenism as William Cavanaugh will still understandably be faithful to the teaching of the Catholic Church. He writes,

> The breaking down of barriers between non-Catholics and Catholics in the post–Vatican II era should be recognized as an unqualified gain. To describe this movement as an embrace of the world by the church, however, is misleading. The ecumenical movement, from the Catholic point of view, is rather a recognition that those who were previously anathematized as belonging to the realm of perdition and not to the

---

[19]"The Gift of the Church," in *The Blackwell Companion to Christian Ethics*, ed. Stanley Hauerwas and Samuel Wells, 2nd ed. (Oxford: Blackwell, 2011), 23-34.

church are now recognized as belonging to the one church of Christ, even though not yet in full communion with the Catholic Church.[20]

Was the grace mediated by my baptism at Jefferson Brethren Church made possible by the fact that somehow, mysteriously, it "subsists" in the Roman Catholic Church? Is this what constitutes its catholicity? If I were to become Roman Catholic, convinced that it alone is the one, true church, they too, like the Methodists, would honor my baptism. They would not ask me to repudiate it. If that is the case, then it seems to pose a difficulty. On the one hand, the Roman Catholic Church acknowledges the catholicity of my baptism on its own terms. On the other, the Roman Catholic Church teaches that this acknowledgment should "impel" me toward the fullness of faith by entering into communion with Rome. But if the first is true, then what is the force of the second? And if I accept the second, how do I not betray the baptism I received at the hands of that Anabaptist preacher, which was received by the United Methodists?

---

[20]William Cavanaugh, *Field Hospital: The Church's Engagement with a Wounded World* (Grand Rapids: Eerdmans, 2016), 43.

5

ASCENSION, COMMUNION, AND THE HOSPITALITY OF THE PRIEST-KING

CHERITH FEE NORDLING

THE TROUBLING DISAPPEARANCE OF THE ASCENDED JESUS

Last fall I taught a new course on the ascended Jesus. For several years the reality that Jesus "ascended into heaven and is seated at the right hand of the Father" has been reframing and reorienting the whole of my Christian understanding, experience, and expectation. I wanted captive conversation partners who would look with me through the lens of this breathtaking reality at the full extent of God's story with us. So I did what academics often do. I created an elective.

When asked over the summer about the course I was prepping, more often than not my answer drew a cocked head, the sound of crickets, and then a "How about those Cubs?" So by early September, when my neighborhood priest asked what I was teaching, and I answered, "A ten-week course on Jesus' ascension," his double take did not surprise me. Rather, it was the straightforwardness of his response. "The Ascension? For ten weeks? I'm not sure what I'd say in a ten-minute *homily*."

My friend is in good company. Despite the fact that for almost two millennia the Feast of the Ascension—like Christmas, Easter, and Pentecost—was among the highest of the church's festival days, the centrality of Jesus' ascension has all but disappeared for most of the church (particularly Protestants), as surely as Jesus did

---

I am deeply grateful to Bethany Joy Kim for her wise, skillful assistance in editing and refining this piece.

when he ascended. If the disciples' initial confusion was quickly resolved through the heavenly testimony and Spirit-baptism at Pentecost, ours remains. If and when we consider Jesus' ascension, our gaze is drawn awkwardly to his mode of departure, rather than to his coronation as our incarnate, exalted priest-king. Though our language—in worship and creed—speaks of Jesus as King and Lord "ascended into heaven and seated at the right hand of Father," we're not sure how to speak about what he's doing and why it matters. When he drops out of sight, so too do the radical implications of his ongoing life for and with us.

Nonetheless, Jesus' ascension is the climax of Scripture's narration of our story as God's people; it is foreshadowed throughout the Old Testament and Gospels and was the key source of hope in the early church. In fact, the language of exaltation in Psalm 110—"The LORD said to my Lord, sit at my right hand until I make your enemies a footstool for your feet"—is the most alluded to Old Testament text in the New Testament. The hope of the suffering New Testament church was that "this same Jesus, who has been taken from you into heaven," is enthroned, exalted, and crowned with the glory and authority befitting YHWH and his image-bearing human children. Indeed, Jesus ascended is quite expressly the crowning event of God's life with us and our life in God.

Accordingly, the New Testament assumes that the ascended Jesus is the climactic lens through which *everything* is to be perceived and understood. He is the orienting center of new creation, embedded in the broader story of God's covenant life with and for us from first creation, and ultimately manifested in the ascended Jesus as Israel's Messiah and the world's new Adam. Why? Because when God the Father "placed all things under his feet and appointed him to be head over everything," he did so "for the church, which is his body, the fullness of him who fills everything in every way" (Eph 1:17-23). In short, what happened to Jesus has in some way already happened to us—"God raised us up with Christ and seated us with him in the heavenly realms" (Eph 2:6).

WHAT HAPPENS WHEN THE ASCENDED JESUS IS NOT IN HIS "PLACE"?

As surely as the ascended Jesus disappeared from the disciples' sight, his ascension has disappeared from much of the church's vision and identity. Without our eyes set on our exalted king, we look to fill the void with our best efforts and self-projections. While historic church practices of the Lord's Supper remind us that our life "is now hidden with Christ in God" (Col 3:3), many of our present Communion liturgies instead focus almost entirely on our sin and Jesus' death on the cross (likewise emphasized in how we share the gospel).

In this liturgical shift, we are often shaped by narratives antithetical to the kingdom of Jesus rather than reordered by the narrative sung over the communion of the saints in the great Eucharistic Prayer. Some of us are far too at home with the privileges of our present condition. Others struggle to anticipate anything beyond present suffering. Still others await a heavenly future that abandons creation, including humankind, and thus feel free to squander creation. These perspectives, however, are difficult to maintain if we indeed set our minds on "things above" (Col 3:2), namely, the incarnate king of heaven who has been made head over everything by our heavenly Father. This is so that the church, God's children and Christ's co-heirs, might manifest the fullness of him who fills everything in every way as we become who we already are in him. The ascended Christ is our loving, living hope. *Homoousios* with us forever, his glorious humanity both guarantees our own future glory and mediates our present broken beauty, both of which we celebrate with him at his table (Rom 8; 1 Cor 11–15; Eph 1–3; Col 3; 1 John).

Our theological amnesia and ecclesial dissociation from our enthroned new Adam have widespread repercussions. Theologies that neglect his ascension become forgetful of who and where Jesus is. They often conflate Son and Spirit, leaving in their wake gnostic Christologies that de-story and disembody Jesus and his people. We are left eschatologically unmoored from an understanding of salvation as "the redemption of our bodies" (Rom 8:23) and thus our final, glorious humanity in communion with God, a cruciform glory that we are already called to enact in the present. Such gnostic and binitarian theologies disregard our union with Jesus by the Spirit and thus disregard the Trinitarian reality grounding the Eucharist.

When Jesus' ascension and coronation fade into the background of our theological imaginations, our narration of the gospel stops at the cross and Jesus' resurrection. That we curtail the gospel to focus only on Jesus' death and resurrection reveals a deep-seated, unconscious gnosticism regarding both Jesus and ourselves. Many of us inadvertently imagine that Jesus shared our humanity only until his salvific work was completed on the cross. This was brought home to me again several years ago when I received an email from some church elders who were wondering whether the ascended Jesus still has a body; after discussion, some decided that he did and others that he didn't, but all agreed that it didn't really matter one way or another. While they were curious as to my opinion, they remarked, "It was not urgent, by the way."

In short, Jesus ascended becomes Jesus disembodied and dehumanized. We say things like "When Jesus was a man . . ." or "When Jesus was alive . . ." as if he shared our humanity only until entering the clouds. Our fuzzy images of Jesus surrounded by clouds drawn from Sunday school are disconnected from the "clouds" described in Acts 1 meant to redirect us to the apocalyptic vision of Daniel 7, which describes "one like a son of man, coming with the clouds of heaven" presented at God's throne room and given eternal kingship and dominion over all things.

Neglecting Jesus' ongoing humanity disorders the proper relation of our present and final humanity in correspondence to him. When "Jesus ascended" equals "Jesus disappeared," the ascension and Pentecost become a kind of baton pass; Jesus left so that the church can get on with doing his work. We tend to think that it is our responsibility to do great things for God rather than finding ourselves united with our king, who is doing great things and invites us to join him. Whether this "responsibility" comes from under-realized eschatologies that focus on the coming kingdom and the saving of disembodied souls, or from over-realized eschatologies that assume the kingdom is present now and that it is our job to make it visible, either way the work is basically ours. In substituting our busy bodies for Jesus' embodied work as prophet, priest, and king, we misunderstand what it means to be Christ's body, the community whose life participates in and with our still-human Lord.

When embodiment, be it Christ's or ours, becomes negligible in this way, we become forgetful of God's relational, triune life revealed in Jesus of Nazareth. With and for us, his whole life, from conception to ascension, has been lived with and by the Holy Spirit in unbroken communion with and in submission to the Father. Without understanding this triune expression of truly human life, we quickly veer off from the incarnate Jesus as our center. It may seem a matter of a few degrees, but without a course correction the result is catastrophically un-Christian. We talk about "Christ in our hearts" as though Jesus is now a disembodied, omnipresent "Christic" spirit. This lays the ground for a binitarianism that neglects the person of the Holy Spirit in favor of an impersonal, sanctifying force that awakens our conscience or our reading of Scripture. The Son is no longer incarnate, and the Spirit is no longer the Lord and giver of life who mediates to us Jesus' real-life presence at the Father's right hand. Furthermore, this binitarianism falsely separates us from the communion of saints, past, present, and future. When Christ and his whole church in heaven and earth, present and absent, are not in view, it is no wonder that we see only ourselves and fall prey to functioning as Christ's replacement.

God's salvation history of making a people for his name is eclipsed by hyper-personalized gnostic "salvation" narratives that emphasize the cross "fixing" the problem of individual sins so that disembodied souls can go to heaven. This individualized "relationship with Jesus" manifests in our treatment of the Lord's Supper as a time for private reflection on our sin and Jesus' death on the cross in ways that suggest that our worth is tied to our agency, to something we must do to validate the invitation and renew our place at the table. When we fail to recognize the full extent of salvation history and instead turn communion into a personal moment to remember our sins and Christ's death, we isolate ourselves from the church's communal life in the triune God, vicariously mediated by our still-human Lord and high priest.

Our salvific hope, however, for which all creation groans, is indeed the "redemption of our bodies," grounded in the fact that "Christ has died, Christ is risen, Christ will come again." This Eucharistic acclamation bears witness to our human realignment as children of God. The Eucharist is meant not just to remember Christ's death but also to celebrate the full extent of the paschal mystery: his resurrection, his ascended reign, our eschatological life united with him, and his final parousia to bring about final new creation.

RECOVERING OUR PARTICIPATION IN THE ASCENDED JESUS

The heart of the gospel involves Jesus *being* the incarnate, ascended Lord. Herein lies all hope of participating in resurrection life with Jesus, sharing by the Spirit in the faithful life, ongoing reign, and priestly ministry of our Lord and elder brother. The early church took for granted that Jesus' ascension was the basis of his lordship. Hope in the crucified Christ came through his resurrection *and* exaltation. As the renewed Word made flesh, he became the first word of renewal, God's final word over death, and the baptizer in the renewing Holy Spirit. "Exalted to the right hand of God, he has received from the Father the promised Holy Spirit and has poured out what you now see and hear. For David did not ascend to heaven, and yet he said, 'The LORD said to my Lord, "Sit at my right hand until I make your enemies a footstool for your feet."' Therefore let all Israel be assured of this: God has made this Jesus, whom you crucified, both Lord and Messiah" (Acts 2:33-36).

This Lord and Christ called forth the identity and loyalty of a suffering church. They belonged to the vindicated, resurrected Lord. They shared the same Father and the same Spirit through whom the Father had raised Jesus from the dead; the same eschatological Spirit who empowered them in life unto death and who would give them their lives back. Their lives corresponded to his ascended lordship. To set our eyes on "things above" is to fix "our eyes on Jesus, the pioneer and perfecter of our faith" (Heb 12:2), with whom we have died and risen in baptism, and with whom we are now seated in glory, to the praise of our heavenly Father. From this New Testament perspective—that bears witness to the first Testament—and from the church's ongoing reflection ever since, the following assertions are made regarding Jesus' ascension.

First, the ascended Jesus is the culmination of the triune God's movement of descent and ascent that structures the divine-creaturely story of salvation history. Jesus' ascension, as enthroned new creation, is salvation's climax and the guarantee of its final consummation. In Israel's first creation narrative God descended by the Spirit to bring forth life from the waters of chaos and speak creation into being through his divine Word. In Daniel's later apocalyptic re-creation vision, the divine Word and image bearing "Son of Man" rises out of the chaos of the powers of this world and ascends to the presence of the Ancient of Days. There he is given all power, dominion, and authority at God's right hand as promised in Isaiah and in Psalm 110. This vision echoes God's original image-bearing children called to exercise their God-given authority as vice-regents for and with creation.

When his exalted children descend into fallenness, God repeatedly descends in mercy, seeking to bring his broken image-bearers into alignment with him as true humanity. God calls Noah and his offspring to rise up on the water out of the chaos of the world around them. God calls Abram up from Ur and ratifies his promise to him on a mountaintop altar. When Abraham's descendants descend into slavery in Egypt, they are brought up again and delivered by YHWH's mighty right hand through Moses, whom YHWH anointed on Horeb, the mountain of God. YHWH then calls Moses to ascend another mountain of his presence, Sinai, to receive the law. Moses' descent therefrom, met by the descent of Israel into idolatry, compels yet another ascent that secures God's continuing presence.

In the land of promise God eventually establishes the throne of David on Mount Zion, the temple-palace hill of the Lord's presence, which Israel ascends in worship. As God's people continually descend into idolatry, which results in exile, God calls them upward through the prophets, who give shape to Israel's hopes for their final ascent into God's kingdom, ushered in through a royal coronation. Finally, descent and ascent are magnificently, everlastingly recapitulated in Jesus Christ. The Son descends to, and fully unites with, sinful old creation, experiencing his sinless exodus on her behalf, carrying her sin as his own as he descends into hell. The

Father calls forth his ascent as the firstborn of a new creation by the resurrecting Spirit. Ultimately Jesus ascends the mountain of the Lord and the temple not made with human hands, to be seated in exaltation at the Father's right hand, "from whence he shall come again to judge the living and the dead."[1] Reflecting on this wonder, Paul exults, and then explains: "'When he ascended on high, he took many captives and gave gifts to his people.' (What does 'he ascended' mean except that he also descended to the lower, earthly regions? He who descended is the very one who ascended higher than all the heavens, in order to fill the whole universe)" (Eph 4:8-9; Ps 68:18).

Second, in this pattern of ascent and descent, exaltation comes expressly through humiliation, thereby revealing the character and extent of God's self-giving love. In the Son's excruciating descent, he sets aside access to his divinely entitled authority in order to enter fully into our condition, coming as God's slave to manifest the true divine character in image-bearing humanity. Suffering as we do and tempted in every way we are, yet without sin, he obeys the Father even unto death. Not just any death, but death on a cross; a horrific, public humiliation uniquely reserved for disobedient slaves and for insurrectionists against earthly powers. Precisely because in Jesus of Nazareth the selfless, sacrificial nature and power of God are undeniably revealed, the Father undoes death and injustice through his Son's unjust death. In Jesus' descent and ascent, God changes the relational, salvific order of heaven and earth, and brings humanity to its telos as children who share in God's divine glory and purposes. "Therefore," on the basis of this faithful witness of true God and true humanity, "God exalted him to the highest place" (Phil 2:5-11). Highest exaltation comes at the cost of utmost humiliation, which is on display in the ascended, incarnate Son.[2]

Third, exaltation through humiliation is essential to Jesus' role as our kingly high priest. In John's apocalyptic vision, the triumphant one standing at the center of the throne is "worthy to take the scroll [from YHWH's right hand] and open its seals" precisely because this lion of Judah is the slain, sacrificed lamb. Only thus can he be both our king and priest, taking what is ours and presenting it acceptable to God. Incorporating images of king, sacrifice, and priest, the writer of Hebrews portrays Jesus as God's final word spoken through the exaltation of his truly human,

---

[1] See Douglas Farrow, *Ascension and Ecclesia: On the Significance of the Doctrine of the Ascension for Ecclesiology and Christian Cosmology* (Grand Rapids: Eerdmans, 1999), for a detailed explication of the biblical pattern of descent and ascent.

[2] A lovely inter-testamental discussion of Jesus revealing YHWH's character and sharing the divine identity this way is found in Richard Bauckham, *God Crucified: Monotheism and Christology in the New Testament* (Grand Rapids: Eerdmans, 1999), 46-61.

image-bearing Son, who ascends and sits down at the right hand of the majesty in heaven only after providing purification for sin (Heb 1:3-4).

Our faithful priest-king vicariously mediates our present and final humanity through his immortal life, standing in for us before the throne, holding our brokenness and perfection in the fellowship of the triune God. By the Spirit he remains united to our suffering and joy, priesting our broken life in his intercessions and also mediating our perfected life until we too receive our glorious humanity. Jesus' priesthood is likened to Melchizedek (Ps 110:4), king of *shalom*, a high priest whose anointing comes directly from God and not through Israel's tribal lineage. Moreover, in the order of Melchizedek, he is our priest forever "on the basis of the power of an indestructible life" (Heb 5:10; 7:16-17). As God's priest, Melchizedek, offered bread and wine to Abram, so too Christ offers himself in bread and wine to us as a sign of our irrevocable, new covenant life in and with him.[3] This indestructible covenant is Jesus Christ, the incarnate, hypostatic union. In sealing us with the eschatological Spirit, God's *arrabon*, Jesus guarantees that we too will share in his glorious human life as children of God, in union with the Father. Sealed to his glorious humanity, we uniquely participate in *koinōnia* with the triune God (Eph 1:11-23; Jn 17).

Fourth, Jesus' exaltation is the eschatological promise and first instance of our human exaltation: he became like us that we might become like him. "In Christ all the fullness of the Deity lives in bodily form," and we "have been brought to fullness" in Christ (Col 2:9-10). Throughout the ages theologians have proclaimed this truth. Ascension "is deification, and deification nothing but the fulfillment of man's creation," since humanity is "uniquely formed by the Word and the Spirit for communion with the Father."[4] John Chrysostom marveled that God's invitation "Sit thou on my right hand" was spoken to the same "nature . . . which heard: 'Dust thou art, and unto dust thou shalt return.'"[5] In the fifth century, Maximus of Turin wrote, "Having fought in man and having conquered through man, Christ made him the inhabitant of heaven and the Lord of earth."[6] Over a thousand years later, John Calvin wrote similarly of how, in the wonderful exchange, Christ takes what

---

[3]Bruce K. Waltke, "'He Ascended and Sitteth . . . ': Reflections on the Sixth Article of the Apostles' Creed," *Crux* 10 (1994): 5-6.

[4]Farrow, *Ascension and Ecclesia*, 40, following Irenaeus.

[5]John Chrysostom, "Sermon on the Ascension," *PG* 50.441-52. Cited by Farrow, *Ascension Theology*, 40.

[6]Cited by Farrow, *Ascension and Ecclesia*, 41.

is ours by sharing in our broken humanity and makes us like him by giving us what is his. And hence we sing today, in the beautiful words of Christopher Wordsworth:

> Thou hast raised our human nature
> On the clouds to God's right hand;
> There we sit in heavenly places,
> There with Thee in glory stand.
> Jesus reigns, adored by angels;
> Man with God is on the throne.
> Mighty Lord, in Thine ascension
> We by faith behold our own.[7]

We were made to bear the divine glory and image and to minister the divine presence upon the earth. In our ascended priest-king, we discover that our calling has not been revoked; it has been restored. As he is crowned with glory and honor, so are we; thus, he guarantees our future as God's image-bearing human children in the age to come. After all, "It is not to angels that he has subjected the world to come," but humanity (Heb 2:5). Hence, we do not yet see any human crowned with glory and honor except Jesus, whose capacity to stand for us came through suffering with us, bringing God's "many sons and daughters, to glory" (Heb 2:10). All the more remarkably, "both the one who makes people holy, and those who are made holy are of the same family. So Jesus is not ashamed to call them brothers and sisters" (Heb 2:11). In Jesus, the Father receives our perfection, even as he loves us into conformity to that perfection.

Fifth, Jesus becomes the baptizer in the Spirit from this position of exaltation. Having joined our humanity to the very life of God in himself, Jesus is present to us by the Spirit. Even as he is absent from us, he holds us with himself in God. As Peter declared, "Exalted to the right hand of God, he has received from the Father the promised Holy Spirit and has poured out" the life-giving Spirit—the same Spirit with whom he was in union with the Father before the creation of the world, by whom he was conceived and conjoined to our humanity in Mary's womb, and by whom he has taken our broken and raised humanity into the very life of God in his resurrected ascension. The Spirit makes possible our union with Christ, both in the relational and ontic mystery of his being *homoousios* with us and with God and in the relational *koinōnia* that unites us with Jesus. He can thus say unequivocally that he will never leave us but will be with us until the end of the age.

---

[7]Charles Wordsworth, "See, the Conquer'r Mounts in Triumph" (1862).

Sixth, Jesus is still active, hence we participate *with* him rather than carrying on his ministry, as though he has "passed the baton" to us. We are seated with him at the Father's right hand, and we share in his power and authority. Since our lives are "now hidden with Christ in God," and "in Christ [we] have been brought to fullness," when he appears we will "appear with him in glory" (Col 3:3-4; 2:10). By the Spirit, we are united with him as co-heirs and children of God, and we are seated with him even now as we wait for our final glory to be revealed. Thus we have been restored as image-bearers and vice-regents of creation, and we receive the power of the Spirit, by whom Jesus did all that he did, so that we may participate with Jesus in his ongoing work as Lord over all things. As von Balthasar writes, "He takes us, as those who have died, risen and ascended with him, into his own movement from the world toward the Father and empowers us to join with him in transforming the old world into a new, divine world, a world of the Spirit."[8] This transformation is grounded in the One who sits on the throne, whose life speaks as the last word over all that is broken. Joined to him, we live the "already–not yet" life of God's eschatological people between two advents, participating with Christ in seeing the inbreaking of the power, beauty, and loving character of God and also lamenting with Christ in deep longing and hope.

Seventh, Jesus is the ascended Lord who will return to bring all things to their consummation and "transform our lowly bodies so that they will be like his glorious body" (Phil 3:21). When he returns to judge the living and the dead, he will restore glorified wholeness to all things, wedding heaven and earth in and by himself. As we await his return, shaped by the full arc of Jesus' life, we practice resurrection between these two human-divine advents. We learn to be human from Jesus' truly human life in submission to the Father by the power of the Spirit. Through the Spirit, we glimpse our place as children with our elder brother at the Father's right hand, and by the Spirit we hear our daily call to exercise that kingdom life on earth. Finally, with the Lord of advent who will bring all things aright, we look forward in the hope of our restored humanity and the restoration of all creation.

In summary, we live as people already marked by and in hope of the final advent in the space opened up by resurrection until the final parousia. We recognize that he is seated at our Father's right hand and that we too have been seated with him. We are heirs of all that he is and all that is his—*panta* and *pleroma*—held in

---

[8]Hans Urs von Balthasar, *Prayer*, trans. Graham Harrison (San Francisco: Ignatius, 1986), 55.

indescribable love and union with the Father and the Spirit, until he returns with his finished kingdom. The love of God in Christ, from which nothing can separate us, *is* our embodied, indivisible, divine-human Lord Jesus. That indivisibility is uniquely held in the Eucharist. Here we reenact our hope for Christ's bodily return and our bodily restoration in an eschatological way. On the one hand, the ascension is marked by Christ's "incomprehensible absence" as "the divergence of his history from ours . . . leaves us gazing, dumbfounded, into the heavens," contributing to the "eschatological tension" we experience. On the other hand, the Eucharist reveals an "equally incomprehensible presence *in* the absence—joining our histories to his in a communion of body and soul" so that we experience hope even in the midst of this present eschatological tension.[9] In this tension between Christ's presence and absence highlighted at his table, ascent and descent intersect in the uniquely dynamic relationship of our priest-king with us as one of us. And as the Father again gives us his Son in the Eucharist—in our feast of remembrance and anticipation of what was, and is, and is to come—we hear our Father joyfully calling us to proclaim in our present lives that one day here on this good earth made new, in our bodies, humanity will dwell fully and freely with him.

PARTICIPATION IN GOD'S KINGDOM OF LEFT-HANDED POWER

The politics of Eucharist. "The celebration of the Eucharist," says Douglas Farrow, "is a political act; in fact, it is *the* political act."[10] In God's name, eating a meal in his presence, God's people participate in the ultimate political reality that interrupts and supersedes all earthly kingdoms—the kingdom of heaven on earth.[11] We pledge our lives in allegiance to the Lord, who has united our human life, death, resurrection, and exaltation to his own. We are a Spirit-people joined to the exalted Jesus who lays this table before us as he calls us to sacrificially lay our lives upon this table with him and let God raise us up. To be seated with him is to take our seat with the slain lamb on the throne, whose descent has made possible our cruciform ascent.

Sharing in Jesus' authority, we receive our mantle as image-bearers, restored children, and vice-regents of God called to bring forth shalom by exercising dominion rather than domination. We participate in God's upside-down kingdom of side-ways or "left-handed power" in service of others. Jesus' ministry and

---

[9]Farrow, *Ascension and Ecclesia*, 65.
[10]Ibid., 90.
[11]Ibid.

exaltation are marked by what Luther referred to as God's "left-handed," cruciform power that submits, comes alongside, and lays itself down for the other. Satan tempted Jesus with a "this-worldly" interpretation of God's right-handed power, but Jesus refused, instead taking on YHWH's divine identity and mission in a decidedly left-handed, submissive manner, thereby revealing to us what politics and power in God's kingdom look like. Jesus was exalted precisely because he refused the temptation to exercise right-handed power in a broken way. It is crucial that we understand that both in his temptation and ascension, Jesus manifests his proper authority from the Father's right hand in a left-handed manner; where one might expect a display of right-handed authority as "power over," he selflessly exercises power in alignment with will of the Father, on behalf of others, for the sake of the world.[12]

By the Spirit, we gather around our Lord 's Table and feast with the only truly human person there has yet been, who fully understands what it is to be tempted by compromised power and pinnacles of easy ascent. This meal is a lifeline to his own person and cruciform power and a witness to the world that all things have been reordered to him. As we participate in the offering of our priest-king, the church becomes with Jesus a community of ascension, "sharing in his heavenly offering to the Father, and manifesting the Spirit who reorganizes created reality around him."[13]

Conformed to the character of our priest-king. As children of our heavenly Father and citizens of his uniquely empowered kingdom, we embody that life together in the image of our priest-king. As we communally partake, we take on the character of our host, conformed to the divine likeness in his human image. We remember who and whose we are, a people for God's name who manifest God's loving character for the sake of his beloved world. As we receive the Spirit-anointed body and blood of the Son into our bodies together, we are re-membered, re-collected, and re-connected as his body. We celebrate our unity in diversity at this table of shared grace and forgiveness. Our practice of communal receiving and giving as God's people reorients us to practice the "one-anothering" life of the church in *koinōnia* with the triune God.

At its nonnegotiable center, the Eucharist reveals the self-giving character of God, whose triune nature is wholly "for the other." This is at the heart of Paul's

---

[12]Robert Farrar Capon, *Kingdom, Grace, Judgment: Paradox, Outrage, and Vindication in the Parables of Jesus* (Grand Rapids: Eerdmans, 2002), 29-30.

[13]Farrow, *Ascension and Ecclesia*, 64.

challenge to the church in Corinth, a people reconstituted by the crucified, ascended Lord; Jew or Gentile, slave or free, woman or man—all belong equally to God and one another as the temple of God's presence. Sharing one loaf, as one body, by one Spirit, they are to live for one another in a manner that upends "earthly things"—every assignment of human privilege or worth through cultural status, ethnicity, or gender, and every assumption of entitlement to things of this world. In this Greco-Roman city and honor-shame culture, eating meals in temples in the presence of the gods as an act of worship and allegiance was a regular occurrence that reinforced cultural privilege in terms of who reclined at table, ate first, and so on. Yet Paul makes utterly clear that God will not let this new people bring the structures, divisions, and priorities of the old order to the table. As they eat in the presence of their Lord and God, they are to look like him together. Hence, to eat in an "unworthy manner" meant to fail to "discern the Body of Christ," to forget who and whose they were under Christ, their head. When they do not look like Christ together at his own meal, his worth and theirs are dishonored (1 Cor 11:17-34).

As we come together around the Lord's Supper and find our place within Christ's body, we are asked to lay down our privilege and divisions, our conflicts and brokenness, and accept Christ's healing as we share the meal offered to us. I was reminded of this one recent Sunday. Frustrated by a personal matter and justifiably angry, I was tempted to nurse my hurt on the way to forgiveness. When my husband asked if I was coming to church, I said that I wanted to "stay home and work it out." "Then I think you need to come to church," he replied. An hour later I found myself at the Lord's Table, readied by the truth-telling hymns, corporate confession, reading of Scripture, singing of psalms, intercessions, homily, and passing of Christ's peace. Together we heard God's salvation story prayed over the meal, sang the Sanctus, declared Christ's death, resurrection, and parousia, were realigned through the Lord's Prayer, and heard the invitation to come, eat, and drink at the table of the Lord, the forgiver of all. With my hands outstretched to receive his body and blood, I saw in my mind's eye, across the round table, those who had wronged me and whom I had sat home wronging in return. Here we were, together, in graced communion, called into life and unity. The Word made flesh pulled me out of my privatized anger and drew me into his redeemed body at his image-bearing table. I stood freely forgiven, free to forgive, and hence more open to being "transformed into his image with ever-increasing glory, which comes from the Lord" (2 Cor 3:18).

Lavish hospitality of the priest-king marked by his table fellowship. The hospitality of our host is unsettling. He invites all to come home and find their story— their identity, their family—with God, his Son, and his other children. As he sets the table, he calls us to lay our lives down as pathways into God's household, barricading nothing and no one from this outpoured grace. The call to lay our lives down around the Lord's Table is always accompanied by the promise of eschatological hope that we too will "know the power of his resurrection" if we submit to the left-handed power of "becoming like him in his death" (Phil 3:10).

Jesus revealed the left-handed power of God's kingdom throughout his ministry. In an honor-shame culture, Jesus' table fellowship uniquely manifested the costliness of sacrificial participation in God's kingdom. Hospitality always demanded payback, and so table fellowship had social boundaries: only those who could reciprocate were invited. Jesus challenged this patron-client system of reciprocity not only by eating with marginalized outcasts but also by eating with the wealthy, challenging them to love people more than position by sharing table fellowship with those who could not repay them. As a result, the powerful ridiculed Jesus as a "friend of sinners." When they invited Jesus to eat with them, they intentionally dishonored him by refusing to wash his feet, attempting to shame him into compliance with communal Jewish honor. Even the rich young ruler, earnestly desiring to follow God, "went away sad," so accustomed was he to seeing his wealth as a sign of God's blessing that he didn't know how to give it away and become poor (Mk 10:22). Contrast Zacchaeus, who was likewise wealthy yet socially marginalized as a tax collector because his wealth signaled his association with the Roman Empire rather than divine blessing. Zacchaeus had no illusions that the right-handed power of wealth and status were signs of God's kingdom, and so he was able to recognize the left-handed power of Jesus' request to stay at his house. In his repentance and giving away of his wealth, he joyfully embraced the upside-down kingdom of God (Lk 19:1-10).

After Jesus' ascension, table fellowship continued to be a space of social disruption as the community of believers was socially reoriented in the new age of the Spirit. Their daily communal sharing of bread leveled out divisions between the rich and poor and set the stage for their sharing of wealth in communal life. Jesus' call to trust God to make all things clean and right in the resurrection, and hence to invite the poor, crippled, lame, and blind ("unclean") to the table (Lk 11:37-41; 14:7-14) was magnified a hundredfold when the Jewish community in Acts was challenged to welcome Gentiles to their table fellowship (Acts 10–11). Even

Peter, who had spent so much time with Jesus, could barely wrap his mind around this invitation. When God called Peter to participate in the Gentile mission by extending this invitation to Cornelius's household, he symbolically invited Peter in a vision to eat unclean foods. Three times Peter refused, and three times a voice from heaven spoke, "Do not call anything impure that God has made clean" (Acts 10:11-16). Compelled by this divine mandate that clearly echoed Jesus' own words concerning God's hospitality and table fellowship (Mt 15:1-20), Peter invited the messengers from Cornelius to be his guests. The next day, he entered Cornelius's house and witnessed God welcome this Gentile household into his reconstituted family through Spirit baptism. When the believers in Jerusalem criticized Peter's table fellowship with uncircumcised Gentiles, Peter recounted that Cornelius's household spoke in tongues just as the believers did when the ascended Jesus poured out the Spirit from his place of exaltation at Pentecost. Thus Peter declared, "If God gave them the same gift he gave us . . . who was I to think that I could stand in God's way?" (Acts 11:17). Just as Jesus showed repeatedly in his ministry that God's kingdom upends every cultural division of hierarchy or privilege, so too the Spirit breaks down barriers and opens wide the doors into God's household.

Like the Pharisees and the leaders of the early church in Acts, we too are tempted to protect the table, thinking that we honor Christ by guarding it, and forgetting that Jesus was extraordinarily unworried about protecting his honor (even in a culture that was far more concerned about honor than our own). We also forget that Jesus is our high priest; making our table fellowship holy is his business. That he is not ashamed to call us brothers and sisters has nothing to do with our own righteousness and everything to do with the reality that he makes us righteous siblings through his vicarious life and the outpoured Spirit of adoption (Rom 8:15).

Jesus invites all to "come." This invitation is both a promise of his Eucharistic presence among us and an eschatological promise of his final coming. In hope, "the Spirit and the Bride say, 'Come!' And let the one who hears say, 'Come!' Let the one who is thirsty come; and let the one who wishes take the free gift of the water of life" (Rev 22:17, 20). With such an invitation and hope, how can we but practice the radical hospitality of Christ?

CONCLUSION

As the reality of Jesus' ascension has been reframing my Christian understanding, a key aspect of that reorientation has been a renewed understanding of Jesus' role as high priest. When my husband and I moved to Chicago several years ago, we began worshiping in a neighborhood community that emphasizes inclusion. At first I struggled, wondering whether the lack of accountability as we gathered around the Lord's Table dishonored Christ. Yet as the woman with the issue of blood who touched Jesus was healed, so too was I reminded that we are healed and cleansed without Jesus becoming unholy in the process. As I prayed weekly, I found myself thanking Jesus for being the hospitable Lord who sets a lavish table and for being our high priest who presents us to the Father as beautiful and holy. One week, however, I found my prayers interrupted by Jesus: "Cherith, it's my greatest delight to be your high priest! And now I want to talk to you about your hands gripping the side of your chair, holding on for dear life. Your hands tell me that you don't quite trust that I'm really here priesting this space; and perhaps I would have less to cleanse in the evangelical church down the road. Relax. My church at all times, in all places, is in need of my priesting, whether her sin appears more covert or overt to you. You don't have to sort it out. Trust that this is what *I* do; it's my joyful, full-time vocation until the day I return for my bride."

As I received the bread and wine that morning, I realized afresh that our obedience doesn't make us righteous. Our righteous high priest is always mediating our whole lives. In Christ, our Father always sees us finished and whole, even as he conforms us daily to the image of his Son by the Spirit. And the Eucharist continually reorders us to our eschatological identity until our Lord's final descent to usher in our exalted homecoming. And so, in communion with the triune God, we thank our ascended priest-king for hosting this feast and pray yet again, "God of abundance, you have fed us with the bread of life and cup of salvation, you have united us with Christ and one another; and you have made us one with all your people in heaven and on earth. Now send us forth in the power of your Spirit, that we may proclaim your redeeming love to the world and continue forever in the risen life of Christ our Savior. Amen."

6

THE GOSPEL WE SHARE AND THE UNITY WE SEEK

Orthodox Eucharistic Ecclesiology

BRADLEY NASSIF

THE PURPOSE OF OUR GATHERING at Wheaton College is to reflect upon the question of the sacramental unity of the church in light of the five-hundredth anniversary of the Protestant Reformation. Since Wheaton is one of the leading centers of evangelical higher education, it seems fitting to address my essay to the evangelical community in our common quest for Eucharistic unity. As an Eastern Orthodox theologian, the position I take in this dialogue is best expressed by Metropolitan Kallistos Ware: "*Before there can be reunion among Christians, there must first be full agreement in faith:* this is a basic principle for Orthodox in all their ecumenical relations."[1] In the pages that follow, I will attempt to explain the essential ecclesiological commitments of the church that require "full agreement in faith" as a precondition for Eucharistic participation.[2] First, I will examine the connections between the Eucharist and Christian identity in Scripture and tradition under the rubric of "Eucharistic ecclesiology." Then I will apply those findings to emphasize the unity we share today as Orthodox and evangelical

---

[1]Timothy (Kallistos) Ware, *The Orthodox Church*, rev. ed. (New York: Penguin, 2015), 303.

[2]For a concise history of Orthodox-Evangelical dialogues up to 2013 with footnotes to further sources, see Bradley Nassif, "Orthodox Dialogues with Evangelical Communities," in *Orthodoxy and Ecumenism: A Handbook of Theological Education* (Geneva: WCC-Volos Academy, 2014), 536-41. Beyond 2013, see the spectacular international accomplishments of the Lausanne-Orthodox Initiative (loimission.net) and its first book, edited by Mark Oxbrow and Tim Grass, *The Mission of God: Studies in Orthodox and Evangelical Mission* (Oxford: Regnum, 2015).

Christians while also identifying barriers that still need to be overcome before there can be full sacramental sharing at the Lord's Table.

EUCHARISTIC ECCLESIOLOGY IN SCRIPTURE AND TRADITION

The discipline of ecclesiology in the Orthodox Church is a relatively recent phenomenon. It was never fully developed in the early centuries of the church and only became a distinct theological discipline in the twentieth century when the nature of the church and its connection to the Eucharist was more fully developed. "Eucharistic ecclesiology" is a label that has been used in modern times to describe the Eucharistic nature of the church. It is not a "new" theology of the twentieth century but simply a modern attempt to articulate what is present in the New Testament and patristic writings. The term was first popularized by the Russian Orthodox theologian Nicholas Afanasiev (1893–1966) in the mid-twentieth century and used as a master theme for his work. Other Orthodox theologians such as John Zizioulas (1931–), Kallistos Ware (1934–), John Meyendorff (1926–1992), and Alexander Schmemann (1921–1983) supported Eucharistic ecclesiology but refined and deepened Afanasiev's insights. In this essay, I use the label "Eucharistic ecclesiology" in a broader sense than Afanasiev's. The basic thrust of Eucharistic ecclesiology is that the Eucharist is the center of worship, and each local church, headed by its bishop or his appointed representative, is created by the Eucharist and is fully catholic. The Eucharist is the sacrament that creates the church and its structures of unity throughout the world.[3] Unity in the faith "once delivered to the saints" (Jude 3) is testified by the church's continuous celebration of the Eucharist. That unity is not simply an agreement in beliefs. The faith itself is taught within the Eucharist. The Orthodox Church maintains that it has kept and passed on that tradition unchanged over the centuries.

St. Paul's letter to the Corinthians. Since Scripture is the internal norm of the church's tradition, I begin with St. Paul as a representative of the apostolic community (a study of other New Testament texts is beyond our allotted space). There we see that Paul does not provide us with a complete systematic theology of the Eucharist per se. Rather, everything that Paul says in his letters is given in the context of a particular dialogue or even a polemic. So when it comes to exegeting

---

[3]Incorporation into the body of Christ comes first through baptism in water and the Spirit (1 Cor 12:13). The Eucharist then "creates" the church by providing a means for ongoing communion with God through participation in the bread and wine. The Spirit's baptism of believers into the body of Christ occurs only once, whereas Eucharistic participation in the body of Christ is ongoing.

Paul's thought on the Eucharist, we need to understand the specific context in which his words occur rather than cite proof-texts from his letters. The main chapters in which Paul deals with the Lord's Supper are 1 Corinthians 10–11. The context of these passages begins back in chapter 8 where Paul deals with the question of whether it is permissible for Christians to eat meat offered to pagan idols. Paul tells the Corinthians that love, not knowledge, should guide their behavior. If a believer who eats meat that had been offered to idols causes another believer to eat idol meat in violation of their conscience, then the Christian is to refrain from eating it. In 1 Corinthians 10:18-22 Paul answers further questions about eating meat offered to idols. The Corinthians wanted to know if it was permissible for them to participate in the actual ritual of pagan worship. To this Paul says, "Absolutely not!" To do so would be to participate in sacrifices offered to demons, and this is completely incompatible with participating in the Eucharist. There is an ontological contrast between participating in meat offered to idols and participating in the bread and wine of communion. "You cannot drink the cup of the Lord and the cup of demons too; you cannot have a part in both the Lord's Table and the table of demons" (v. 22).

Paul begins his argument against participating in pagan idolatry in 1 Corinthians 10:1-13. There he focuses on the deliverance of the Israelites through the sea under Moses. Paul warns the Corinthians against imitating the rebellion of the Israelites who, although "baptized into Moses" (i.e., incorporated into the community of God's people), were destroyed in the wilderness. Just as the Israelites were miraculously sustained in the wilderness by God, so also the Corinthians can be sustained by their obedience to God. In verses 1-5 Paul interprets the exodus event typologically. He shows how the Israelites were sustained by manna from heaven and the water that came from a rock that accompanied them on their journey. He says, "They all ate the same spiritual food and drank the same spiritual drink; for they drank from the spiritual rock that accompanied them, and that rock was Christ." Notice the expressions "spiritual food," "spiritual drink," and "spiritual rock." In Paul's understanding, these are typological images that point forward to the Eucharist. There is not the slightest question about it. These expressions emphasize the divine origin of the food and water that sustained the Israelites by the grace of God as they wandered in the desert. Yet the books of Exodus and Numbers say nothing about the rock "following" them. The idea of the rock accompanying the Israelites is midrashic. It comes out of Rabbinic interpretation in which the idea that the rock followed the Israelites through the wilderness consistently appears. Paul takes up this particular emphasis to stress two things: First, that there is a continuing *divine presence* with the Israelites that is manifested particularly through the act of consuming what was necessary to sustain physical life, namely food in the form of manna and liquid in the form of water that came forth from the rock. Second, when Paul emphasizes that the rock followed them, he is also saying that Christ himself was *present* among the people of Israel in pre-incarnate form. This is one of the most explicit passages in Paul's writings that confirms the pre-existence of Jesus Christ in the desert wanderings of Israel. It is based on the nature of a typological correspondence between the past and the future—a relationship I would like to explain in greater detail because it contains the notion of *ontological participation* that Paul will develop Eucharistically in 1 Corinthians 10:16.

What is often overlooked, even by many biblical scholars today, is that the whole point of typology is to emphasize a double dimension. Old Testament types not only look *forward* to their antitypes (fulfillments) in the New Testament. Types also permit their future fulfillments to actualize themselves in the *past*. In other words, the movement in typology is not only from the past to the future; it is also a movement from the future to the past. In 1 Corinthians 10:2-4, the manna and the rock not only point prophetically to Jesus Christ, but Paul also declares with virtual identity "that rock was Christ" (1 Cor 10:4). So what Paul was saying is that the Israelites had everything. Not only did they have food and water, but they actually had Christ himself walking with them as they wandered through the desert. And yet they displeased God—a theme Paul will go back to when addressing the abuses of the agape meal and Lord's Supper in 1 Corinthians 11:17-34.

This way of bringing together a typological correspondence between past and future realities in 1 Corinthians 10:2-4 stands at the very foundation of all Orthodox sacramental theology. The manna given by God is not simply a prophetic image pointing forward with no inherent sacramental value of its own. Instead, the manna, in an incomplete yet prophetic way, actually embodies the reality of Christ himself. The same is true of the rock. Moreover, the mutual indwelling between type and antitype applies not only on the horizontal plane but also in the vertical perspective as found, for example, in the Gospel of John's bread of life discourse (Jn 6:1-15, 25-59) and the epistle to the Hebrews (9; 12:18-25). The earthly church that we now participate in is seen as a type of the heavenly Jerusalem, yet the heavenly kingdom is also present in the earthly reality of the church. Similarly, our present Eucharistic participation points toward the future messianic banquet

(Rev 19:9) and also participates in that eschatological banquet as a reality made present in the bread and wine of the Eucharistic celebration of the local church. The eschatological kingdom and the eschatological Eucharist are both "fulfilled" in the church but are not yet "consummated" in their full dimensions. That will only take place in the eschaton.

Thus, in 1 Corinthians 10:14-17 Paul develops the participatory elements of the exodus typology of 1 Corinthians 10:2-4 and applies them to the Eucharist: "Therefore, my dear friends, flee from idolatry. I speak to sensible people; judge for yourselves what I say. Is not the cup of thanksgiving for which we give thanks a participation in the blood of Christ? And is not the bread that we break a participation in the body of Christ? Because there is one loaf, we, who are many, are one body, for we all partake of the one loaf."

I will not attempt an exegesis of the "real presence" of Christ in the Eucharist in the writings of Paul, John, or the Synoptic Gospels. Critical scholars such as Joachim Jeremias, Oscar Cullmann, and Louis Bouyer have demonstrated the many images, allusions, and descriptions of the Eucharist throughout the pages of the New Testament. The only point that needs to be made here is that the Orthodox Church has been content to affirm the Eucharistic mystery without explaining it. The exact nature of the real presence of Christ in the Eucharist has never been explained or debated as it was in the Christian West. Nevertheless, it is imperative that we understand that when St. Paul speaks of "unity" here in 1 Corinthians 10:14-17, he is speaking about unity within the "body of Christ" (*sōmatos tou Christou*). This body is expressed both ecclesially and Eucharistically. In this passage, "body of Christ" is probably not primarily Eucharistic but refers mainly to the church, just as it does in 1 Corinthians 11:29 when Paul warns the Corinthians against taking communion "without recognizing the body of the Lord." This most probably means "not being properly concerned for the rest of the members of the church." Yet we would probably be mistaken if we excluded from Paul's thought an inclusive reference to participation in the real presence of Christ in the elements of the Eucharist when he speaks of "the body of Christ" in 1 Corinthians 10:16. There is likely also an allusion to the Eucharist when Paul speaks of "the body of the Lord" in 1 Corinthians 11:29. Nevertheless, Paul continues his thought by affirming that the Eucharist creates the church. It is our means for "participating" (*metechomen*) in the body of Christ (1 Cor 10:17). In 1 Corinthians 10:17 Paul says that because there is "one bread" (*heis artos*), there is "one body" (*heis soma*), for "we all partake [*metexomen*] of the one loaf."[4] Notice that *the bread creates the body*; the body does not create the bread. The one Eucharist creates the one church every time the Corinthians gathered together to partake of it in worship. Constantine Campbell, an evangelical New Testament grammarian, acknowledges this in his exegesis of 1 Corinthians 10:16-17: "It seems that partaking in the 'bread' that is Christ's body actually *produces* the body. That is, believers constitute the *one body* by sharing in that *one bread*; stated otherwise, by partaking in the body of Christ, believers become part of the body."[5] This means there is *no division* in the Eucharistic bread. The Eucharist gives a theological identity to the unity of the church. It is clear that Paul is talking about one universal Eucharistic bread and not many breads. Those who partake of the Eucharist in Corinth (or Philippi, Galatia, Ephesus, or any other location) are all participating not in different Eucharistic loaves that somehow symbolize Christ's body; they are participating in that one body which is communicated to us through the very substance of the bread. There is one body and one loaf given in each local church. This unity between the local church and the Eucharist forms the very foundation of the *one faith* of the Orthodox Church that is commonly shared in each local Eucharistic community throughout the world today, whether in Antioch, Constantinople, Moscow, or Warrenville, Illinois. Such is the Eucharistic ecclesiology of the apostle Paul given in the mid-50s when 1 Corinthians was penned. As we will see, the continuity of this apostolic faith was passed on unchanged in the life of the post-apostolic churches as manifested by Ignatius of Antioch.

St. Ignatius of Antioch. Writing to the Smyrneans around AD 107, Ignatius reflects a continuation of the Pauline vision by affirming that church unity is grounded in the Eucharist. He further states that the Eucharist is headed by the bishop, who is an image of Christ and God:

> Avoid divisions as the beginning of evils. All of you follow the bishop as Jesus Christ followed the Father. . . . Let no one do anything that pertains to the church apart from the bishop. Let that be considered a valid Eucharist over which the bishop presides, or one whom he has delegated. Wherever the bishop appears, there let the people be, just as wherever Christ Jesus may be, there is the catholic church.[6]

---

[4]Elsewhere in Paul, all Christian unity (whether Eucharistic or ecclesial) is grounded in the "unity of the Spirit." All the faithful hold in common "one Lord, one faith, one baptism" (Eph 4:5).

[5]Constantine Campbell, *Paul and Union with Christ* (Grand Rapids: Zondervan, 2012), 271 (emphasis his).

[6]Ignatius of Antioch, *Epistle to the Smyrneans* 3. Also in *Epistle to the Magnesians* 6.1 and *Epistle to the Philadelphians* 4. Adolf von Harnack and other scholars have claimed that Ignatius was the inventor

The term "catholic" (*katholikos*) is not a reference to the modern Roman Catholic Church. In Ignatius, it means "according to the whole, that which is complete, full and lacking in nothing." The term is used in a qualitative sense, not a quantitative one. This catholicity or fullness is rooted in every local church that is in communion with its local bishop. The connection between the bishop and the catholic church in Ignatius and other early Christian writers (e.g., 1 Clement 34:6-7) is grounded in the Eucharistic celebration of each local church (*epi to auto*) in its worship. There is no elaborate explanation of what we today call Eucharistic ecclesiology in Ignatius, but Ignatius clearly builds his understanding of the church around that concept. The unity of the local church and its oneness in the sacrament are expressed by the congregation's communion with its local bishop. But then each local parish must also be in communion with other local parishes, whether they be in Alexandria, Jerusalem, or elsewhere. These "structures of unity" are expressed when each bishop from each local community is in communion with other bishops and their local communities. That is why it is important for each member of the local church to be in communion with his or her bishop. The structures of unity

---

or promoter of the office of one bishop over one church (the "monepiscopate" or "monarchical episcopate" as it is called—an unfortunate title since it speaks more of dominance than servanthood). If correct, we have a major innovation in church government that is different from what we find in the New Testament and illustrates what New Testament scholars have called "early catholicism" (German: *Frühkatholizismus*). Thomas Robinson, however, explains why the charge that Ignatius was innovating with the office of bishop cannot be sustained. (1) Ignatius shows no awareness of a need to explain his use of the term *bishop*. The churches he addresses in Asia Minor understood him because the office had already been established. (2) Ignatius's amanuensis (secretary), Burrhus, was a leader of the church at Ephesus. Nothing in Ignatius's letters suggests an awareness of the need to clarify the term *bishop*. (3) Ignatius identifies several people from the five churches of Asia by name and rank as "bishop, presbyter or deacon." He does not appoint them as bishops but recognizes them as already existing. If he were appointing them as bishops, instead of recognizing them as already existing, he would have needed to say more to this effect. Ignatius is thus defining the nature of the church, not instituting the office of bishop (Thomas Robinson, *Ignatius of Antioch and the Parting of the Ways* [Peabody, MA: Hendrickson, 2009], 99-102). I would add two further observations to Robinson's views: (1) There is no evidence of any outcry against the so-called monarchical episcopate in the second century. If it was new and innovative, one would have expected to see at least some opposition to it, but we have no evidence of that. (2) It is likely that the office of bishop was already inherent in the primitive Eucharistic ecclesiology that we find present in the church of Jerusalem led by Peter in fulfillment of the words of Jesus (Mt 16:18; Lk 22:32; Jn 12:15-17). The one Eucharist that was presided over by the one master was taken over by Peter, who served as an image of the Lord at the Last Supper. This organizational pattern of the Jerusalem church may have become a model for other local churches founded by the apostles. It is true that there was no uniform pattern of church government in the New Testament, and gaps do exist in our knowledge of how the monarchical episcopate developed. However, the model of Peter presiding over the Eucharist in the Jerusalem church, along with the trajectory we see developing toward the monarchical episcopate in the pastoral epistles, leads to the natural expression of one bishop over each church as found in Ignatius by the early second century.

are preserved when a new bishop of a neighboring community is ordained. According to Hippolytus, *Apostolic Tradition* 2, and later ecclesiastical canons, a new bishop must be ordained by at least two or three neighboring bishops of the same faith as a sign of the ordained bishop's and community's continuity with the apostolic tradition. Over the centuries, the Eastern Orthodox Churches have retained this ancient approach to unity. It is but one example of how the church has preserved a consistent and continuous tradition of faith that has been passed down from apostolic times.

For Orthodoxy, catholicity is manifested in each local church, which implies both universality and particularity. The catholic church resides in each local community. For example, Holy Transfiguration Antiochian Orthodox Church in Warrenville, Illinois, to which I belong, becomes "the" universal church in all the fullness of its Eucharistic celebration every bit as much as the Patriarch of Antioch's church in Damascus, Syria. The emphasis in this ecclesiology is placed upon unity in Christ, who is the one who unites all of these local communities into his one resurrected and glorified body. Consequently, it is through our communion in Christ's body and blood that ecclesial oneness is sustained. Ignatius describes the Eucharistic unity of this communion of local churches when he says: "Be careful therefore to use one Eucharist so that whatever you do it may be according to God. For there is one flesh of our Lord Jesus Christ, and one cup for union with his blood, one altar, as there is one bishop with the presbytery and the deacons my fellow servants."[7]

In Eucharistic ecclesiology, apostolic succession belongs to the entire *community* of each local church headed by their own bishops, and not to the bishops alone. Moreover, bishops are not "successors to the apostles" in a one-to-one correspondence, since the original apostles were eyewitnesses to the resurrection and performed itinerant ministries rather than local ones. Bishops are apostolic successors only to the extent that they transmit and safeguard the original apostolic deposit in the context of their local communities, and to the extent that their ordinations occur within the Eucharistic context of a local apostolic church. Apostolic succession, therefore, is not defined in individualistic terms, or simply as a succession of persons, but as a succession of *communities* to which the individual bishops belong in unity and communion with one another. Each Eucharistic community continues in historical succession and maintains an ongoing connection to

---

[7] *Epistle to the Smyrneans* 8; *Epistle to the Ephesians* 20:2.

other communities of the same faith, thus safeguarding continuity with the church's apostolic origins, theology, and lifestyle. Such are the ecclesial structures and perspectives that enable communion among the local Orthodox churches throughout the world today.

The Eucharist and church councils. A brief word is in order concerning the relation of the Eucharist to the conciliar structures of church unity. Here we must guard against separating the dogmatic conclusions of the early ecumenical councils (AD 325–787; other councils could be added) and the visible, historic churches that produced them. The great tradition, in other words, must not be separated from the great church to which it belongs. It is vital to understand the ecclesiology that lies behind the gathering of bishops in the ecumenical councils.[8] We see very clearly that there was a *pre-existing, sacramental unity* among local churches that was already in place by the time the Councils were convened even though dogmatic disagreements and schisms were alive and well. Through the power and guidance of the Holy Spirit, the bishops and churches were sufficiently united in sacramental unity to enable them to gather for a common confession of faith. Of major concern to the Councils was the preservation of Eucharistic communion between the local churches. Those who opposed conciliar decisions broke communion with the sacramental communities that were united by a commonly shared Eucharist.[9] Although most evangelical communities today share in the early church's affirmations of the Nicene Creed and Chalcedonian Definition of faith, they are historically and sacramentally disconnected from the Eucharistic communities that originally gathered together under their bishops in council. It is not enough to accept the doctrines explicitly mentioned in the Nicene Creed or Chalcedonian Definition. One must accept the whole catholic faith of the church, as the Nicene Creed itself

---

[8]George Florovsky, "The Authority of the Ancient Councils and the Tradition of the Fathers," in *Bible, Church, Tradition: An Eastern Orthodox View* (Belmont, MA: Notable & Academic Books, 1979), 93-104. Florovsky observes that the ecumenical councils were not to be seen as institutions but as *charismatic* witnesses to the gospel. See John Meyendorff, "What Is an Ecumenical Council?," in *Living Tradition* (Crestwood, NY: St. Vladimir's Seminary Press, 1978), 45-62; and Alexander Schmemann, "Towards a Theology of Councils," in *Church, World, Mission* (Crestwood, NY: St. Vladimir's Seminary Press, 1979), 159-78.

[9]Another sign of the Orthodox Church's recognition of sacramental unity with specific churches is the liturgical use of the diptychs, which developed by the fourth century and continues into modern times. They are called diptychs because they contain two lists of names (the living and the dead) written on two tablets. The lists contain the names of an apostolic succession of local bishops, saints, theologians, and others that would be read aloud by a deacon in church as an expression of the local church's theological and sacramental unity. For a concise summary of Robert Taft's work on the diptychs, see Paul Meyendorff, "Church and Eucharist in the Orthodox Tradition," in *Eucharist and Ecclesiology: Essays in Honor of Dr. Everett Ferguson* (Eugene, OR: Wipf & Stock, 2016), 33-47.

confesses: "and we believe in one, holy, catholic and apostolic church." A breach in this communion manifests theological, sacramental, and ecclesial disunity that must be healed before there can be full Eucharistic sharing. Of course, unity in faith is not to be confused with total agreement in theological opinions. A diversity of opinions on various issues has always existed in Christian history. But it is not always easy to distinguish essential from non-essential matters, as Ulrich Zwingli discovered when Martin Luther broke fellowship with him over the real presence of Christ in the Eucharist during the Marburg Conference in 1529. Even Luther agreed that a common confession of faith was essential for Eucharistic sharing. In his *Smaller Catechism* of 1529, question 305, Luther said, "When asked, 'Who must not be given the sacrament?' Luther replied that it should not be given 'to those of a different confession of faith, since the Lord's Supper is a testimony of the unity of faith.'"[10] That is why Eucharistic division strikes at the very heart of the church's faith. Since Orthodox and evangelical Christians are separated from one another, there cannot be a sharing of communion even occasionally or by so-called Eucharistic hospitality. Whenever the Eucharist is taken, it manifests the particular church and faith to which one belongs. That is why according to Scripture, the church fathers, and the ecclesiastical canons of the Orthodox Church, there can never be intercommunion, but only full communion or no communion.

The Eucharist and the spiritual authority of saints. For the Orthodox, the people of God are a visibly structured community. The visible church and its equally visible communion are expressed through visible Eucharistic fellowship and church leadership. Sacramental structures of communion are essential to unity in the faith as taught by Paul, Ignatius of Antioch, and Irenaeus in his refutation of the Gnostics (*Against Heresies* 3). Also, there has always existed the paradox of a simultaneous existence of both sacramental and charismatic leadership. There is a formal absence of clericalism and authoritarian concepts of the church in the Eastern Orthodox tradition, though in practice abuses of authority have undoubtedly occurred. That is why an appeal to the authority of bishops in the Eucharistic ecclesiology of the church is a proper but inadequate criterion by itself for discerning the true boundaries of the church. One must also consider an internal tension that exists within the church from time to time between the institutional life of the clergy and the authority of the Holy Spirit working through the lives of saints. For example, St. Symeon the New Theologian (AD 949–1022), perhaps the

---

[10]Quoted in an appendix of primary sources in John H. Armstrong, *Understanding Four Views on the Lord's Supper* (Grand Rapids: Zondervan, 2007), 166.

greatest of the Byzantine mystics, seems to formally deny the authority of the clergy in his opposition to bishop Stephen of Nicomedia when he condemned Symeon for elevating a personal experience of God over the administrative hierarchy of the church. Symeon preached that a conscious experience of God's grace in the heart was an essential requirement for all Christians, including bishops, in order for there to be authentic spiritual leadership in the church. A "baptism in the Holy Spirit," as he called it, was needed, which resulted in a "new birth" that was grounded in the sacrament of water baptism and nourished by the Eucharist. Any bishop who was not "consciously aware" of the Holy Spirit in his life was not a true bishop, but a man-made one. The life of St. Symeon demonstrates that there exists in the church spiritual leadership whereby all those who have experienced the Holy Spirit consciously are the true spiritual witnesses of the church. "Do not say, 'It is impossible to receive the Holy Spirit'; . . . 'Do not say, then, that one can possess Him without knowing it.' . . . This is a thing never impossible, my friends, but on the contrary altogether possible for those who so wish." Again: "Do not try to be a mediator on behalf of others until you have yourself been filled with the Holy Spirit, until you have come to know and to win the friendship of the King of all with conscious awareness in your soul."[11]

Father John Meyendorff explains that neither bishops nor charismatic saints were allowed to monopolize the spiritual and doctrinal leadership of the church, but both coexist together:

> The institutional and sacramental authority of the bishops and the spiritual authority of the saints coexist in the catholic Church, and the tensions which occasionally arise between them cannot justify the suppression of either one. The authority of the Church does not suppress the authority of the Spirit, and the spiritual leaders understand their leadership only in the context of the sacramental communion of the Church.[12]

There are important implications of this Spirit-ecclesiology for advancing Orthodox-evangelical unity in the sacraments. First, a common experience of the Holy Spirit is a bond that unites all true believers. Those Orthodox and evangelicals who have had this experience possess an innate recognition of the Spirit in the life

---

[11]"Hymn 27," in *Symeon the New Theologian: The Discourses*, trans. C. J. DeCatanzaro (Mahwah, NJ: Paulist Press, 1980); "Letter 1," in *The Epistles of St. Symeon the New Theologian*, trans. H. J. M. Turner (Mahwah, NJ: Paulist Press, 2009).

[12]John Meyendorff, *The Byzantine Legacy in the Orthodox Church* (Crestwood, NY: St. Vladimir's Seminary Press, 1982), 213.

of each other. A conscious experience of God in the heart may take place in the form of a sudden, dramatic conversion or a slow, gradual awareness. A conscious awareness of the Lord's presence may manifest itself in the sense which John Wesley called a "personal assurance" of salvation, a charismatic or Pentecostal experience of the Holy Spirit flooding the soul, or a quiet, conscious awareness of God's presence in the heart as a result of gradual spiritual growth over time. Regardless of the manner, the result is the same: a conscious awareness of the indwelling Holy Spirit is a precious bond of unity between Orthodox and evangelical Christians. A commonly shared experience of the Holy Spirit is a major link that binds Orthodox and evangelicals together and provides a solid foundation on which to work towards Eucharistic unity.

For the Orthodox, the normal context in which the Holy Spirit is given to a new believer is the rites surrounding baptism (baptism, chrismation, and communion being a three-part act of a single rite of initiation).[13] When an evangelical wishes to join the Orthodox Church, and an Orthodox priest recognizes as valid his or her previous baptism that was performed in the name of the Trinity, the church is recognizing that person as already belonging to Christ even before being admitted formally to the church.[14] Simply stated, if a person is "in Christ," they can be nowhere else but "in the church." Why, then, should not all evangelicals who have been baptized the same way be allowed to take Communion in the Orthodox Church and vice versa? Is not a common baptism proof of an already existing unity?[15] To that, one may ask, Baptism into which church? To say that we are all baptized into the one invisible body of Christ is not enough for sharing communion,

---

[13]However, the mainstream of the Orthodox catholic tradition recognizes the freedom of the Spirit in bestowing new life and that God is not limited to a sacramental box. He may give the Holy Spirit before, during, or after baptism as testified to in the book of Acts as well as in the diverse liturgical practices of the early church. It is a well-known fact that during the days of John Chrysostom in the fourth century, the church of Antioch did not practice anointing with oil (i.e., chrismation) after baptism. It was done before baptism was administered. So the connection between baptism and the Holy Spirit was essentially one sacramental act regardless of whether anointing with oil was done before or after baptism.

[14]See the qualifications for baptism in Bradley Nassif, "The Evangelical Theology of the Eastern Orthodox Church," in *Three Views on Eastern Orthodoxy and Evangelicalism*, ed. James Stamoolis (Grand Rapids: Zondervan, 2004), 75-81.

[15]Canon 95 of the Sixth Ecumenical Council (Quinisext or Trullo in AD 680/1), and Canon 7 of the Seventh Ecumenical council (AD 787) are the classic ecclesiastical canons that recognize the effectiveness of irregular baptisms performed by those outside the canonical boundaries of the church. Relevant also to this essay is the BEM (Baptism, Eucharist, and Ministry) document *One Baptism: Towards Mutual Recognition (A Study Text)*, Faith and Order Paper No. 210 (Geneva: World Council of Churches, 2011). BEM is one of the most significant statements the Faith and Order Commission of the World Council of Churches has produced. A number of leading Orthodox theologians were

for the church does not exist solely as an invisible community of believers that transcends time and space. Rather, it is visibly manifested as a concrete local church. One cannot be baptized into the body of Christ without belonging to a local church. Yet that is the very problem we face because our local churches are visibly separated from one another. The same holds true for the Eucharist. It is offered in local churches that are visibly divided. Spiritual unity without visible and theological unity is not sufficient grounds for Eucharistic sharing.

THE GOSPEL WE SHARE AND THE UNITY WE SEEK

As shown above, the main concern of Orthodox ecclesiology is to ground the nature or being of the church in the Eucharist. Eucharistic ecclesiology, however, has not been without weaknesses in the manner of its presentation. An ecclesiology that is based almost exclusively on the Eucharist is clearly missing something. Attempts have been made, therefore, to counterbalance Eucharistic ecclesiology with baptismal ecclesiology.[16] Such correctives are warranted but do not seem to go far enough. There remains a more fundamental deficiency in the way the Orthodox have presented both Eucharistic and baptismal ecclesiology. That deficiency neglects or underestimates *the centrality of the gospel* in baptism and the Eucharist. Modern ecclesiology, like modern church practice, has minimized or simply taken for granted the centrality of the gospel in the life of the church, especially its sacraments. This is no small matter because St. Paul considered the gospel to be of "first importance" in the church (1 Cor 15:1-4). I have demonstrated elsewhere how the Christian gospel occupies a central place in the Eastern Orthodox tradition. It permeates the church's theology, spirituality, and worship.[17] Far greater weight must be given to the gospel as the basis and precondition for baptism and the Eucharist. Perhaps we can

---

involved in its construction. See *Orthodox Perspectives on BEM*, ed. N. M. Vaporis (Brookline, MA: Holy Cross Orthodox Press, 1985); and *Greek Orthodox Theological Review* 30, no. 2 (1985).

[16]Maximos Aghiorgoussis, "Some Preliminary Notions of 'Baptismal Ecclesiology': Baptism and Eucharist, Constitutive of the Church as Communion," in *In the Image of God* (Brookline, MA: Holy Cross Orthodox Press, 1999), 75-113; John Erickson, "The Local Churches and Catholicity: An Orthodox Perspective," *The Jurist* 52 (1992): 505; Paul Meyendorff, "Towards Baptismal Ecclesiology," in *Liturgies in East and West: Ecumenical Relevance of Early Liturgical Development*, vol. 6, ed. Hans-Jurgen Fuelner (Zurich: Lit Verlag, 2013), 287: Stanley Harakas, "The Local Church: An Orthodox Perspective," *Ecumenical Review* 29 (1977): 141-53. Professor Serge Verhovskoy provides an oral critique of Eucharistic ecclesiology on cassette tape recordings held in St. Vladimir's Seminary Library.

[17]"The Evangelical Theology of the Eastern Orthodox Church," in *Three Views on Eastern Orthodoxy and Evangelicalism*, 25-114; Bradley Nassif, "Orthodox Spirituality: A Quest for Transfigured Humanity," in *Four Views on Christian Spirituality*, ed. Bruce Demarest (Grand Rapids: Zondervan, 2012), 27-55; Bradley Nassif, "The Beauty of Holiness: Deification of the Passions in the Liturgy of

refer to this biblical emphasis as "kerygmatic (gospel) ecclesiology." Father Theodore Stylianopoulos, a prominent Orthodox New Testament scholar, avers, "At the core of the Orthodox tradition, whether we turn to the Eucharist or the lives of the great saints, the same truth has primacy, namely, Christ and the Gospel. . . . The challenge of rediscovering the centrality of the Gospel, as well as of energizing the evangelical ethos deeply enshrined in the Orthodox tradition [is our highest task]."[18] Notice that the gospel is not absent from the Orthodox Church. On the contrary, it is everywhere present. What is missing in the church today is the primacy of the gospel and the proclamation of it in every life-giving action of the church. The failure of Orthodox scholars and pastors to give the gospel its rightful place in their theological writings and pastoral ministries has, by default, minimized the prospects of Christian unity as well as spiritual renewal within the Orthodox Church itself. Ecumenically, this means we Orthodox have often inadvertently contributed to our disunity with evangelicals because we have not given sufficient attention to the role of the gospel in the church's theology, worship, and spiritual life even though it is fully and formally present in the liturgical services, the writings of the church fathers, and icons, hymns, and dogmas. A recovery of the primacy of Christ and the gospel will joyfully lead us to affirm and support evangelical communities that do likewise. Naturally, a critical question arises concerning the extent to which Orthodox and evangelicals share the same gospel. David Bebbington, the British authority on evangelicalism, lists four identity markers that unite all evangelicals: an emphasis on the life, death, and resurrection of Jesus Christ as God's provision for the forgiveness of sins; the Bible as the inspired Word of God; the need for all men and women to commit their lives to Christ in repentance and faith; and missionary outreach to non-Christians. Those beliefs alone, however, do not make an evangelical; rather, what makes the members of this movement "evangelical" is the particular *emphases* given to them. In the end, evangelicalism is largely a set of emphases that is shared across denominational boundaries. While Orthodoxy shares these same principles of the gospel, the church emphasizes and develops them in ways that are in fact quite different than evangelicals—theologically, liturgically, spiritually, and missiologically. "The

---

St. John Chrysostom," in *The Spirit, the Affections, and the Christian Tradition*, ed. Dale M. Coulter and Amos Yong (Notre Dame, IN: University of Notre Dame Press, 2016), 65-86.

[18]Theodore G. Stylianopoulos, *The Way of Christ: Gospel, Spiritual Life and Renewal in Orthodoxy* (Brookline, MA: Holy Cross Orthodox Press, 2002), 49. See also Theodore G. Stylianopoulos, "Fostering an Evangelical Ethos," in *The Apostolic Gospel* (Brookline, MA: Holy Cross Orthodox Press, 2015), 87-94; and "The Gospel as the Basis of Unity," in *The Making of the New Testament* (Brookline, MA: Holy Cross Orthodox Press, 2014), 45-60.

Orthodox Church has comprehended the larger cosmic and ecclesial consequences of that commonly shared faith in a way evangelicalism has not. Orthodoxy embraces all the principles of the gospel that evangelicals hold but transcends them in the outworking of their implications."[19] Nevertheless, Orthodox and evangelicals should be able to work together in a limited way in the area of missions and evangelism. Perhaps the best model for that is an often forgotten one that Billy Graham called "cooperative evangelism." Graham successfully used cooperative evangelism in his evangelistic campaigns with the Russian Orthodox and Romanian Orthodox churches many years ago. High-ranking Orthodox patriarchs and bishops publicly supported Billy Graham's outreach in those countries on the condition that all Orthodox people who came forward to dedicate their lives to Christ under Graham's preaching would be directed back to an Orthodox Church for follow-up. Converts who might have come from an evangelical background would likewise be directed to a Bible-believing evangelical church for discipleship. The success of this model is that it promotes genuine evangelism that is church based while avoiding the problem of proselytism (i.e., sheep stealing, or leading others away from their own churches to join another).[20]

Evangelism raises the all-important question, What is the church here for? Kallistos Ware has answered,

> The Church is here to preach the Gospel of Christ, to announce the good news of the Son of God, crucified and risen. Such an answer is true but incomplete. For our task as Christians is more than to preach and to announce; we are here not merely to *say* but to *do*. To do what? "The tradition which I handed on to you came to me from the Lord himself: that the Lord Jesus, on the night of his arrest, took bread and, after giving thanks to God, broke it and said: 'This is my body, which is for you; do this as a memorial of me'" (1 Cor 11:23-24).[21]

As stated at the beginning of this essay, for the Orthodox there can be no reunion among Christians until there is first a full agreement in faith. That plea for theological integrity is one of the most valuable contributions the Orthodox have

---

[19]Nassif, "Evangelical Theology of the Eastern Orthodox Church," 83.

[20]Carl Braaten, a Lutheran theologian, writes, "The whole gospel of God includes both Christ and the church. The church is part of the gospel because Christ is the head of the church and the church is the body of Christ. The head and body belong together, forming the whole Christ" ("The Church Is Part of the Gospel," in *Evangelicals and Nicene Faith: Reclaiming the Apostolic Witness*, ed. Timothy George [Grand Rapids: Baker Academic, 2011], 95).

[21]Kallistos Ware, "Church and Eucharist, Communion and Intercommunion," *Sobornost* 7, no. 7 (1978): 551; Thomas Hopko, "Catholicity and Ecumenism," in *All the Fullness of God* (Crestwood, NY: St. Vladimir's Seminary Press, 1982), 98-102.

made to ecumenical dialogue because it reminds us that we are not really one church. How, then, can we take communion together if we believe so differently about such things as the real presence of Christ in the Eucharist? Or that the Eucharist creates one visible, local church headed by bishops in apostolic succession? Or that your local evangelical church does not share the same faith as my bishop? Or that I cannot honestly recognize the Pope of Rome as the chief bishop? To take communion together would pretend that Christianity has already been united when we know very well it has not. It is not enough to reply that the Eucharist is Christ's and does not belong to us or the bishop, because the Eucharist is bound to the whole content of the faith and visible structure of the church. Hence, "These three forms of unity—oneness of Eucharistic communion, dogmatic oneness, oneness round the bishop—are complementary and interdependent, and each loses its true meaning if divorced from the other two."[22]

A WAY FORWARD

Having explained above some of the defining characteristics of Eucharistic ecclesiology, it is my hope that this exposition of the Orthodox faith will help evangelicals to better understand the perspective from which the Orthodox Church experiences the Eucharist. How, then, might Orthodox and evangelicals move forward in our common quest for Eucharistic unity? Rather than drawing up a list of doctrines we must all agree on before taking communion together, I suggest a more fruitful and catholic way forward is to agree on a common path by which together we can discern the fullness of Christian unity. That path returns us to the first millennium of Christian history, a time in which the church was most united. The first thousand years of Christian history will provide the standards by which a common faith may be discovered—a time when the church was essentially undivided, with all the qualifications that entails. It was an era before Eastern and Western Christianity split in the eleventh century, and Catholicism and Protestantism divorced in the sixteenth-century Reformation. In the first millennium, true Christian identity was an essential concern to the "one, holy, catholic and apostolic church." However we end up interpreting the events of the first thousand years of church history, authentic Christianity involved diversity as well as continuity with the apostolic witness as given in the canonical Scriptures, the dogmas and disciplinary canons of local and ecumenical councils, and the consensual teachings, worship,

---

[22]Ware, "Church and Eucharist," 555. Credit belongs to Ware for much of this paragraph.

and spiritual experience of the church fathers and saints. The Christian way of life was a mosaic of integrated doctrine, worship, ethics, and spiritual life. It was more akin to an icon than a *summa theologica*.

A precedent for returning to the past for contemporary guidance was set by the examples of the late Robert Webber and Thomas Oden, who invited their evangelical family members to recapture their "common roots" by returning to the early centuries of Christian history. Long before Webber and Oden made their pleas, Father George Florovsky had called Protestants in the ecumenical movement to "return to the Fathers." Florovsky's "neo-patristic synthesis" meant not simply quoting the Fathers' sentences or listing their doctrines but acquiring their whole mindset (*phonema*). Florovsky also reminded us that the study of history requires the intellectual virtues of patience and humility. We must listen attentively to the past and be willing to reconsider our own views in light of new information. Our study of the undivided church today is vital, therefore, not only for the task of restoring lost unity but also for the church's witness to "one bread, one body, one faith."

7

CHRIST THE
URSAKRAMENT

KATHERINE SONDEREGGER

IN ONE OF THE MOST ASTONISHING PASSAGES in an astonishing letter—in truth one of the most astonishing passages in all Holy Scripture—the apostle Paul tells the church in Corinth that "God made Christ, who knew no sin, to be sin for us, that we might become, in him, the righteousness of God" (2 Cor 5:21). Now, I believe that a full Christian lifetime could be spent in reflection and deep prayer on this verse; I don't pretend here to do justice to it as a wellspring of Christian confession about the lordship and saving work of Jesus Christ. But I do think that we may well learn from the apostle Paul here a lesson and touchstone for proper teaching about Christian sacraments—and in those sacraments, the deeper unity of the church of God. This verse, and the daring exchange it teaches—sinless for sin, the righteous one for the unrighteous—can guide and quicken our intellect as we turn it, unveiled, toward the glory found in the face of Jesus Christ. As the sinless one become sin, Christ is the primal sacrament.

Perhaps a word first about this odd term, *Ursakrament* in German, or "primordial sacrament" in English, would be helpful here. Like many of its kin, this term of art arose in the midst of perplexity and debate within the church and between the church and the world. How should we understand the relation between Christ and the sacraments of the Christian faith? That is the foundational question lying at the heart of *Ursakrament*. Now, no one needs to be told that a seemingly innocent question of this sort is far from simple or innocent! We might even consider it a kind of *casus belli*, sounded from the far battlegrounds of the sixteenth century. In this anniversary year of the Reformation, the *Lutherjahr*, it is proper for us to remember the ecumenical gift but also the ecumenical danger and caustic

power of this question about the relation of Christ to his sacraments: it is as mighty as a two-edged sword. (But even here, we should say, God works for our good: "From Conflict to Communion," a statement issued jointly by the Lutheran World Federation and the Pontifical Council for Promoting Christian Unity, will guide the *Lutherjahr* in its world-wide commemoration; it is an ecumenical achievement.)[1] Still, we must say that the sacraments of the church are famously the source of our deepest unity and of our deepest divisions. "Visible unity," the lofty goal of the faith and order movement, encompasses a dream for shared word and table, a true *communicatio in sacris*. As is painfully clear, sacramental worship in common is not yet the gift or practice of Christ's one, holy, catholic, and apostolic church. In this sense, the great ecumenist Geoffrey Wainwright says, all our worship, doctrine, and ecumenical life together is "pre-conciliar."[2] We all stand on Mount Nebo here, spying that land of unity, the fertile hills and vineyards of Canaan, but we do not yet cross over or inhabit that promised land.

The Jesuit systematician Karl Rahner once mused that the decrees and doctrines and practices of the divided churches in the West may be more polarizing, alienating, and jarring in the *post*-Reformation era than in the long centuries leading up to the break.[3] We are more bitterly atomized and at odds now than we were in Luther's day: that is Rahner's speculation. Luther himself was born and catechized in a united Latin church; Calvin, a scant generation later, came of age in a ruptured one. Luther's anguished treatise "On the Babylonian Captivity of the Church" is unthinkable without Christendom; Calvin's majestic *Institutes* is unthinkable without division. A divided church was a fact by the 1550s, and even if reluctantly, Calvin seemed to say, we must bow down to it all the same. And perhaps, if Rahner's reflections are accurate, we must bow still lower today. After a generation of great ecumenical progress—my own beloved Episcopal Church is now in full communion with the Evangelical Lutheran Church of America, a rich harvest of these fertile years—some say that we have entered an "ecumenical winter." It seems that we live now in the world of Calvin, not Luther, a world of unrepentant disunity under the chastening and directing hand of the *providentia Dei*. So, I do not want

---

[1] *From Conflict to Communion: Lutheran-Catholic Common Commemoration of the Reformation in 2017: A Report of the Lutheran-Roman Catholic Commission on Unity* (Leipzig: Evangelische Verlaganstalt, 2013).

[2] Geoffrey Wainwright, *Doxology: The Praise of God in Worship, Doctrine, and Life* (New York: Oxford University Press, 1980), 315.

[3] For one celebrated discussion, see Karl Rahner, *Foundations of Christian Faith*, trans. W. V. Dych (New York: Crossroads, 1978), 346-69.

to paper over a deep divide here or avert my eyes from a wound that must be dressed and healed—that is not how Christians confess the truth in love.

But such a somber warning can never be the whole story for a Christian! Far from it, for we receive this ministry from our good Lord, so we do not lose heart. Indeed, I want to advance what the ecumenical theologian Mitzi Budde calls the "rich ecumenical harvest" of working papers, joint agreements, and scholarly monographs of the present day—the feast made up of the World Council of Churches' paper "The Church: Toward a Common Vision"; the "Declaration on the Way: Church, Ministry and Eucharist" issued by the US Catholic Bishops and Evangelical Lutheran Church of America; and "Christian Witness in a Multi-Religious World," a statement published by the World Council, the Pontifical Council for Interreligious Dialogue, and the World Evangelical Alliance.[4] A rich harvest, indeed! So, in that spirit of hope and concord, I want to place this matter of Christ's ordaining of the sacraments in a larger room, a larger nave, one that is oriented toward visible unity and hopes in it. Let us turn toward the true light who is Christ breaking over our darkened sanctuaries, illuminating them with his mysterious and glorious oneness. Christ, as the primordial sacrament, just *is* this land of peace, and he calls us, even now, all the more so now, to visible unity. So I want to offer the notion of Christ as *Ursakrament* as grounds for common life together under this saving person and work, and as grounds for hoping to one day enter into the true freedom of *communicatio in sacris*. I want to offer, that is, an extended meditation on Paul's rich evocation of the mystery who is Christ: "I want hearts to be encouraged and united in love," Paul writes, "so that they may have all the riches of assured understanding and have the knowledge of God's mystery, that is, Christ Himself, in whom are hidden all the treasures of wisdom and knowledge" (Col 2:2-3). Christ is mystery, *sacramentum*, wisdom itself.

Now, no discussion of the term *Ursakrament* could be complete without a word of thanks for the remarkable work of the distinguished Flemish theologian Edward Schillebeeckx. "Primal sacrament" finds its first home in the world of Roman Catholic theology and worship. Like Rahner, Schillebeeckx served as

---

[4] *The Church: Towards a Common Vision*, Faith and Order Paper No. 214 (Geneva: World Council of Churches, 2013); *Declaration on the Way: Church, Ministry and Eucharist*, Bishops' Committee for Ecumenical and Interreligious Affairs, United States Conference of Catholic Bishops and the Evangelical Lutheran Church in America, 2015; *Christian Witness in a Multi-Religious World: Recommendations for Conduct*, Pontifical Council for Interreligious Dialogue of the Holy See, World Council of Churches' Programme on Interreligious Dialogue and Cooperation, and the World Evangelical Alliance, 2011.

peritus, theological advisor, to the assembled bishops at the Second Vatican Council; like Rahner again, he found deep kinship with the liturgical renewal movement we associate with Maria Laach and the *nouvelle théologie*. In his early work, *Christ: The Sacrament of Encounter with God*,[5] Schillebeeckx brought a rich and sophisticated Thomism into the *ressourcement* theology of these liturgical pioneers, sharing with them the hallmarks of personalism, existentialism, and a good helping of the Christ mysticism that washed through these pre-war movements. Here is Schillebeeckx on Christ as *Ursakrament*: "Because the saving acts of the man Jesus are performed by a Divine Person, they have a divine power to save, but because this divine power to save appears to us in visible form, the saving activity of Jesus is *sacramental*." And then, a central definition: "For a sacrament is a divine bestowal of salvation in an outwardly perceptible form which makes the bestowal manifest; a bestowal of salvation in historical visibility." A good Dominican, Schillebeeckx makes every word count: this brief section is something like a string of technical insights and terms in the *aggiornamento* of Christology and sacramental theology. He sums up these complex notions in a short definition: "The man Jesus, as the personal visible realization of the divine grace of redemption, is *the* sacrament, the primordial sacrament, because this man, the Son of God himself, is intended by the Father to be in his humanity the only way to the actuality of redemption."[6]

The sacramental reality of Christ is strongly personal and person-forming: "Human encounter with Jesus is the sacrament of the encounter with God, or of the religious life as a theological [we might say 'self-involving' now] attitude of existence towards God."[7] I do not mean by such a short introduction to imply that I have sounded the fathoms of Schillebeeckx's work; this is a beautifully technical and complex retrieval of Thomistic Christology. But I do want to linger here on several elements of this book and this concept central to our task today.

Note that Schillebeeckx anchors his doctrine of the *Ursakrament* in the *person* of Jesus Christ. His theology makes a pronounced emphasis upon the doctrine of incarnation, the event, if we may style it so, of the Word become flesh. Note that opening phrase, pregnant with a Cyrillian Christology: "The saving acts of the man Jesus are performed by a Divine Person, the Son of God." More strong still is

[5]Edward Schillebeeckx, *Christ: The Sacrament of the Encounter with God*, trans. P. Barrett (New York: Sheed and Ward, 1963).
[6]All citations from Schillebeeckx, *Christ*, 15.
[7]Ibid., 15-16.

the note of personal unity in the *encounter* we have with the living Christ: He is "the personal visible realization of the divine grace of redemption, . . . an invitation to a personal encounter with the life-giving God, because personally that man was the Son of God."[8] Or to express this in crisp summary: "The incarnation of the divine life therefore involves bodily aspects."[9] Now this is a central element in the sacramental theology of the entire renewal movement because it ties sacraments not principally to an *action* or *word* of the earthly Jesus but rather to the very reality, the very God-manhood of the incarnate Word. In Schillebeeckx's view, Jesus is not the *instituter* of the Eucharist nor the *commander* of baptism in the first-order or primary sense. Of course, Jesus in his ministry and teaching *does* institute the sacraments, but that is a secondary act, an outworking of Christ's own reality as mystery and sacrament. Schillebeeckx's principal point is this: the Son of God in the flesh simply *is* the sacrament of redemption. Note that strong "is of identity": to teach and confess the doctrine of the incarnation is to lay out before the intellect and before the world the mystery of God us-ward. Or, to speak in the idiom of the sacraments themselves, Jesus Christ is the *presence* of God in this world, the saving *Christus praesens*.

Schillebeeckx makes use of creedal and Pauline language to express the notion of the hypostatic union as sacrament. He says in many variants that Jesus Christ, the man Jesus, is the *visible* form of the invisible God. Perhaps we could think of an analogy here drawn from our own inner lives. The way we express or make visible our inner thoughts, our emotions and dreams, is to *enact* them by word or gesture—a hand that caresses or strikes, a word that consoles or shames. The inner becomes outer, and real to us, as it becomes visible and manifest—or better, becomes *flesh, body*. Anticipating the Lutheran ecumenist Robert Jenson here—perhaps influencing him—Schillebeeckx describes the body as "availability" or "manifestation," the rendering tangible and visible of the inner spiritual life of a human creature.[10] The pronounced *metaphysical* account at work here is unmistakable. The incarnation is the utterance of the eternal Word in *bodiliness*. When we think of Christ as saving, sacramental presence, Schillebeeckx warns, we are not to turn our attention first to miracles, exorcisms, or symbolic or prophetic acts; we are not searching for the founder, of a religion here—not first, not principally.

---

[8]Ibid., 15.

[9]Ibid.

[10]See, for example, Robert Jenson, *Systematic Theology*, vol. 1 (New York: Oxford University Press, 1997), 201-6.

Rather we fundamentally seek and encounter mystery. We stand before the living Son of God made flesh, who is visible in this one human body. All treasures of wisdom and knowledge are laid up in him, this very one.

The natural home for the incarnate sacrament, then, is *actualism,* the act or *event* of Jesus Christ—though that diagnosis may startle at first. With our ears trained to the Chalcedonian master terms of relation—without separation, without division; without confusion, without mixture—we find it nearly irresistible to reach for stable, conceptual, and non-historical categories as analytic aids. But this, modernists such as the Russian theologian Sergei Bulgakov warn, is to use the mechanical and the inert as guides to the living, the spiritual, and the personal. Not so should we think of Christ, the living one![11] Schillebeeckx shares with his near contemporary, Karl Barth, the conviction that Chalcedonian Christology can hardly be captured by a static and abstract depiction of natures in relation.[12] Rather, the doctrine of the incarnation is principally and truly a *history,* an *event* in which the downward rush of the divine Son meets the prayer, obedience, and upward praise of the human life, the *eschatos Adam,* fully open to God. Schillebeeckx says, "The redeeming mercy of God himself [comes] to meet us from a human heart. But as well as this movement down from above, . . . there is in the man Jesus also a movement up from below . . . in a word, the man Jesus' love of God."[13] In a luminous summary, he sets out an actualist Christology: "This incarnation of God the Son is a reality which grows." That's a lovely phrase, isn't it? It is dynamic to its very core. "It is not complete in a matter of a moment," Schillebeeckx continues; not complete, "for example, at Jesus' conception in Mary's womb or at his birth. The incarnation is not merely a Christmas event. To be man is a process of becoming man; Jesus' manhood grew throughout his earthly life, finding its completion in the supreme moment of the incarnation, his death, resurrection and exaltation. Only then is the incarnation fulfilled to the very end."[14] These are jewel-like phrases—intense, compact, saturated. What we are to see here is the primal category of *encounter,* the fundamental memory of the church as it is caught up in the exchange of prayer and blessing that is the grace of the man Jesus—the event he simply *is.* Now this means that the central categories of Christian thought are rendered mobile and vital. They unfold much as a human life does; their *nature* is to

---

[11]See Bulgakov's withering assessment of (some) patristic metaphysics in *Lamb of God,* trans. B. Jakim (Grand Rapids: Eerdmans, 2008), 2-19, esp. 10-13.

[12]See the influential opening framework of *Church Dogmatics* IV/1, trans. G. Bromiley and T. F. Torrance (Edinburgh: T&T Clark, 1956), 157-210.

[13]Schillebeeckx, *Christ,* 17-18.

[14]Ibid., 18-19.

develop, expand, and ripen. Such dynamism however is hardly *shapeless*. "Actualism" as a metaphysical term can convey an air of unstructured and undisciplined motion, as if movement alone were sufficient to actualize an objective category. But not so for Schillebeeckx! As with Rahner, Schillebeeckx sees dynamic life in service of a *telos*, a goal that at the end declares what the final truth of the whole is. A life is "finalized" at death—that is, it becomes definite, complete, utterly self-same. It is at rest. This is why for these existential and personalist theologians, Christ's human nature, given and assumed at the annunciation, is fully itself, fully *realized*, at the passion, where the cross declares and defines just who this man is. The resurrection and ascension are vindications of this realized life. That is why these theologians can speak so freely of "the man Jesus" and "the Son of God" without fretting about the unity of Christ's person: there is a way of God with human creatures—the divine way of love—and there is a way of the creature with God, the God-intoxicated life that just is Jesus' humanity. The unity of these ways we call "encounter," and that just is the mystery of Christ. As Paul teaches us, we have died, and our life is hid with Christ in God.

So we need not look for particular incidents in the life of Christ to confirm or express his God-manhood, though to be sure, his life is saturated with it and unthinkable without it. We need not say, here is the divine nature in act, and here the human; here is exaltation and glory, and here lowliness, abasement, and suffering. No, the incarnate person of Christ is one living whole, given temporal extension from Bethlehem to a hill outside the city wall. To borrow a phrase from contemporary philosophy, we might say, *mutatis mutandis*, that Christ's human nature is an "extended simple."[15] In just these ways, we should say, Jesus Christ in his person is the sacrament of God, the mystery and love of God made visible, final, and embodied in our midst.

Now, notice how our discussion of sacraments and their relation to the person of Christ has been altered by such a scheme. Christ is the embodied love of God; to encounter him is to encounter and be drawn by the loving summons who is God; and just this is to receive the saving grace of the redeemer. This is a strongly christocentric account of the sacraments. Note that we do not have a doctrinal *locus*, the person of Christ, and then a second, his sacraments. He is not one person, one incarnate Lord, and *then* the giver of gifts to his people. We are not to distinguish person and work in this way; Schillebeeckx mirrors Barth on this central insight. The sacraments of the church are distinct from Christ, his personal reality,

---

[15]For an illuminating theological application, see Martin Pickup, "The Trinity and Extended Simples," *Faith and Philosophy* 33, no. 3 (2016): 414-40.

in a *notional* way only. We are not to imagine that Christ bestows upon his disciples a separate gift, something like a strong-box willed to an heir, along with the keys to the lock, which the heir opens, uses, explores, and exploits as it pleases the lonely survivor. No, despite the many years and bitter controversies in the divided churches over the sacramental means of grace—and for that matter, the "power of the keys"—the sacramental theologians of the twentieth century did not imagine that sacraments could be cordoned off into a sacred room, a sacristy, under the watchful eye of prelacy of some sort and set far apart from the person and living sovereignty of Jesus Christ. No, this is not the way of God us-ward! Just this is the force of calling him the primal sacrament of God.

In contrast to all that stark divide between person and act, Schillebeeckx lays before us a dynamic unity of Christ with his disciples; so close, indeed, that he can call the church—indeed I believe his view demands this—the "extension of the Incarnation" on earth. In his hands, the sacramental theology of the church, its means of grace and mediation of divine love, is not a distinct treatise or power or faculty; no, it is an ever-deeper reflection upon the mystery of Christ and his sacramental reality as it radiates out over this fallen world. Now some of Schillebeeckx's contemporaries and heirs would be rather wary of such christological or ecclesial exuberance. Herbert Vorgrimler, the former Catholic Bishop of Münster, would demur here; the church, he says, cannot be the continuation of the incarnation; nothing else but Christ alone is that. Karl Rahner distinguishes carefully between the *Ursakrament*, Christ himself, and the church as fundamental sacrament or *Grundsakrament*.[16] And many heirs of the Reformation would be reluctant to so strongly assimilate the church to the person of its Lord, especially those who see in the church and its councils assemblies that "have erred and do err," as the *Thirty-Nine Articles* famously expresses. Indeed, in the recent major document of the World Council of Churches, "The Church: Towards a Common Vision," this disagreement is frankly acknowledged: "Some communities believe that this [distinct holiness] can be suitably expressed by speaking of the 'Church as sacrament,' others do not normally use such language or reject it outright."[17]

Yet we should not overstate this difference. For it is the proud legacy of the Genevan Reform and the Radical Reformation to name the dominical sacraments,

---

[16]See, for example, H. Vorgrimler, *Sacramental Theology*, trans. L. Maloney (Collegeville, MN: Liturgical Press, 1992).

[17]*The Church: Towards a Common Vision*, 15.

Eucharist and baptism, as sacraments of the church and to find Christ present not in the *sacramental elements* but instead in the assembly: the whole people of God standing in grateful encounter before its living Lord, caught up in the Spirit of Christ poured out on the people. No need to pick out a "moment of consecration," a defined mode of presence, a complex account of validity and intention; Christ comes to his faithful, gathered in his holy name, and *manifests himself* as Savior. That is a sacramental theology, a sacramental ecclesiology that could be embraced by a remarkable array of Christians, from some evangelicals and Baptists to many liturgical theologians at work on present-day prayer books and Vorgrimler himself, who spies in the Second Vatican Council a way at last to free sacraments from their captivity to canon law and set them free as the world's blessing.

So we might now ask, How can this rich legacy of Christ as *Ursakrament*, the visible means of grace in the world, guide our ecumenical work today? You will notice that I have concentrated here on *theologians*, not ecclesial statements or bilateral agreements. That is not because I have little interest in the official documents, nor the world-wide, patient work of ecumenical bodies; far from it! In truth I think it will be only through delicate and sophisticated statements approaching consensus—what ecumenical documents now term "convergence"—that final, visible unity under the lordship of Christ will be received and confirmed. But there is a special place, I believe, for close, ecumenical assessment of particular theologians, for it is in their unified vision, and also in the studied assembly of church teaching and reading of Scripture, that the *force* of a doctrine, its contours and sharp edges, can be made plain. Indeed it is my hope that this more extended reflection upon Schillibeeckx will clarify and distinguish the other major doctrines of the church proposed as engines of "convergence" in recent official ecumenical statements. Consider once again the force of Schillebeeckx's claim that Christ in his person is the eternal sacrament, and his community, the church, is the extension of the mystery of salvation.

Here we have a vision of the church that is a creature—if we may style it thus—of the *mysterion*, the presence of Christ to his lost world. This stands in marked contrast to the recent Lutheran-Roman Catholic statement, "Declaration on the Way: Church, Ministry, and Eucharist," a convergence statement that eloquently sums up a half-century of dialogues between the two principle antagonists of the sixteenth-century debates. Here is the principal ecclesial agreement: "Catholics and Lutherans hold in common that the Church on earth is gathered by the proclamation of the gospel of God's saving mercy in Christ, so that the gospel, proclaimed in the Holy Spirit by the apostles, remains the church's normative origin and binding foundation."[18] This captures the *apostolicity* of the church, its essential and enduring relation to the preaching of the apostles. The documents make this explicit: "The primacy of the gospel is a well-known emphasis of the Reformation, expressed by calling the church 'a creature of the Gospel' *creatura Evangelii*. Vatican II manifests as well the conviction that 'the gospel is for all time the source of life for the Church' and its preaching is the 'chief means' of founding the Church. . . . Thus, proclaiming the gospel is a fundamental reality permanently defining the church."[19] The kerygmatic identity of the church is taken to be its *origin*: the church is *founded* by "Christ's apostles proclaim[ing] the gospel of Christ by announcing his saving death and resurrection. When people heard this and accepted it in faith as a message of merciful salvation for themselves, congregations were constituted from Jerusalem as far as Rome and beyond."[20] And this document does not stand alone. The World Council of Churches' statement "The Church: Toward a Common Vision" echoes this primacy of preaching amidst a broader sounding of communion, mission, and service. This disagreement about the origin and character of the church—in sacramental mystery or in apostolic preaching—goes to the heart of the *historical* or *actualist* claims that structure the whole of Schillebeeckx's Christology. It marks a crisp dividing line between the doctrine of the incarnation as the metaphysical *being* of the church and, in contrast, the church's essential reality in the preaching, witness, and martyrdom of the apostolic age.

Just so, the ecclesial unity we seek will be stamped, on one hand, by the originating force of the personal unity of Christ, and, on the other, by the common preaching of the college of the apostles, the faith once delivered to the saints. We might express this distinction, again, in Pauline language: shall we know the church, its sacraments and Lord, *kata sarka*; or shall we know them so no longer? Or, to express this distinction using the language of one final recent ecumenical study, "Who Do We Say We Are? Christian Identity in a Multi-Religious World": "Our primary identity as Christians lies in the fact that we are 'people of the resurrection.'"[21] Is that in truth the origin and proper identity of the church—a creature of the resurrection; or is it, rather, to know Christ and him crucified? Much in the task, hope, and identity of the ecumenical movement turns on these governing texts, distinctions, and confessions!

---

[18] *Declaration on the Way*, 26.
[19] Ibid.
[20] Ibid.
[21] "Who Do We Say We Are? Christian Identity in a Multi-Religious World," *Ecumenical Review* 66, no. 4 (2014).

For Edward Schillebeeckx, the church just *is* the mystery, the *sacramentum* of Christ. It is not that he denies the apostolic kerygma or, even less, the complete paschal mystery of Christ's dying and rising. It is rather that the covenant, the saving mystery, is *complete* in Jesus Christ himself. This is the Anselmian or "objectivist" note in Schillebeeckx's Christology. Were Jesus Christ the only human creature, *per impossibilia*, he would remain the fullness of the church and its saving gifts, for he just is the historical visibility of grace. Like Schleiermacher, Schillibeeckx holds that the disciples, crowds, hungry, and lost are drawn already, in the earthly halo of Christ's life, into the luminous and perfect presence of God. In his flesh he is the light of the world. The cross renders this light unmistakably clear, definite, and searing. But the whole aim of the Christian life is to enter that light, to stand *there*. We are caught up into the love who is God by this earthy, embodied life; he is the living sacrifice, whole and acceptable to God. A seamless garment extends from the incarnate life, definitive and hallowed in its death and rising, to the world drawn to the redeemer, from the beginning to the end of time. The separate sacraments articulate and are borne along by the saving act of Christ's personal unity. The historical, earthly life of Jesus Christ, his fleshiness, glorified in his ascended life, is in just this way the sacramental unity of the whole world.

Not so for the church that is the "creature of the Gospel." A rupture marks the world's history before and after the empty tomb. The resurrection propels the once-terrified disciples out into the Roman empire to the waiting hearts and ears of believers—the nascent church—but also to the bitter opposition and fear that made them martyrs for the faith, the seed-bed of the church. These early witnesses preach the "word of Christ," the saving word *about* him, that Jew and Gentile may be drawn to and in him and his pardon, presence, and renewal. The church is born of that word. The gift of those early assemblies is the written word, the liturgy, the rites, and sacraments that sustain the faithful from age to age. But even as an Abelardian account of Christ's saving work rests upon the distinction between and the movement from Christ to his people, so this kerygmatic account of the church rests upon the distinction between Christ's risen authority and the heralds and shepherds he commissions and commands. Unity here stems upon the coherence, consistency, and faithfulness of the proclaimed word, the ready ear of the preachers and teachers for the Spirit's instruction about Christ. The "witness, worship, and service" of the faithful—the *martyria, leiturgia,* and *diakonia* of the church—must be ever awakened, chastened, and renewed so that the world may see the risen Christ in the sanctified lives of pardoned sinners, the Christians of every land, nation, and tongue. This is the church built upon the prophets and apostles; its sacraments are the rites of those faithful in the apostles' teaching, the breaking of the bread, and the prayers. The church as creature of the gospel proclaims Christ as the answer to sin, the deliverer of a lost and fallen world.

Now, consider the contrast Schillebeeckx's *mysterion* poses. The church born of Christ, the *Ursakrament*, casts the world's struggle with sin in a different light and leads the fallen world to a different remedy. As primal sacrament, Christ enters into the sinful economy of the earth in a strikingly odd and mysterious manner. He is the mystery hid for long ages and generations but now manifested to the saints. Schillebeeckx takes up anew the Thomistic teaching of "natural sacraments" in the peoples of every culture: burdened by sin, they seek expiation, and in their longing for healing and deliverance they are met by the God who wills all to be saved and come to the knowledge of the truth. Even as Israel is given rites of sacrifice and grain offering—sacraments of the old law—so the family of humankind is sheltered by a gift of grace that "by the hand as it were" leads them to the mysterious grace of the unknown God. All this is foretaste and foreshadow of the one who will be the final sacrifice, the one who expiates the sin of the world.

Now I would I like to advance a step beyond Schillebeeckx and invite a Pauline reading of Christ's sacramental reality that Schillibeeckx might well reject. I dare to extend the notion of *Ursakrament*, however, because I believe that in this somber Pauline darkening, the strength of this ecclesiology announces itself. It becomes ground for our greater unity in church and sacrament. In this Pauline key, Christ, the primal sacrament, becomes sin *for us*. We might say that this just is *sacrament* in the full and mystical sense: that the divine exchange who is Christ takes on the world's sin—its bitter loss and denunciation of God; its enmity and greed; its violence and callousness—and makes it his own. He becomes *that*. He, the unblemished victim, becomes the defiled, broken, scattered, and lost. This is his history, the mystery of his life. He is the sacrament of the life for others. He is the *telos* of the world and its longing just because the ancient struggle for the good—and the even more ancient struggle for the wrong—finds its fulfillment in the Son of God assimilating their very suffering into his own marrow. Thus the world is *one*: one history, one longing, one search for deliverance from cruelty and death. But it is a victorious unity too, for Christ is the mystery of this exchange, the righteous for the unrighteous, the sinless for the sinner. Just so we can warrant the Rahnerian and Reformation distinction—a vital one, I say—between Christ as primal sacrament and the church as foundational; even, I would say more, a sinful foundation, even if graciously preserved from fatal error. In this Pauline exchange, the church in its sinful divisions, fragility, faithlessness, worldliness, and, yes, its violence, remains the effective sign of Christ, its mystery and Lord; for even there, at the uttermost edge of the sea, Christ, the sinless one, is manifest as the sin of the world taken up and taken over by good. The church, I would say, is the "creature of the Passion."

Our little sacraments are just this, the creatures of our sinful yet graced lives, grown from the good earth but under the condition of sin. The sacraments receive our sins by the laying on of our hands and are taken up by Christ, who in becoming this sin, redeems, hallows, and makes it his very own body. Even as the holiness code taught the priest to lay the sins of Israel on the head of the animal victim by resting a priestly hand on the victim's head, so the minister and priest of the church lays hands upon the bread, water, and wine that the sins of the church and the world may be laid upon the altar to be assumed by, wed to, and exchanged for the sinless sacrament. His holiness becomes ours, and our defilement becomes his. This is the wonderful exchange, the *commercium admirabile*, and the church that issues from its side is the creature of the incarnation, the creature of the saving mystery of God. The notion of the church as sacrament, drawn deep into the primal mystery who is Christ, is one yet distinct. The church remains visible within the fallen world and partakes of its soil. It is of the earth, and its deep divisions are also a sign of its distinction from its Lord. Yet because he *becomes* sin, he, the unexcelled light, remains one with it—the great eccleisal miracle of grace. We may grow ever closer, one to the other, not because principally and primally we follow the apostles' teaching more faithfully, enter more deeply into Easter life, or give ourselves ever more freely to self-giving love; though these are great goods to be desired! Our convergence stems rather from the sovereign sacramental exchange that is present and patient and almighty in our midst. This is the church's *holiness*; its catholicity and apostolicity do not precede but rather follow from it. Our growing unity, the church's oneness, is the reality of the primal sacrament, the mysterious oneness of Christ manifest to us and for our sake. Even today he becomes sin for us that we may become the righteousness, the perfect peace and unity, of God. We exhibit until the day he comes the holy death of Christ, his body given up for the sake of the world. May the church become ever more one, as Christ is one, and may the saving mystery of his presence be known and adored, here and always, to the ages of ages.

8

VISUAL ECUMENISM

The Coy Communion of Art

MATTHEW J. MILLINER

The first Protestants split from the Latin church
that had, of course, already been in schism with the
Orthodox church for almost five hundred years. In light of
this reality, all Christians must be considered schismatics;
no Christian church is immune from this accusation,
including Catholics and the Orthodox.

RONALD RITTGERS

As long as and to the extent that the
maximum solution must be regarded as a requirement
of truth itself, just so long and to just that extent will
there be no other recourse than simply to strive
to convert one's partner in the debate.

POPE BENEDICT XVI

*The Law is the Word in which God teaches and tells us what we are to do
and not to do, as in the Ten Commandments. Now wherever human nature
is alone, without the grace of God, the Law cannot be kept, because since
Adam's fall in Paradise man is corrupt and has nothing but a wicked desire
to sin. . . . The other Word of God is not Law or commandment, nor does it
require anything of us; but after the first Word, that of the Law, has done this
work and distressful misery and poverty have been produced in the heart,
God comes and offers His lovely, living Word, and promises, pledges, and
obligates Himself to give grace and help, that we may get out of this misery
and that all sins not only be forgiven but also blotted out. . . . See, this divine
promise of His grace and of the forgiveness of sin is properly called Gospel.*

MARTIN LUTHER

ON THE LEFT OF LUCAS CRANACH the Elder's 1529 *Law and Gospel*
panel, threatening expectations steer a helpless streaker to his unwelcome end
(fig. 8.1).[1] The demands made upon him are legitimate, but his future skeleton's
promise of inevitable death and a ram-headed devil—whose stomach is a second
mouth—makes fulfilling his obligations impossible. God is there, of course, but
only in the distance—present via unfulfillable demands. Moses spells them out,
pointing to the letter of the law. His prophetic companions evince shock and
concern at the sinner's shortcomings—not unlike our twenty-first century social
media outrage at every moral failing. Indeed, there are modern versions of the
Mosaic tablets as well: Thou shalt succeed professionally, display unimpeachable
sensitivity to every subset of human culture, exhibit an ideal body fat percentage,
and be the very picture of work-life balance.[2] These too are a species of what Martin
Luther called the law.

---

[1] The law-gospel images referenced throughout this essay (the Gotha, Prague, and Weimar versions
in particular) are readily available online, especially through the extraordinary Lucas Cranach Project. The Gotha (named for its present location) described at the outset can be viewed here: www
.lucascranach.org/DE_SMG_SG676. Images can also be viewed in the video that was the first
version of this chapter: www.youtube.com/watch?v=6yMrGXZdu1k.

[2] For a similar application of Luther's insights, see William McDavid, Ethan Richardson, and David
Zahl, *Law and Gospel: A Theology for Sinners (and Saints)* (Charlottesville, VA: Mockingbird
Ministries, 2015).

Figure 8.1. Lucas Cranach the Elder, *Law and Gospel*, Gotha, 1529

On the right side of Cranach's panel, however, expectation is met by fulfillment. Demands are replaced by declaration. The tree of death that divides the panel blossoms into the tree of life as the law is fulfilled to the jot and tittle on behalf of the sinner. At the very moment of realization that it was done *for him*, a Super Soaker of imputing blood jet streams from Christ's side-wound to seal the transaction, splashing on the sinner's head. The devil and death are detained by the deputized Lamb of God, who neutralizes their power. As Luther put it in the Heidelberg disputation, "The Law says, 'do this' and it is never done; the Gospel says 'believe this' and everything is already done."[3] But, arguably, the paintings and prints of Lucas Cranach the Elder have been as effective at disseminating this message as has the discursive theology of Luther.

The distinction between law and gospel, called the "most important pictorial subject conceived to illustrate Lutheran doctrine,"[4] is the visual center of the evangelical tradition, which has recently enjoyed much positive reassessment.[5] Distinguishing

---

[3]Timothy F. Lull, ed., *Martin Luther's Basic Theological Writings* (Minneapolis: Fortress, 1989), 47.

[4]Timo Trümper, "Art in the Service of Politics: Cranach and the Reformation," in *Martin Luther and the Reformation* (Dresden: Sandstein Verlag, 2016), 236.

[5]Steven Ozment's *The Serpent and the Lamb* (New Haven: Yale University Press, 2011) rescues Cranach from contextual reductionists and from those who have dismissed his images as "laborious

law from gospel is—according to Luther—"the highest art in Christendom,"[6] and Lucas Cranach the Elder put the *art* in this highest art in Christendom. It could have been otherwise. When Martin Luther was summoned to Worms, his fellow reformer Andreas Karlstadt began to tear down the images in Wittenberg. Cranach, who had settled in Wittenberg before Luther, was horrified.[7] Luther's Reformation was about to cause Cranach to lose his livelihood. Fortunately, however, Luther returned to Wittenberg—against the counsel of his protector Frederick the Wise—to refute Karlstadt and partner with Cranach.[8] The theologian and the artist, the religious and political "swashbucklers" required of the age,[9] became co-conspirers in the propagation of Luther's message. And not just Luther's, one might say, but Paul's.[10]

Tragically though, as inter-Christian warfare accelerated, the law-gospel tradition quickly calcified into a polemic.[11] In the hands of Lucas Cranach the Younger, this visual template, intended as a mnemonic image (*Merkbild*) to propagate the gospel,[12] was weaponized to attack the Pope and his minions.[13] In one

---

allegories" (esp. 6-24); Bonnie Noble's *Lucas Cranach the Elder* (New York: University Press of America, 2009) shows how Cranach's imagery "does not replicate the precise meaning of its textual sources; rather it appropriates meanings of its own based on the properties of its own meaning" (28). An equally original approach is taken by Matthew David Rosebrock, "The Highest Art: Martin Luther's Visual Theology in *Oratio, Meditatio, Tentatio*" (PhD diss., Fuller Theological Seminary, 2017).

[6]Martin Luther, "The Distinction Between the Law and the Gospel: A Sermon Preached on January 1, 1532," trans. Willard L. Bruce, *Concordia Journal* 18, no. 2 (1992): 153.

[7]Cranach arrived in 1505, Luther in 1512. Trümper, "Art in the Service of Politics," 231.

[8]Ozment, *Serpent and the Lamb,* 137.

[9]Ibid., 24. "Cranach was quick to recognize in Luther the perfect ally for the coming confrontation with Protestant iconoclasm, while Luther was no less prescient in picking Cranach as his secular guide and worldly mentor on the political fronts of Saxony, Rome, and Vienna" (133).

[10]The question as to whether Luther's distillation of Paul is sufficiently Pauline is admittedly enormous, calling to mind a massive rift between the forensic (Protestant) and ontological (Catholic) readings of Paul. Rather than wading into the new versus old perspective debates, Peter Leithart's suggestion of "deliverdict," which combines forensic and ontological aspects, is instructive (Peter Leithart, *Delivered from the Elements of the World* [Downers Grove, IL: IVP Academic, 2016], 180-83). Also of interest is Kevin Vanhoozer's suggestion that "*sola gratia* has ontological and not merely soteriological significance" (Kevin Vanhoozer, *Biblical Authority After Babel* [Grand Rapids: Brazos, 2016], 50). I aim to show here that a similar conciliating reading of Luther can be found through the lens of art history.

[11]Cranach the Elder's first attempt at such polemics, interestingly, was with Karlstadt himself! (Ozment, *Serpent and the Lamb,* 123-24). Carlos Eire's description of such propaganda is instructive. Luther "was not responsible for all that was printed, or even a fraction of it, but he was inextricably connected to it, and he benefited from it" (Carlos Eire, *Reformations: The Early Modern World, 1450–1650* [New Haven: Yale University Press, 2016], 184).

[12]Trümper, "Art in the Service of Politics," 237.

[13]I am in debt to Jonathan Anderson, during a conversation in front of Lutheran prints at the Los Angeles County Museum of Art, for the apt word "weaponize."

particularly outrageous woodcut from the mid-sixteenth century, the gospel side is replaced with Martin Luther's pure preaching, and the law side with the papacy roasting in hell.[14] That the law and gospel tradition has been used in this way cannot be ignored.

Nevertheless, perhaps these images can be read backward instead of simply forward in time. Lucas Cranach the Elder was deeply shaped by the Catholic visual culture that preceded him and to which he continued to contribute alongside his involvement with Luther. Cranach himself, supplying "both Rome and Wittenberg with their preferred religious artworks," has been described as "ecumenical in an age that was not."[15] Not surprisingly, therefore, echoes of the law and gospel tradition can be found in Catholic and Orthodox visual culture as well. Pursuing this evangelical visual heritage in non-Lutheran contexts, I contend, is one way of seeking church unity where sacramental communion has failed.

Evangelicals who are proud of the law-gospel visual tradition might be surprised to learn that "present[ing] the dry Tree of Death and the green Tree of Life within an integrated image . . . would have a direct application to the spiritual life of the individual soul" was a formula that dates back at least to the early twelfth century.[16] To choose just one place where it appeared well before Cranach, consider the famous missal presented by Berthold Furtmeyr to the Archbishop of Salzburg in 1481.[17] Here the same law-gospel distinction is laid out sacramentally, an appropriately feminine distillation of Cranach's formula. On the right, Eve has been given the first law ("thou shalt not eat"), and yet she eats. As with Cranach, this is no distant event but a present reality, as contemporary persons—fifteenth-century folk—take up Eve's suggestion. Death, almost straddling his victims, holds them hostage as a result.

But on the left side is gospel. The tree is the no longer the tree of the knowledge of good and evil but the tree of the cross, as made clear by the crucifix nestled in

---

[14]Lucas Cranach the Younger's "The False Church and the True Church" (ca. 1549) can be found in *Renaissance and Reformation: German Art in the Age of Dürer and Cranach* (Berlin: Staatliche Museen, 2016), 91, or in high resolution at Google Arts and Culture: www.google.com/culturalinstitute/beta/asset/the-false-and-the-true-church/3gHrD-YpBcBEug.

[15]Ozment, *Serpent and the Lamb*, 1.

[16]Jennifer O'Reilly, "The Trees of Eden in Mediaeval Iconography," in *A Walk in the Garden: Biblical Iconographical and Literary Images of Eden*, ed. Paul Morris (Sheffield: Sheffield Academic Press, 1992), 186.

[17]Ibid., 195. The image can be found in the following database: daten.digitale-sammlungen.de/~db/0004/bsb00045166/images/index.html?fip=193.174.98.30&seite=127&pdfseitex. See also Joseph Leo Koerner, *The Moment of Self-Portraiture in German Renaissance Art* (Chicago: University of Chicago Press, 1993), 377.

its host-bearing branches. The dispenser of the good news in this case, however, is not John the Baptist but Mary, who distributes the sacrament in an undeniably priestly fashion. Or perhaps she is the personified *ekklēsia*. Either way, not only did Luther have a career-long love of the Virgin Mary,[18] she has a clear place in many of Cranach's law-gospel panels as well.[19] It should be evident from such pre-Reformation imagery that "studied allusion to themes in Romans 5–8 does not represent an exclusively Lutheran interest, of course, but arises from the late mediaeval concern with the program of justification."[20] Moreover, if the "cross and the Last Supper are the alpha and the omega of . . . Lutheran theology as a whole,"[21] then Furtmeyr's Salzburg miniature—a law-gospel missal we might call it—is perhaps equally "Protestant."

Should this be the case, then Cranach's law-gospel distinction may have been less branding Lutheranism than it was catechizing people into a transconfessional grammar of the gospel. As Cranach's law-gospel panels spread in so many versions, including frontispieces to new translations of the Bible and theological treatises, countless prints, and even domestic wooden chests,[22] the best of pre-existing Catholic theology was being disseminated as well. Which is to say, while verbal systems increasingly polarized the confessions, art may have been surreptitiously uniting them.[23] As art historians have been pointing out for some time, "The terms 'Anabaptist,' 'Lutheran,' 'Calvinist' and 'Catholic' do not entirely hold water because the religious doctrine, as it emerges in the rhetoricians' poems and plays [and paintings], is never entirely pure."[24] Or, to borrow the words of Sarah Hinlicky Wilson, "profound Christian art will not stay obediently within the boundaries we impose upon it."[25]

---

[18]Susanne Kimmig-Völkner, "Luther, the Virgin Mary, and the Saints: Catholic Images as a Key to Understanding the Lutheran Concept of Salvation," in *Martin Luther and the Reformation: Essays* (Dresden: Sandstein Verlag, 2016), 261-69.

[19]In the Prague version (discussed below), Mary is nearly as prominent as Christ.

[20]O'Reilly, "Trees of Eden," 198. O'Reilly claims the same Augustinian tones are reflected in late fifteenth-century manuscripts of Augustine's *City of God*.

[21]Noble, *Lucas Cranach the Elder*, 84.

[22]The range of such variations is well illustrated in Ernst Grohne, *Die bremischen Truhen mit reformatorischen Darstellungen und der Ursprung ihre Motive* (Bremen: Geist, 1936), 65-87.

[23]Not all art, of course. As mentioned above, images were undeniably weaponized as well.

[24]Koenraad Jonckheere, *Antwerp Art After Iconoclasm: Experiments in Decorum, 1566–1585* (New Haven: Yale University Press, 2012), 47.

[25]Sarah Hinlicky Wilson, "Death and Ecumenism in Flannery O'Connor's Fiction," paper delivered at the Strasbourg Institute for Ecumenical Research, August 2015. www.strasbourginstitute.org/en /summer-seminar-2015-ecumenism-in-the-arts/shw-flannery-oconnor/.

VISUAL ECUMENISM

This is not to suggest that art is any kind of substitute sacrament. Baptism and Eucharist are the church's chief symbols of unity. "Because there is one bread, we who are many are one body, for we all partake of the one bread" (1 Cor 10:17). And yet—to state the obvious—Orthodox, Catholic, Protestant, and Pentecostal Christians in the twenty-first century, even when they acknowledge the legitimacy of baptisms beyond their confessional boundaries, cannot share the Eucharist.[26] On the eve of his conversion to Catholicism, John Henry Newman claimed that if St. Athanasius or St. Ambrose were to "come suddenly to life, it cannot be doubted what communion he would take to be his own."[27] But if one takes into consideration the competing claims of the Orthodox Church, it can very much be doubted.[28] Attempts to save appearances by claiming the church "as such" to still be unified are unconvincing when two churches make the same such pronouncement.[29] The Reformation historian Ron Rittgers is right to see here an "impossible choice between two mothers."[30] With due respect to Newman, it is a far safer bet to say that if *Paul* were to come suddenly to life, whose pleas for unity pervade his epistles, it cannot be doubted that he would be horrified by our divisions.

---

[26]See for example, John Paul II's 2003 encyclical *Ecclesia de Eucharistia,* where "communion with [the Roman Pontiff] is intrinsically required for the celebration of the Eucharistic Sacrifice." This clearly rules out non-Catholic Christians, even should they believe in the real presence (www.vatican.va/holy_father/special_features/encyclicals/documents/hf_jp-ii_enc_20030417_ecclesia_eucharistia_en.html).

[27]John Henry Newman, *Essay on the Development of Christian Doctrine* (Garden City, NY: Image, 1960), 113.

[28]I am in debt to George Hunsinger for this observation.

[29]For a book-length attack on the idea of the church "as such" to be united, see Ephraim Radner, *A Brutal Unity: The Spiritual Politics of the Christian Church* (Waco, TX: Baylor University Press, 2012). "The sole Church of Christ [is that] which our Savior, after his Resurrection, entrusted to Peter's pastoral care, commissioning him and the other apostles to extend and rule it. . . . This Church, constituted and organized as a society in the present world, subsists in (*subsistit in*) the Catholic Church, which is governed by the successor of Peter and by the bishops in communion with him" (*Catechism of the Catholic Church* [New York: Doubleday, 1995], §816). "The Orthodox Church is the true Church of Christ established by our Lord and Savior, the Church confirmed and sustained by the Holy Spirit, the Church of which the Savior himself said, 'I will build my church and the gates of hell shall not prevail against it' (Mt 16:18)" ("Basic Principles of Attitude to the Non-Orthodox," Russian Orthodox Church Department for External Church Relations, https://mospat.ru/en/documents/attitude-to-the-non-orthodox, 1.1). Even with the famous "softenings" of *Lumen Gentium*'s subsistence language or Philaret of Moscow's (d. 1867) "purely true" versus "impurely true" Christianity (Metropolitan Hilarion Alfeyev, *Orthodox Christianity*, vol. 2 [Crestwood, NY: St. Vladimir's Seminary Press, 2012], 408), convergences are, of course, insufficient to permit communion.

[30]Ronald Rittgers, epilogue to *Protestantism After 500 Years* (New York: Oxford University Press, 2016), 336.

In the wake of this failure, however, art may have fostered a coy communion where the sacraments have faltered. If, as the Princeton Proposal for Christian Unity laments, "Great divisions remain, and few see a way forward," images may offer one of those directions.[31] To suggest art has brought churches together in the way that the law-gospel panels propagated the best of late medieval Catholic theology is not to say that art affords adequate communion. We are rightly warned against "generic endorsement of the arts as inherently sacramental activities."[32] When this is done, "their essential connection to the work of Jesus Christ easily fade into the background or disappear entirely."[33] But like a motorcycle weaving between lanes of a traffic jam, art may have a nimbleness to outmaneuver sacramental and verbal theological gridlock.

And indeed, verbal theology—frequently holding the sacraments hostage within conceptual frameworks—remains a primary obstacle to unity. This accounts for the exhaustion that has marked many ecumenical discussions. Formal documents are produced but seem to have little effect. William Abraham bluntly declares, "Ecumenism is now braindead. . . . The best and brightest in the younger leadership of the church have abandoned the ecumenical seas and gone sailing in other waters."[34] As Brian Daley puts it, there is "a kind of spiritual and mental exhaustion in the face of the difficulties that prevent real communion among the churches, and a willingness to settle simply for practical cooperation in external programs."[35] R. R. Reno even concedes that "any progress toward Christian unity will undermine and diminish the sophisticated theological systems born in the polemical centuries that followed the Reformation."[36]

But the same essay collection intimates other strategies less encumbered by the verbal traditions. Brian Daley explains that the chief way the patristic era spoke of

---

[31]Carl E. Braaten and Robert W. Jenson, eds., *In One Body Through the Cross: The Princeton Proposal for Christian Unity* (Grand Rapids: Eerdmans, 2003), 7.

[32]Daniel J. Treier, Mark Husbands, and Roger Lundin, *The Beauty of God: Theology and the Arts* (Downers Grove, IL: InterVarsity Press, 2007), 10.

[33]Ibid. Timothy Verdon is much more sanguine in this respect but carefully ensconces sacramental art in a liturgical matrix: "Images made in [the liturgy's] service thus automatically become part of a *proclamation* that is also an *encounter,* in direct analogy with the sacraments, the signs of salvation and new life instituted by Christ. It is in fact from the sacramental liturgy that sacred images draw their 'power,' their 'presence,' their 'reality'" ("Art and the Liturgy," in *The Ecumenism of Beauty*, ed. Timothy Verdon [Brewster, MA: Paraclete, 2017], 90).

[34]William J. Abraham, "Ecumenism and the Rocky Road to Renewal," in *The Ecumenical Future*, ed. Carl E. Braaten and Robert W. Jenson (Grand Rapids: Eerdmans, 2004), 178.

[35]Brian E. Daley, SJ, "Rebuilding the Structure of Love: The Quest for Visible Unity Among the Churches," in *Ecumenical Future*, ed. Braaten and Jenson, 102.

[36]R. R. Reno, "The Debilitation of the Churches," in *Ecumenical Future*, ed. Braaten and Jenson, 69.

the church is through images, because the mystery of the church "cannot be exhaustively plumbed by a single idea or expressed in a single term, but that it must be teased out in an almost inexhaustible stream of images and analogies, which release to us new aspects of the one mystery."[37] "The fathers," he continues, "think and write about the church almost exclusively in the language of *symbol*."[38] Daley would not be the first to see need for a degree of responsible demurral from verbal precision. A theologian as skilled as Pavel Florensky argued for "pneumatic incoherence," including a "deliberate dismantling of logical articulation[s]."[39] And Aquinas himself acknowledged the limits of verbal constructions when he complained, "If we take careful note of the statements of the Greeks we shall find they differ from us more in words than in meaning."[40]

To interrogate, without abandoning, logocentric systems is often to see that divided Christians can share, and have been sharing, visual traditions in ways that most theologians have ignored.[41] Any degree of reading in ecumenical documents will quickly encounter the plea for "visible unity."[42] What the authors intend is a sacramental unity that can be seen by the world. But until we reach that goal, we may have achieved visible unity in a different way, if we will permit art history to do serious theological work. There are countless places one could go to point to this dynamic, whether the *Simultankirche* in Germany, where Charles V gave Catholics the right to worship in the same church with Lutherans;[43] the double-nave

---

[37]Daley, "Rebuilding the Structure of Love," 96-97.

[38]Ibid., 95.

[39]Ephraim Radner, *Spirit and Nature: The Saint Médard Miracles in Eighteenth-Century Jansenism* (New York: Crossroad, 2002), 371-72. Radner is elaborating on Florensky's essay "On the Holy Spirit" in *Ultimate Questions: An Anthology of Modern Russian Thought*, ed. Alexander Schmemann (Chicago: Holt, Rinehart, Winston, 1965). Fascinating as it is that Florensky beat Derrida to the logocentric punch, when Florensky went to art history, he fell into the old confessional grooves, dismissing print culture as irreducibly Protestant and sculpture as necessarily Catholic, a facile dichotomy disrupted by recent developments in the history of art. See Pavel Florensky, Donald Sheehan, and Olga Andrejev, *Iconostasis* (Crestwood, NY: St. Vladimir's Seminary Press, 2000), 113.

[40]*De Potentia,* cited in Marcus Plested, *Orthodox Readings of Aquinas* (New York: Oxford University Press, 2012), 25.

[41]One exciting, recent exception is Verdon, *Ecumenism of Beauty.*

[42]The New Delhi World Council of Churches 1961 assembly put it, "The unity which is both God's will and his gift to his Church is being made visible as all in each place who are baptized into Jesus Christ confess him as Lord and Saviour" (www.oikoumene.org/en/resources/documents/assembly/1961-new-delhi/new-delhi-statement-on-unity).

[43]Interestingly, this offers a rare bright spot in Radner's mostly dark book, *A Brutal Unity* (Waco, TX: Baylor University Press, 2012). There are many churches in the Rhineland that function in the same way today. Even the villain of Radner's narrative, Ephipanius of Salamis, has been subject to a sort of visual ecumenism, showing up in frescoes in both the Catholic and Orthodox churches in Famagusta, Cyprus. Maria Paschali, "Blurring the Lines: Devotional Imagery and Cultural Identity in

churches of Crete where Orthodox and Catholic Christians worshiped together;[44] the paintings on Mt. Athos inspired by Protestant prints;[45] the works of Polish sculptor Paul Landowski, who carved both the Catholic Jesus that overlooks Rio's Guanabara Bay *and* the famous depiction of the Reformers in Geneva;[46] or the ecumenical responses to the beheading of non-Chalcedonian Coptic Christians on the beach of Libya.[47] But to provide focus to this proliferation, my aim in this chapter, as we've seen, is to isolate a particularly cherished evangelical visual tradition, the law-gospel panel, revealing its non-Protestant appearances. We might call such convergences an appetizer enjoyed in anticipation of a time when Protestant, Pentecostal, Catholic, and Orthodox Christians can finally dine as one.

CAMOUFLAGE CRANACH CONTINUED

As the church history charts given to visitors of Orthodox monasteries or polemical websites will tell you, the Orthodox stand aloof from Western rational conflicts centering on law and gospel.[48] But if the law-gospel distinction is indeed fundamental to Pauline thought, perhaps it can be found in the Orthodox visual tradition as well. Consider, for example, the quintessential Orthodox icon found at the foot of Mt. Sinai in St. Catherine's monastery, the Sinai Pantocrator (fig. 8.2). It was rediscovered in the mid-twentieth century at the Princeton/Michigan Sinai expedition where it was recognized as a masterpiece of late antique realism that would soon be eclipsed by increasingly spiritualized abstraction. It has since emerged in popular visual culture as a deeply authentic Christ image—strangely consistent with other depictions, including the shroud of Turin. Perhaps the law-gospel distinction can be seen here as well, though—in a move that will please any Barthian—the distinction is grounded in the person of Christ.[49]

Late Medieval Famagusta," paper presented at the Byzantine Studies Conference, Fordham University, 2015.

[44]Olga Gratziou, "Cretan Architecture and Sculpture in the Venetian Period," in Anastasia Drandaki, *The Origins of El Greco: Icon Painting in Venetian Crete* (New York: Alexander S. Onassis Foundation, 2009), 22-23.

[45]Exhaustively analyzed and illustrated in Paul Huber, *Apokalypse: Bilderzyklen zur Johannes-Offenbarung in Trier, auf dem Athos und von Caillaud d'Angers* (Patmos: Aufl, 1989).

[46]Matthew J. Milliner, "Towards a Visual Ecumenism," paper presented at Duke University, 2015.

[47]Matthew J. Milliner, "Towards 2017," paper presented at George Fox College, 2016.

[48]See, for example, the timeline at the Antiochian Orthodox Archdiocese's website: www.antiochian.org/orthodox-church-history.

[49]For a helpful overview of Barth's demurral from traditionally Lutheran takes on law and gospel, see I. John Hesselink, "Law and Gospel or Gospel and Law?—Karl Barth, Martin Luther, and John Calvin," *Reformation and Revival Journal* 14 (2005): 139-71.

Figure 8.2. Replica of the Sinai Pantocrator flanked by traditional Deësis imagery from Stavronikita monastary on Mt. Athos

On Christ's left side (our right) looms the book and the severe gaze. Faced with Christ's standards for holiness in the Sermon on the Mount, who can stand? But of course, his demands are never meant to drive us away from Christ but toward him. On Christ's right (our left), we see the merciful gaze, the hand that was pierced for us raised in blessing. In this face, not just in the psalm, "righteousness and peace have kissed each other" (Ps 85:10). Indeed, as one recent evangelical points out, a frequently employed Hebrew term for grace (*ḥēn*) "connotes the favor that an inferior finds in the eyes of a superior," and the facial and ocular aspects of grace in Scripture (Num 6:25; Ps 80; 2 Cor 4:6) are abundant.[50] As Luther puts it, "Before receiving the comfort of forgiveness, sin must be recognized and the fear of God's wrath must be experienced through the preaching or apprehension of the Law, that man may be driven to sigh for grace and may be prepared to receive the comfort of the Gospel."[51] All of this happens in the Sinai Pantocrator, but with a single look.

---

[50]Vanhoozer, *Biblical Authority After Babel*, 56.

[51]Ewald M. Plass, ed., *What Luther Says: An Anthology*, 3 vols. (St. Louis: Concordia, 1959), 2:738. Compare the words of the Byzantine writer Nicholas Mesarites regarding the face of Christ: "These eyes to those who have achieved a clean understanding, are gentle and friendly and instill the joy

Interestingly, later Pantocrators—in the domes at Lagoudera in Cyprus or Daphne in Greece for example—seem to lose this dynamic, instead choosing between severity and mercy. But the Sinai law-gospel dynamic does endure, however, in Byzantine mosaics and iconostases wherever the Deësis theme appears (see fig. 8.2), which shows Christ flanked by Mary on his right and John the Baptist on his left. In the famous Hagia Sophia Deësis, for example, John the Baptist is on the law side (Mt 11:11), near the book, and Mary, representing the incarnation, is on the side of the gospel. The traditional interpretation of such imagery is that they are meant to urge supplication to John the Baptist and Mary at the last judgment.[52] But perhaps a simpler and more straightforward reading of the motif is that the classic Byzantine Deësis communicates the law-gospel dynamic so pervasive in the epistles of Paul.

Reformed theologian Michael Horton's disagreement with Orthodox theology centers on precisely this point: "Discerning in [the] New Testament lines of thought a clear distinction between law and gospel—that which commands without promise or assistance and that which gives without command or judgment—Reformation theology observes in Orthodox theology a serious confusion on this point."[53] But without denying that this confusion can emerge in Orthodoxy (and in Reformed theology as well!), the Orthodox Deësis may show that the law-gospel distinction has been hiding in plain sight.[54] As Johann Huizinga puts it, "What matters is not primarily the dispute among keen-minded theologians, but the ideas that completely dominate the life of fantasy and thought as it is expressed in art."[55]

---

of contrition in the souls of the pure in heart. . . . To those who are condemned by their own judgment, [the eyes] are scornful and hostile and boding of ill." "Nicholas Mesarites: Description of the Church of the Holy Apostles at Constantinople," XVI, 3-5, ed. and trans. Glanville Downey, *Transactions of the American Philosophical Society* 47 (1957): 872-73.

[52]Perhaps this is why in one of Cranach's law-gospel prints at the British Museum (1530), Cranach actually includes the Deësis on the law side of the panel where it symbolizes the inaccessible God. Fortunately, however, this is not the version that endured (www.britishmuseum.org/research /collection_online/collection_object_details.aspx?objectId=1421368&partId=1&people=128204&p eoA=128204-2-60&page=3).

[53]Michael Horton, ed., *Three Views on Eastern Orthodoxy and Evangelicalism* (Grand Rapids: Zondervan, 2004), 136.

[54]To be sure, this dynamic can work in reverse. Despite suggestions that John Climacus's *Heavenly Ladder* is not Pelagian (see the introduction to John Climacus, *Ladder of Divine Ascent* [Mahwah, NJ: Paulist, 1982], 16), the *illustrations* of the ladder, which show Christ at the top as monks work out their own salvation without him, are very Pelagian indeed!

[55]Johann Huizinga, Rodney J. Payton, and Ulrich Mammitzsch, *The Autumn of the Middle Ages* (Chicago: University of Chicago Press, 1996), 237. Or for a more recent expression of the same notion: "The theological view needs to be combined with visual studies in order to address the problem of how a visual image can intuit a theological dogma, analyzable in conceptual terms" (Clemena

Even where Orthodox formal theology may seem at complete odds with Reformed dogmatics, the dynamic of Christ's severe requirements driving us to his mercy may be what people actually *saw*. Or to put it another way, iconostases, if they include a Deësis as they so frequently do, are irreducibly evangelical.

LAW AND GOSPEL IN CATHOLIC FLORENCE

Thus far we have examined covert Cranach law-gospel templates in late medieval manuscripts and icons that predate the contentious sixteenth century. As confessions became polarized in the wake of the Reformation, however, one would think that fleeting connections between the evangelical visual tradition and other confessions would decrease. Nevertheless, in the very midst of these tensions the law-gospel dynamic emerges within squarely Catholic turf. Art historians have uncovered a "world of reforming activity in [early modern Catholicism], some of it very sympathetic to Protestant positions."[56] Moreover, such connections are discernible not only in minor artists but in the most celebrated Renaissance names of the sixteenth century. In fact, with due respect to Lucas Cranach the Elder, the most beautiful and expansive law-gospel painting was completed in 1558 by Jacopo Pontormo and completed by Agnolo Bronzino, artists working for Catholic patrons in the heart of Medici Florence.[57] The fresco program was tragically destroyed in 1742 during an attempted restoration of the Medici chapel just behind it, but survives in a 1598 engraving and in preparatory sketches at the Uffizi. Modern art historians have been exploring the Protestant aspects of this lost program for nearly seventy years.[58]

Perhaps because it was crypto-Lutheran, Pontormo's program was criticized for lacking the honesty (*onestà*) and reverence (*riverenza*) demanded by the Catholic Reformation.[59] In the most well-known art historical source for this period, Giorgio Vasari criticized Pontormo's "mass of dead and drowned bodies," claiming the painting

---

Antonova, *Space, Time, and Presence in the Icon: Seeing the World with the Eyes of God* [Burlington, VT: Ashgate, 2010], 166).

[56]Nagel, *Controversy of Renaissance Art*, 198.

[57]I am in debt to Christopher Castaldo for informing me of this in his 2016 Wheaton Theology Conference paper, now published as "The Bible and the Italian Reformation," in *The People's Book: The Reformation and the Bible* (Downers Grove, IL: InterVarsity Press, 2017), 171-87.

[58]This 1598 engraving was published by Charles de Tolnay in 1950. Kurt Forster further established the connection of the series to the *Beneficio di Cristo* and the reforming impulse of Juan de Valdés (Kurt W. Forster, *Pontormo. Monographie mit kritichem Katalog* [Munich: Bruckmann, 1966]). The scholarly history is nicely summarized and expanded in Chrysa Damianiki, "Pontormo's Lost Frescoes in San Lorenzo, Florence: A Reappraisal of their Religious Content," in *Forms of Faith in Sixteenth-Century Italy*, ed. Abigail Brundin and Matthew Treherne (Burlington, VT: Ashgate, 2009), 77-118.

[59]Damianiki, "Pontormo's Lost Frescoes," 113.

as a whole lacked "the order of the scene, measure, time, variety . . . nor any rule or proportion."[60] But what may be behind such critiques, other than rivalry between competing artists, is concealment. The conceit of stylistic critique—at the very birth of modern art history—may have been an attempt to suppress theological content.[61]

Pontormo, it has been argued, was chosen for this series precisely because of his sympathies with the Italian Reform movements.[62] The reason was admittedly political. Cosimo I de' Medici, in direct competition with the powerful Farnese family of Rome, deliberately allowed Lutheran ideas in his city, where the memory of Savonarola's reform had not disappeared.[63] Pierfrancesco Riccio, who held the position of major-domo for Duke Cosimo de Medici, had clear Protestant affinities, and his library contained a manuscript of the *Beneficio di Cristo,* banned in 1549 for its downright Lutheran content,[64] alongside the writings of the Italian reformer Juan de Valdés.[65] Another influence on Pontormo may have been Benedetto Varchi, whose Protestant sentiments were disseminated through a sermon printed in Florence in 1549.[66] These undeniably Lutheran influences each could have influenced Pontormo's program at San Lorenzo.[67] He chose to centralize a benevolent Jesus, to eliminate purgatory and the Virgin Mary, and to offer a clear and direct law-gospel appeal in an age of distracting artistic embellishment.[68] By piecing together the last frescoes from surviving sketches, we can gain a sense of what the original program revealed (fig. 8.3).

---

[60]Ibid., 83-84.

[61]Or perhaps Vasari was rendering Pontormo a favor: "In attributing Pontormo's failure in this late work to his intellectual and spiritual regression, and to his exhaustion owing to hard work, Vasari found a way of protecting both Pontormo and Cosimo from later accusations of complicity with Protestant heresy" (ibid., 91). Confinement of the critique to the aesthetic realm "may have been responsible for their survival up to the mid-eighteenth century despite their reputation as being heterodox" (ibid., 84).

[62]Ibid., 80.

[63]Ibid., 88-89. As Cosimo wrote in a letter to Ambrogio of Gumppenberg, "I always have been, and always will be, a good Christian . . . ready to give to the Lutherans, too, all possible favours" (Cosimo I de' Medici, *Lettere,* ed. Giorgio Spini [Florence: Vallecchi, 1940], 97).

[64]Because the text was necessarily published anonymously, it has been attributed to various authors. The current consensus is that it was composed by Benedetto Fontanini (who was first identified as Benedetto da Mantova) and refined by the poet Marcantonio Flaminio (Castaldo, "Bible and the Italian Reformation," 176).

[65]Damianiki, "Pontormo's Lost Frescoes," 85.

[66]Ibid., 87. See Salvatore Lo Re, "Jacopo da Pontormo e Benedetto Varchi: una postilla," *Archivio Storico Italiano. Deputazione di Storia Patria per la Toscana* 150, no. 1 (1992): 139-62.

[67]Ibid., 85. Caponetto claims that the first eighteen articles of Valdés's *Catechismo* directly correspond to Pontormo's frescoes (Salvatore Caponetto, *La Riforma Protestante nell'Italia del Cinquecento* [Turin: Claudiana, 1992]). Damianiki claims the entire *Catechismo* can be seen reflected in the program ("Pontormo's Lost Frescoes," 88).

[68]Ibid., 91.

Figure 8.3. Tentative reconstruction of Pontormo's lost San Lorenzo fresco based on Damianiki

In Valdés's *Catechismo* (patterned after Luther's Small and Larger Catechisms) and in the *Beneficio di Cristo,* the flood is emphasized at length to express the hopeless state of the human condition without Christ.[69] Not surprisingly then, the flood is a key feature on the law side of Pontormo's fresco series as well.[70] Pontormo embroils the viewer in drowned, contorted bodies, offering a set up for the marvelous uplift of ascended souls, visually imitating the law-gospel rhetoric of a good Lutheran sermon.[71] The most Cranachian moment, however, is when the

---

[69]Ibid., 108.

[70]Indeed, Lucas Cranach the Elder used the theme as well in one of his versions of the panels, namely the Schneeberg altarpiece, which illustrates the flood on the exterior panel.

[71]Ibid., 113. For an earlier confirmation of Damianiki's law-left and gospel-right reconstruction, see Janet Cox Rearick, *The Drawings of Pontormo* (Cambridge, MA: Harvard University Press, 1964), 327.

flanking walls culminate with law on the left, with Moses stunned by the accusing finger of God, and the gospel on the right, where New Testament writers are buoyed by a trumpeting angel, corresponding nicely with the second and third chapters of the *Beneficio di Cristo* and Valdés's *Catechismo*.[72] Damiankiki even suggests that Pontormo's centralized Jesus, which bears resemblance to Cranach's, might be offering a refutation of Michelangelo's more severe last judgment.[73]

MICHELANGELO AMONG THE SPIRITUALI

And yet, near the time he was completing the Last Judgment, Michelangelo was being swept up in reforming currents as well. Archival breakthroughs have persuasively established that Michelangelo was drawn to Protestant ideas, which came to him through his spiritual friendship with a powerful noble woman, Vittoria Colonna and her circle of Reformers who met outside the centers of power in Viterbo.[74] They were known as the *Ecclesia viterbiensis*, or *Spirituali* ("the spiritual ones") in contrast to their opponents, the *Zelanti*.[75] Even if this reform circle did not realize the desired formal reconciliation with Protestants, there were other ways to express their sympathies for notions of grace, namely by shattering the contractual system of artistic production through free gifts of poetry and art. Alexander Nagel sees the poems freely given by Vittoria Colonna to Michelangelo, and the drawings given by him to her, as directly reflecting the culminating passage of the *Beneficio*: "The remission of sins would not be a gift and a grace but a payment, if God granted it to you because of the worth of your works. But I repeat that God accepts you as just and does not impute your sins to you through the merits of Christ, which are given to you and become yours through faith."[76]

---

[72]Damianiki, "Pontormos's Lost Frescoes," 110-11.

[73]Ibid., 115-18.

[74]The archival breakthroughs were published in Massimo Firpo and Dario Marcatto, eds., *Il processo inquisitoriale del cardinal Giovanni Morone* (Rome: Istituto storico italiano per l'età moderna e contemporanea, 1981–1989). See also Sergio Pagano and Concetta Ranieri, *Nuovi documenti su Vittoria Colonna e Reginald Pole* (Vatican City: Archivio Vaticano, 1989). These discoveries are reflected in English in (among other publications) Alexander Nagel, *Michelangelo and the Reform of Art* (New York: Cambridge University Press, 2000); Antonio Forcellino, *Michelangelo: A Tormented Life*, trans. Allen Cameron (Malden, MA: Polity, 2009); Abigail Brundin, *Vittoria Colonna and the Spiritual Politics of the Reformation* (New York: Taylor & Francis, 2016); Christoph Luitpold Frommel, *Michelangelo's Tomb for Julius II: Genesis and Genius* (Los Angeles: J. Paul Getty Museum, 2016); and Sarah Rolfe Prodan, *Michelangelo's Christian Mysticism: Art, Poetry and Spirituality in Sixteenth Century Italy* (New York: Cambridge University Press, 2014).

[75]Castaldo, "Bible and the Italian Reformation," 174.

[76]Cited in Nagel, *Michelangelo and the Reform of Art*, 172, with original Italian on 266.

The gift giving in the Viterbo circle directly reflected these ideas, such that "even the exchange of courtesies and the practice of gift giving were, semiplayfully, couched in the terms of the debate over grace."[77] In a series of letters between Vittoria and Michelangelo, dating from between 1538 and 1546, we see just such playful language at work. Presented with a gift (perhaps a poem) by Colonna, Michelangelo struggled with a desire to offer some kind of payment, but then yielded. "Having recognized and seen that the grace of God cannot be bought, and that to have it with discomfort is a grave sin, I say the fault is mine and willingly I accept these things."[78] The grace circulating in the *Spirituali* liberated him from the sense of obligation—noted even by Vasari[79]—under which he labored over a long artistic career. Michelangelo, in turn, scolded Vittoria Colonna for going through an intermediary, his friend Tommaso de' Cavalieri, to urge him to finish a drawing for her. He was, in fact, preparing something even better, and her refusal to make a direct appeal to him had "spoiled" the gift.[80] The friendship between Michelangelo and Vittoria was a kind of tutorial in unmediated grace that drew on the language of Italian reforming texts.

But the Reformation influence on Michelangelo did not just appear in private correspondence and drawings. It influenced his most famous formal commissions as well. The same notions of unmediated grace emerged in Michelangelo's frescoes in the Vatican's Pauline chapel[81] and most dramatically in the tomb of Pope Julius II (in office 1503–1513). Michelangelo's initial plans for the tomb date to the early sixteenth century, decades before the Reformation.[82] After an initial sketch, the tomb quickly mushroomed into a gargantuan scheme that would rival the imperial funerary monuments of the Caesars—a spectacular confluence of Michelangelo's and Julius's ambitions.[83] A figure of Julius II would cap the massive structure, and below him would be Victories standing astride reconquered papal lands interspersed with larger-than-life male nudes, which may have symbolized the arts Julius patronized so abundantly.[84] Moses, Paul, and allegorized figures of the contemplative

---

[77]Ibid., 172.

[78]Ibid.

[79]"It seemed to him, when someone gave him something that he was put under a permanent obligation" (cited in Nagel, *Michelangelo and the Reform of Art*, 172-73).

[80]Ibid., 175.

[81]For unmediated grace reflected in this late fresco, see Forcellino, *Michelangelo*, 224.

[82]Frommel, *Michelangelo's Tomb for Julius II*, 24.

[83]John T. Paoletti and Gary M. Radke, *Art in Renaissance Italy*, 4th ed. (New York: Prentice Hall, 2012), 400.

[84]Ibid.

and active life, reflective of Julius II's spiritual and earthly interests, would be included as well. Moreover, the entire tomb was to be placed prominently in St. Peter's basilica, whose reconstruction—which helped ignite the Reformation—was spearheaded by Julius II.[85] By any account this sepulchral ambition was unrealizable. Despite Michelangelo's long life, only six of the sixteen male nudes were even started, to say nothing of the additional figures. Which is to say, the original tomb of Julius II was the quintessence of Michelangelo's youthful arrogance.

Julius II, however, died in 1513, which left Michelangelo in the position of having been paid handsomely for a tomb that he never created. Michelangelo attempted to sublet the projects to assistants to no avail. By 1532, nearly three decades after the commission was conceived, legal consequences were threatened were he not to complete the project.[86] And so Michelangelo was forced to finish. But the years 1532 through 1545, when the tomb was completed, coincided with the more mature Michelangelo's association with the *Spirituali*. Michelangelo therefore fulfilled his obligations to depict his friend, but not as Julius II, "The Warrior Pope," might have wanted.

Figure 8.4. Michelangelo's Tomb of Julius II, showing Moses turned away from the chain altar

---

[85]The tomb's importance is conveyed by the fact that the Sistine Chapel itself was a side project born from Julius's frustration that Michelangelo had not completed his tomb!
[86]Frommel, *Michelangelo's Tomb for Julius II*, 68.

The sculpture was not placed under St. Peter's basilica as planned. Instead, it is tucked away in the side of a church that is itself tucked away in Rome: *San Pietro in Vincole* (St. Peter in Chains), where Julius was titular cardinal before his elevation to the papacy. There Julius was especially fond of the relic of the chains.[87] Legend related that in the fifth century, Eudoxia, the wife of emperor Valentinian III, had been given the chains of Peter's Jerusalem imprisonment by her mother as a gift. When Pope St. Leo I compared them to the chains of St. Peter's Roman imprisonment, the two miraculously fused together. As a result, the chains marked "the symbolic unity of the empire under a new Christian faith."[88] But Michelangelo did not flatter his deceased patron by having his central figure of Moses look upon the chains as planned. Late in the game, he wrenched the head of Moses to look away from the altar (fig. 8.4).[89] The result is a statue that "rebels against the original project."[90]

Indeed, if Michelangelo's Moses symbolizes law—including the law of ambition that drove Michelangelo's early career—perhaps we can see in this figure a record of shocked conversion when faced with a different set of gospel ideals. Indeed, at St. Peter in Chains, the polished ambition of Michelangelo's youthful sculptures are wrenched to an unsettling halt. It might even be possible to see here an echo of the 1529 Prague version of the Lucas Cranach the Elder's law-gospel panel (fig. 8.5).[91] In this version, the subject who had been split onto both sides merges into once central figure, as if to illustrate our condition as sinners always bent toward self-justification, in constant need for reminders of grace. While a direct Cranach-Michelangelo influence here is unlikely, it is at least interesting that Cranach's central figure, overshadowed by a scolding Moses, is similarly twisted in Michelangelo's famous tomb.

But further investigation into the tomb of Julius II makes the Protestant connection here even less of a stretch. The latest sculptures in the series to be completed, from 1542 to 1545, show the most influence from the reforming circles.[92] The male nudes and conquering victories are eliminated, but the image of the active and contemplative life—now reinterpreted—remained.[93] The figure of the active life

---

[87]Ibid., 55.

[88]Forcellino, *Michelangelo*, 220.

[89]Ibid., 222. A surviving fragment of a letter to Vasari testifies to this sudden shift. Frommel, *Michelangelo's Tomb for Julius II*, 55. Michelangelo is on record joking to his friend Tomasso Cavalieri, "You didn't know that Moses intended to speak to us the other day and that he turned in order to understand us better." But the humor might have concealed a deeper motivation.

[90]Forcellino, *Michelangelo*, 222.

[91]Available at www.lucascranach.org/CZ_NGP_O10732.

[92]Forcellino, *Michelangelo*, 62.

[93]Ibid., 211.

Figure 8.5. Lucas Cranach the Elder, *Law and Gospel*, Prague, 1529

shows a female figure's hair merging with a torch. Vittoria Colonna and the circle of Viterbo used this flaming hair analogy to illustrate thoughts of charitable intelligence that plan deeds of service.[94] In addition, the *Beneficio di Cristo* uses the analogy of fire to describe the natural relationship between faith and works: "This is justifying faith. It is like a flame of fire which only bursts forth in its brightness. It is like the flame that burns the wood without the help of light; yet the flame cannot be without the light. In similar fashion it is true that faith alone consumes and burns away sin without the help of works, and yet that same faith cannot be without good works."[95]

This mediating position, which might be called a Joint Declaration on the Doctrine of Justification (1999) *avant la lettre*, could have done much to reconcile warring Protestants and Catholics were it heeded. Standing to the left of Michelangelo's Moses, moreover, was a figure who stood apart from works completely. The sculpture

---

[94]Ibid., 212.
[95]Don Benedetto, *The Benefits of Christ* (Vancouver: Regent College Publishing, 1984), 130. This English edition offers a more accessible abridged text.

of the contemplative life was "in all probability the last statue made for the tomb and indeed the last sculpture Michelangelo ever completed,"[96] and may also have been a portrait of Vittoria Colonna herself.[97] It might be called Michelangelo's last free gift to his spiritual mentor and friend.

Through association with the *Spirituali*, the greatest sculptor of the Renaissance had clearly been changed by the message of grace, which he even dared insert into the radically reworked tomb of Julius II. But soon came the backlash. Cardinal Giampietro Carafa—the worst enemy of the *Spirituali*—was elected Pope Paul IV (in office 1555–1549), cancelling Michelangelo's commissions his first day on the job.[98] The severity of Paul IV's persecution of Reformers meant Michelangelo had to cover his tracks. Hence, in Michelangelo's dictated biography, the connections to *Il Beneficio di Cristo* in the tomb of Julius II were concealed with benign references to the more acceptable Dante.[99] According to Forcellino, the election of Cardinal Carafa to the papacy may have even been the prompt for Michelangelo's famous attack on his own deposition, which stands in Florence's *Opera del Duomo* museum today. Michelangelo's prominent self-portrait as Nicodemus within this sculpture, which "reveals his guilt over not having the courage to celebrate more openly his dangerous religious beliefs,"[100] offered evidence of reforming sympathies that had to be destroyed.

PERSONALIZED LAW AND GOSPEL IN WEIMAR AND BEYOND

One last version of Cranach's law-gospel template remains to be considered. Described as the supreme image of the Reformation, the Weimar altarpiece was completed not by Lucas Cranach the Elder but by his son (fig. 8.6).[101] Following the tested formula, Lucas Cranach the Younger depicted the damned sinner in the distance, but the sinner saved by grace takes the form of a moving portrait of the painter's own father at the foot of the cross.[102] This portrait of Lucas Cranach the Elder is flanked by John the Baptist, who points to Christ, alongside his dear friend Martin Luther. As in the original law-gospel formula from Gotha, Jesus' imputing blood pours from his side to fall on Lucas Cranach the Elder's forehead. His acquiescent expression conveys that he "is saved not by action but

[96]Frommel, *Michelangelo's Tomb for Julius II*, 67. Frommel discerns a possible pun between the first four letters of Vittoria Colonna's name and the title of the sculpture: Vi(ta) Co(ntemplativa).
[97]Ibid.
[98]Forcellino, *Michelangelo*, 284.
[99]Ibid., 283.
[100]Ibid., 288. "Nicodemus . . . came to Jesus by night" (Jn 3:1-2).
[101]Available at www.lucascranach.org/DE_PPW_NONE-PPW001A.
[102]Noble, *Lucas Cranach the Elder*, 149.

Figure 8.6. Lucas Cranach the Younger, altarpiece in St. Peter and Paul, Weimar, 1555

by passive acceptance of grace."[103] Which is to say, the Weimar altarpiece offers less an abstract discussion of law and gospel than an illustration of the doctrine's direct, personal realization.

This personal thrust causes one scholar to contrast the Weimar altarpiece to earlier crucifixions that only gestured at the possibility of salvation. "The blood splashing on Cranach's head and Luther's text assure the viewer that this is not what the artist hopes for but, rather, what he is guaranteed."[104] Even so, both German and Italian reform circles of the sixteenth century would have agreed that to see *someone else* experiencing this guarantee is inadequate. The *Beneficio* concludes with a personal appeal to not believe in remission of sins in general, but to "apply this belief to your own case, and believe without doubt that through Christ all your iniquities are pardoned."[105] With such personal application in mind, one analogue to the Weimar law-gospel panel is on offer in a famous piece of modern Catholic kitsch.

---

[103]Ibid. Luther incidentally does not receive it, as he had been dead for a decade and was resurrected for this portrait (ibid., 148). Noble adds very insightfully, "Cranach is the naked sinner to be sure, but his artistic personality remains intact. . . . Cranach as naked sinner does not dissolve his personality into a theological concept" (ibid., 151).

[104]Ibid., 153. It is interesting to note that the blood spurts directed toward Dominican brothers at San Marco in Florence are less plenteous than Cranach's more consistent stream. I am in debt to John Walford for this comparison.

[105]Cited in Nagel, *Michelangelo and the Reform of Art,* 172.

The image I refer to (fig. 8.7) can be traced to Sister Faustina Kowalska (1905–1938), who shares many parallels with Martin Luther. She gave endless, scrupulous confessions, such that her confessor sought to offload his burden by asking her to keep a journal, which is why we know so much about her.[106] As with Luther, it was the message of undeserved grace and mercy that set Sister Faustina free. At one point Christ said to her, "The flames of mercy are burning Me—clamoring to be spent; I want to keep pouring them out upon souls; souls just don't want to believe in My goodness."[107] Though she did not enjoy a collaborator as talented as Lucas Cranach the Elder, a visual component to Faustina's piety came when she sought an artist to replicate her vision of Christ. The painting did not live up to her heavenly vision, which caused her to weep, but consolation came from Jesus himself: "Not in the beauty of the color, nor of the brush lies the greatness of this image, but in My grace,"[108] which nicely corresponds to Lutheran understandings of sacred images.[109] The painting survived communist occupation, spawned several versions, and after a time of suppression, emerged to prominence when a Polish pope made Sister Faustina the first canonized saint of the twenty-first century.

As in the Weimar altarpiece, the streams of imputing righteousness are here aimed at the subject—but in this case the subject is not a historic personage, but the viewer. As one devotional guide puts it, "the Divine Mercy Image is not just a picture of Jesus for *us to look at*. It's, in a very real sense, an icon that helps us see with our inner eyes *the way God looks at us*."[110] If anything, the divine mercy image is *more* evangelical than Cranach's wonderful Weimar altarpiece. It is a visual altar call urging the viewer to receive the imparted righteousness of Christ, just as Lucas Cranach the Elder does in the Weimar altarpiece itself.[111] There is also an unexpected resonance with women's ordination that surrounds

---

[106]Catherine M. Odell, *Faustina: Apostle of Divine Mercy* (Huntington, IN: Our Sunday Visitor, 1998), 87.

[107]Ibid., 74.

[108]Ibid., 313.

[109]For Luther, sacred images must be "rough-hewn so as to be grasped by simple people ('*groben volk*'). They also must *look* rough-hewn so that the simple recognize them for what they are: not representation of reality, but mere indications of what cannot be represented" (Joseph Leo Koerner, *The Reformation of the Image* [Chicago: University of Chicago Press, 2004], 248).

[110]Vinny Flynn, *Seven Secrets of Divine Mercy* (San Francisco: Ignatius, 2015), 109. There is a remarkable confluence between this popular devotional publication and the learned explorations of Jean-Luc Marion in "Seeing, or Seeing Oneself Seen: Nicholas of Cusa's Contribution in De visione Dei," *The Journal of Religion* 96, no. 3 (2016): 305-31.

[111]The word *impartation* is employed by George Hunsinger to convey the same Protestant insights without falling into the over wrought debates between imputation and infusion. See "Ninety-Four

Figure 8.7. Shrine of Divine Mercy in Lombard, Illinois, with "Jesus, I Trust in You" in Polish at base of painting

devotion to the image of divine mercy.[112] But the clearest Lutheran touchpoint comes from the legible message that accompanies all versions of the image, a prompt for personal devotion: What could be more indicative of the central thrust of the Reformation than the message "Jesus, I trust in you"?

In the divine mercy image, moreover, the connection to sacraments—the subject of this volume—grows very close indeed. If "the pale ray stands for the Water which makes souls righteous [and] the red ray stands for the Blood which is the life of souls,"[113] then here is something of a sacramental analogue that Protestant, Catholic, Orthodox, and Pentecostal Christians can actually share. If Simone Weil, without orally receiving the Eucharist, "feasted on the Host ardently with her eyes in adoration, practicing as a paradoxically non-Christian Christian what medieval believers called spiritual Communion,"[114] then perhaps the visual

---

Theses on Justification," in George Hunsinger, *Evangelical, Catholic and Reformed* (Grand Rapids: Eerdmans, 2015), 233-44. Thank you to Keith Johnson for this reference.

[112]Sister Faustina heard these words in her heart: "Eternal Father, I offer You the Body and Blood, Soul and Divinity of Your dearly beloved Son, Our Lord Jesus Christ, for our sins and those of the whole world" (Diary 475, cited in Odell, *Faustina*, 109, 183). These words are repeated by all present during any Novena to the image.

[113]Diary 299, cited in Odell, *Faustina*, 79.

[114]Anne Astell, *Eating Beauty: The Eucharist and the Spiritual Arts of the Middle Ages* (Ithaca, NY: Cornell University Press, 2016), 6.

ecumenism offered by images like the divine mercy can temporarily satisfy woe-fully divided Christians as well.[115]

CONCLUSION

I have attempted to show in this chapter that three versions of Cranach's law-gospel visual formula—Gotha, Prague, and Weimar—have a vibrant life within non-Lutheran confessional traditions. The Gotha version can be seen in a certain form in late medieval manuscripts, in Orthodox icons of Jesus, and most explicitly in Pontormo's lost program in Florence. A less direct but still viable candidate for the Prague version is on offer in Michelangelo's twisted head of Moses in the tomb of Julius II, which was inspired in part by reform circles in Italy. Finally, the Weimar law-gospel version can be viewed, to a degree at least, in the divine mercy image that non-Catholic Christians can celebrate as well.

While this may appear to be a colonizing of other traditions with Protestantism, it is intended as a way of stripping Protestantism of any sense of exclusive pos-session of the law-gospel message, enabling us to see it elsewhere.[116] Evangelicals, therefore, can be at home with certain medieval Catholic devotional manuals, Russian Orthodox Cathedrals, some monuments of Renaissance Catholicism, and even modern Catholic kitsch. But nor is this to suggest that the Reformation was unnecessary because evangelical insights have covertly resided in other traditions all along. Were it not for the Reformation, Pontormo and Michelangelo could not

---

[115]Legitimate questions about the complexion of the figure can be met with two observations. First, Sister Faustina was dissatisfied with the image—it is an inadequate replication. In addition, it was created by Eastern Europeans who understandably used their visual norms. While the image's global proliferation among a variety of races should not be ignored, we can also hope for supple-mentary images that show different views of Christ, whose ecclesial body includes Eastern Euro-peans, and every other race as well.

[116]A similar dynamic can be observed in devotional literature as well. The success of much Catholic and Orthodox devotional literature is often the result of a remarkably Lutheran approach. "I am totally unable to root out my resentments. They are so deeply anchored in the soil of my inner self that pulling them out seems like self-destruction" (Henri Nouwen, *The Return of the Prodigal Son* [New York: Image, 1994], 76). See also Jacques Philippe's section subtitled "From Law to Grace: Love as a Free Gift," in *Interior Freedom* (New York: Scepter, 2007), 111. For Orthodox equivalents, see the *Philokalia* section titled "On Those Who Think They Are Made Righteous by Works: Two Hundred and Twenty-Six Texts," or Orthodox prayers such as the following (brought to my atten-tion by Christopher Iacovetti): "O Saviour, save me by Thy grace, I pray Thee. For if Thou shouldst save me for my works, this would not be grace or a gift, but rather a duty. . . . Let faith instead of works be imputed to me, O my God, for Thou wilt find no works which could justify me. But may my faith suffice instead of all works, may it answer for, may it acquit me, may it make me a partaker of Thine eternal glory" (John Hutchison-Hall, *Daily Prayers for Orthodox Christians* [n.p.: St. Eadfrith Press, 2012], 11-13).

have produced their celebrated masterworks, for in both cases Protestant influence is very difficult to contest. But even where the law-gospel message emerges "spontaneously," so to speak, in late medieval manuscripts, the Orthodox Deësis, or in the vision of a scrupulous Polish nun, there is, for this viewer at least, a peculiar debt to Protestantism as well. For without the Reformation's recovery of the law-gospel dynamic for the sake of the whole church, I for one would not have known what to look for. Grateful for this retrieval, in Catholic and Orthodox regions where Protestants might expect to hear only law, we might learn to see gospel instead.

9

THE EUCHARIST, THE RISEN LORD, AND THE ROAD TO EMMAUS

A Road to Deeper Unity?

MATTHEW LEVERING

THE GREAT PROTESTANT THEOLOGIAN HANS FREI, in his influential essay on the Gospel accounts of Jesus' resurrection, remarks upon the evident fact that these accounts are not what we would expect from historians trained in the modern academy, and indeed they are even a bit sketchy when measured by the standards of ancient historiography. Frei attributes this to the evangelists' efforts to record something that was historical but that, at the same time, was a mystery far beyond any other event of history. He states, "The text is not a photographic depiction of reality, for not only are the accounts fragmentary and confusing, but they depict a series of miraculous events that are in the nature of the case unique, incomparable, and impenetrable—in short, the abiding mystery of the union of the divine with the historical, for our salvation from sin and death."[1] The evangelists describe this "abiding mystery" in a manner that makes clear that their principal aim does not consist in proving the historicity of Jesus' resurrection, although they are not unconcerned with its historicity. What then is their principal aim? They offer faith-filled testimony to the truth of Jesus' resurrection, testimony

---

[1] Hans W. Frei, "Of the Resurrection of Christ," in *Reading Faithfully*, vol. 1, *Writings from the Archives: Theology and Hermeneutics*, ed. Mike Higton and Mark Alan Bowald (Eugene, OR: Cascade, 2015), 187.

that functions as an invitation to faith in what Frei describes as "the mystery of Christ's resurrection as a real event."[2] In my view, Frei here articulates a core element of the accounts of Jesus' resurrection appearances. Namely, their teaching about the reality of the risen Jesus' unique appearances to his disciples is not simply reportage but also includes the expectation that the risen (and now ascended) Jesus will make himself present to his followers "to the close of the age" (Mt 28:20). Because the resurrection of Jesus is both a "real event" and a "mystery," the first disciples were uniquely witnesses to the event, but all generations are called to encounter the risen Lord.

The Emmaus road narrative in the Gospel of Luke constitutes a prime example of the way in which Jesus' resurrection appearances, while unique, open up the prospect of Jesus' ongoing presence "to the close of the age." In Luke 24, the risen Jesus meets two disciples—Cleopas and his companion—on the road to Emmaus, but they do not recognize him. The risen Jesus first opens the Scriptures to them and shows them that the suffering of the Messiah was fitting, prior to the Messiah's exaltation. But Cleopas and his companion still fail to recognize the risen Jesus. It is only when he breaks bread with them that they finally recognize him—at which point he vanishes from view, since they no longer need to see him in the flesh (now that they recognize that he is truly risen). Once they have recognized him, they recall that their hearts burned within them "while he opened to us the scriptures" (Lk 24:32).

By teaching Cleopas and his companion how to read the Old Testament so as to recognize the necessity that the Messiah should suffer and then rise from the dead, the risen Jesus shows later believers one path for comprehending the truth of his resurrection: reading and understanding the Old Testament. In this essay, however, I will focus on a second path to which the risen Jesus directs believers: "the breaking of the bread" (Lk 24:35). The experience of Cleopas and his companion differs radically from that of later believers, insofar as Cleopas and his companion actually walked and sat at table with the risen Jesus in his glorified flesh. Now that Jesus has ascended to the right hand of the Father, this direct experience is no longer available to believers. Even so, just as believers can still learn to recognize the risen Jesus through reading the Old Testament, so also believers can still come to recognize that Jesus is truly risen by participating in "the breaking of the bread."

---

[2] Ibid.

For a sacramentally inclined Christian, the phrase "the breaking of the bread" tends to call to mind the Lord's Supper or the Eucharist. Yet, Christian biblical scholars today disagree about what "the breaking of the bread" signifies in the Gospel of Luke. Specifically, is "the breaking of the bread" a sacramental meal that accords with Jesus' commandment at the Last Supper to "do this in remembrance of me" (Lk 22:19)? Or does the evangelist (and/or Cleopas and his companion) have primarily in view a parallel with the miraculous feeding that Jesus undertook during his public ministry?

At issue is whether Jesus intended to leave us the Lord's Supper or Eucharist as one of the primary modes by which we can seek and find the answer to the question posed by N. T. Wright in his superb *The Resurrection of the Son of God*, "Did Jesus of Nazareth . . . really rise from the dead?"[3] For St. Augustine, the Emmaus road narrative describes the way in which receiving the Eucharist opened the eyes of the two disciples to the presence of the risen Jesus.[4] Through the Eucharist, they were able to perceive the reality of Jesus risen—in their case (unlike ours), a reality that was directly before their eyes rather than sacramentally veiled. More recently, the *Catechism of the Catholic Church* argues in light of the Emmaus road account, "The liturgy of the Word and liturgy of the Eucharist together form 'one single act of worship.' . . . Walking with them he explained the Scriptures to them; sitting with them at table 'he took bread, blessed and broke it, and gave it to them.'"[5] Like Augustine, the *Catechism* assumes that Luke 22:19 has the sacrament in view.

Can the truth of Jesus' resurrection be known not solely through historical study but also through the Lord's Supper or Eucharist? Does the risen Jesus manifest himself to us in the Eucharist (even if less directly than he did to Cleopas and his companion), so that we thereby come to know that Jesus is truly risen? If so, then despite ongoing disputes about the nature of the Eucharist, Catholics and Protestants may find that we have each met the risen Christ "in the breaking of the bread," and we may draw closer to each other on this basis of this shared encounter with the risen Christ.

In what follows, I address this topic by means of three steps. First, I examine four views of the Emmaus road narrative. I treat two Protestant biblical scholars,

---

[3]N. T. Wright, *The Resurrection of the Son of God* (Minneapolis: Fortress, 2003), 3.

[4]See Thomas Aquinas, *Catena Aurea: Commentary on the Four Gospels Collected Out of the Works of the Fathers*, vol. 3, part 2, ed. John Henry Newman, trans. Thomas Dudley Ryder (Albany, NY: Preserving Christian Publications, 1995), 779-80.

[5]*Catechism of the Catholic Church*, 2nd ed. (Vatican City: Libreria Editrice Vaticana, 1997), §§1346-47. The first interior quotation comes from *Sacrosanctum Concilium* §56.

Joel Green and I. Howard Marshall, and two Catholic ones, Luke Timothy Johnson and Joseph Fitzmyer. Second, in light of the work of Stefan Alkier, I argue that we should *expect* the Lord's Supper to be a central place where believers truly meet the risen Christ so as to apprehend the truth of his resurrection. As a third and final step, I offer an example of the interior encounters of St. Gertrude the Great with the risen Christ during the liturgy of the Eucharist. I propose that Gertrude may exemplify the way in which the "breaking of the bread," as a place of encounter with the risen Christ, serves believers' apprehension of the truth of the Gospels' proclamation that Jesus Christ is risen.

FOUR VIEWS ON THE EMMAUS ROAD ACCOUNT AND THE LORD'S SUPPER OR EUCHARIST

For readers of Luke–Acts, the statement of Cleopas and his companion that the risen Jesus "was known to them in the breaking of the bread" (Lk 24:35) will inevitably resonate with other meals that are significant in Jesus' ministry, and especially with his feeding miracle and with his Last Supper. Recall that in his miracle of feeding the crowd, Jesus took five loaves and "looked up to heaven, and blessed and broke them, and gave them to the disciples to set before the crowd" (Lk 9:16). In his Last Supper, Jesus "took bread, and when he had given thanks he broke it and gave it to them, saying, 'This is my body which is given for you. Do this in remembrance of me'" (Lk 22:19). Note that the language of Luke 24:30—"he took the bread and blessed, and broke it"—has parallels with both of these meals, as well as with the standard description of the communal meal of Christians that we find in Acts, namely, "the breaking of the bread" (Acts 2:42). The "breaking of the bread" appears to be the weekly enactment of the Last Supper in remembrance of Jesus. This is implied by Acts 20:7, "On the first day of the week, when we were gathered to break bread," and it seems also to be possibly present in Acts 27:27, where Paul "took bread, and giving thanks to God in the presence of all he broke it and began to eat" (Acts 27:35).

Joel Green. Given the two especially important meals—the feeding miracle and the Last Supper—contemporary biblical scholars disagree about which meal provides the primary context for the Emmaus road narrative. The Methodist biblical scholar Joel Green favors the primacy of the feeding miracle. In his commentary on Luke 24, Green notes that the journey to Emmaus of the two followers of Jesus indicates "the beginnings of the drift away from high hopes and the community of discipleship," the breaking up of the community of Jesus' followers due to their disappointment about Jesus' death and their (seeming) disbelief of the women's testimony.[6] When the risen Jesus joins them on the road, the two followers—apparently taking to a new level the misunderstandings that had characterized the disciples during Jesus' earthly ministry—turn out to be "incapable of recognizing Jesus."[7] Green notes that Luke 24:16's "reference to their 'eyes' is reminiscent of the correlation of 'sight' with comprehension, faith, and salvation elsewhere in the Gospel."[8] Like Cleopas and his companion, whose "eyes were kept from recognizing" Jesus (Lk 24:16), the male disciples who went to the tomb of Jesus found it empty but "did not see" Jesus (Lk 24:24). Their failure to see relates to the fact that for the Old Testament "'a suffering Messiah' would be an oxymoron."[9]

When he addresses the meaning of Luke 24:30-31 and Luke 24:35—where Cleopas and his companion suddenly recognize the risen Jesus "in the breaking of the bread"—Green argues that the key link is to Luke 9:16, the miraculous feeding. He begins by noting the importance of meals in the Gospel of Luke, where meals (hosted by Jesus) often are "the site for revelatory discourse and the prospect of genuine fellowship characteristic of the kingdom of God."[10] According to Green, Jesus' actions at the Emmaus road meal are "most reminiscent of his similar actions in 9:16 in the account of the miraculous feeding."[11] It might seem that the motifs of sudden recognition and presence/absence fit more closely with the Eucharistic blessing, breaking, and distributing of the bread that we find in Luke 22:19. Green, however, holds that the Emmaus road event is fundamentally a *revelatory* one: the disciples recognize that Jesus is not dead but risen. The Last Supper was not revelatory in this way, but the event of the miraculous feeding was so.

As Green explains, "Prior to the feeding, Luke records misconceptions about Jesus' identity, including the possibility that Jesus is a prophet"—whereas after the miraculous feeding, "Peter acknowledges that Jesus is the Messiah."[12] For Green, it is decisive that Peter's confession occurs directly after Jesus has performed his miraculous feeding of the five thousand. Green correlates this meal, which in a certain way reveals that Jesus is the Messiah, with the Emmaus road meal, which reveals that Jesus is risen. Green points out that prior to the miraculous feeding,

---

[6]Joel B. Green, *The Gospel of Luke*, NICNT (Grand Rapids: Eerdmans, 1997), 844.
[7]Ibid., 845.
[8]Ibid.
[9]Ibid., 848.
[10]Ibid., 849.
[11]Ibid.
[12]Ibid.

the disciples had not really understood Jesus' true identity. After the miraculous feeding, the disciples understand Jesus to be the Messiah, but they do not really understand that he will have to suffer. Jesus tries to explain it to them; after Peter's confession that Jesus is the Messiah, Jesus immediately teaches that "the Son of man must suffer many things, and be rejected by the elders and chief priests and scribes, and be killed, and on the third day be raised" (Lk 9:22). As we learn when Jesus prepares to go to Jerusalem to be killed, however, in fact the disciples "understood none of these things" (Lk 18:34). Jesus tells the disciples that he must "be mocked and shamefully treated and spit upon," and must be killed and rise again on the third day, but, as Luke says, the meaning of "this saying was hid from them, and they did not grasp what was said" (Lk 18:34).

Therefore, Green holds that at the center of the Emmaus road account is the revelation not simply of the Messiah (which was the revelation given by the miraculous feeding in Lk 9:16) but now of the *suffering* Messiah. Recall that in his conversation with the risen Jesus, Cleopas had expressed sadness because he "had hoped that he [Jesus] was the one to redeem Israel" (Lk 24:21). Cleopas did not understand how the Messiah could suffer and die. The risen Jesus, still unrecognized, has to teach Cleopas from the Scriptures that it was "necessary that the Christ should suffer these things and enter into his glory" (Lk 24:26). As with the miraculous feeding that instructed Jesus' disciples about his messianic status, so also the actual revelation that Jesus, having suffered and died, is indeed the Messiah comes about through "the breaking of the bread" (Lk 24:35).

In connecting these two revelatory moments regarding Jesus' messianic status—Luke 9 and Luke 24, the feeding of the five thousand and the Emmaus road event—Green also highlights the centrality of Scripture for the final revelation of the identity of the suffering Messiah. He points to "the crucial function of scriptural interpretation for the new insight of the disciples, even if the revelatory moment is 'the breaking of the bread.'"[13] He observes that the puzzlement of Cleopas and his companion gives way to understanding when they become "able to articulate the reality of the divine presence among them, transforming them, as they had the Scriptures interpreted to them during the journey."[14] Revelatory teaching involves scriptural interpretation at its heart, since the need is to understand Jesus' identity as the Messiah who suffers and dies. Whereas the disciples prior to

---

[13]Ibid., 850.
[14]Ibid.

Emmaus had not been able to understand this truth about the Messiah, they are now able to do so: "their eyes were opened and they recognized him" (Lk 24:31).

When Cleopas and his companion return to Jerusalem after the Emmaus road event, they find that the risen Jesus has also appeared to Peter. The whole community of Jesus' followers now calls Jesus "Lord," which Green understands to signify "their conversion to the belief that the heinousness of his crucifixion is no contradiction of his status as the one through whom the gracious benefaction of God would continue to be made available."[15] On this view, the revelatory event of the Emmaus road, which ends in a meal, parallels the revelatory event of the miraculous feeding insofar as its outcome and purpose have to do with instructing the community of disciples about the truth of Jesus' messianic lordship.

Green is aware that some scholars connect the Emmaus road account with Jesus' Last Supper and with the church's celebration of the Eucharist or the Lord's Supper. However, Green argues that in the Emmaus road account, "the breaking of the bread" simply refers to the meal that Cleopas and his companion shared with Jesus. He explains that "'the breaking of the bread,' which signals the beginning of the meal, is metonymic for the meal as a whole."[16] Of course, the Emmaus road meal was no normal meal, because it was a revelatory meal. In Green's view, the meal that Cleopas and his companion shared with the risen Jesus "provides a bridge from table fellowship during Jesus' ministry to the celebratory meals characteristic of the early church in Acts."[17] He notes that such "celebratory meals" are mentioned in Acts 2:46-47, which describes the disciples, after Jesus' ascension and Pentecost, "attending temple together and breaking bread in their homes" and partaking "of food with glad and generous hearts, praising God and having favor with all the people." Again, these meals are not *mere* meals any more than meals were during Jesus' ministry. The meals now "signify the coming near of salvation" in an eschatological sense.[18]

In a footnote, Green cites the Methodist biblical scholar I. Howard Marshall's *Last Supper and Lord's Supper*. As Green notes, Marshall supports the view that the phrase "the breaking of the bread" means "Eucharist." Here Green disagrees with Marshall, on the grounds that Marshall's "view is based on the problematic identification of κοινωνία with 'common meal' rather than with the more probable

---

[15]Ibid., 850-51.
[16]Ibid., 851n42.
[17]Ibid., 851.
[18]Ibid.

'sharing of possessions' [see Acts 2:42]."[19] Furthermore, Green adds that Marshall himself does not think that a "sacrament" of the church is being described in Acts 2:42. Green points out that the connection to the Lord's Supper also presupposes that Acts is concerned with "the presence of Jesus at the meal," a presence that in fact Acts 2 (like Acts 20:7 and 27:35) never mentions.[20]

Luke Timothy Johnson. In his commentary on the Gospel of Luke, the Catholic biblical scholar Luke Timothy Johnson agrees with much of Green's analysis. Commenting on Luke 24:30, which states that the (as yet unrecognized) risen Jesus "took the bread and blessed, and broke it, and gave it to them," Johnson points out the link to the miraculous feeding of Luke 9:16. Although Johnson also makes a connection to the Last Supper (Lk 22:19), he suggests that the connection to the miraculous feeding is stronger, at least linguistically. Comparing Luke 9:16 and 22:19 with Luke 24:30, Johnson observes, "In both accounts [9:16 and 22:19] as here [24:30], Jesus 'took' bread (*lambanō*). Here and in 9:16, he 'blesses' (*eulogeō*), whereas in 22:19 he 'gives thanks' (*eucharisteō*)."[21] This seems a reason for linking the Emmaus road meal more closely with the miraculous feeding.

Commenting on Luke 24:32, where Cleopas and his companion are reflecting on their experience of recognizing the risen Jesus (who has now vanished), Johnson underscores the significance of their recollection of Jesus' opening the Scriptures to them. Much like Green, Johnson comments that "as they perceived the true, messianic meaning of the Scripture, they were also able to 'see' Jesus in the breaking of the bread."[22] The "messianic meaning of the Scripture" involves a suffering Messiah, and until Cleopas and his companion recognized this, they were unable to recognize the risen Jesus.

Unlike Green, however, Johnson holds that Luke 24:30 does indeed refer also the Last Supper. He observes that when Luke reports that the risen Jesus "was known to them in the breaking of the bread" (Lk 24:35), Luke employs "the phrase *klasis tou artou*, which recurs in Acts 2:42 as the ritual meal of the community (see also Acts 2:46; 20:7, 11; 27:35)."[23] Johnson is careful to say "the ritual meal of the community" rather than to load his text with all the implications we associate with "sacramental" or "Eucharist." But he nonetheless insists upon the connection of the Emmaus road experience of the risen Jesus with the Christian "ritual meal," which

---

[19]Ibid., 851n42.
[20]Ibid.
[21]Luke Timothy Johnson, *The Gospel of Luke*, Sacra Pagina 3 (Collegeville, MN: Liturgical Press, 1991), 396.
[22]Ibid., 397.
[23]Ibid.

can only be the celebration of the meal that Jesus commands when he says at the Last Supper, "This is my body which is given for you. Do this in remembrance of me" (Lk 22:19).

According to Johnson, the evangelist Luke holds that the experience of Cleopas and his companion bears upon "the *mode* of Jesus' presence to humans after his resurrection," including the fact that the risen Jesus can now "be recognized in the ritual gestures of the community fellowship meal."[24] Here, Johnson is agreeing with St. Augustine, although he does not cite him. Johnson makes clear that through "the ritual gestures of the community fellowship meal"—in "the breaking of the bread" (Lk 24:35)—believers can now encounter and recognize the living Lord Jesus. The truth of the resurrection of Christ, the truth that Christ has been raised, can be known experientially by participating together in the ritual meal, because the risen Christ wills to make himself present to us in this mode (among other modes).

At the same time, Johnson strongly agrees with Green's emphasis on the disciples' gradual discovery of the fact that suffering belongs to messianic identity. Johnson remarks that "there is an even broader framework within which the 'necessity of the Messiah to suffer and enter his glory' [Lk 24:26] is to be understood: the writings of the Torah, and the pattern of prophetic sending and rejection to be found in those writings."[25] Jesus is not simply a man who has been raised; he is the Messiah of Israel, and thus what happens to him must accord with the messianic prophecies and the entire pattern of salvation revealed in the Scriptures (the Old Testament). A suffering Messiah was originally unthinkable for the disciples. They needed to have their eyes opened so that they could understand the teaching of the Scriptures (the Old Testament) about the Messiah and recognize the crucified and risen Messiah. Johnson states that in the Emmaus road account, Luke is suggesting that "the 'opening of the eyes' to see the texts truly and the 'opening of the eyes' to see Jesus truly are both part of the same complex process of seeking and finding meaning."[26]

Why, however, could they not simply recognize Jesus, who after all was walking with them? Johnson holds that Luke is describing an interpretive circle between early Christian experience and early Christian employment of Scripture: "Without 'Moses and the prophets' they would not have had the symbols for appropriating

---

[24]Ibid., 398.
[25]Ibid., 399.
[26]Ibid.

their experience. Without their experience, 'Moses and the prophets' would not have revealed those symbols."[27] Green does not go quite so far in this hermeneutical direction. Rather than talking about "symbols for appropriating their experience," Green simply suggests that Cleopas and his companion originally believed that Jesus' death meant that he was not "the one to redeem Israel" (Lk 24:21), the Messiah. They could not recognize the risen Jesus until they recognized scripturally that the Messiah did indeed have to suffer and die. Only then could encountering the crucified Messiah, now risen from the dead, make any sense or be an option for their minds.

Joseph Fitzmyer. More forceful in his use of Eucharistic language is the Catholic exegete Joseph Fitzmyer. In his Anchor Bible commentary on the Gospel of Luke, Fitzmyer describes the Emmaus road account as a "circumstantial narrative" (a category adapted from C. H. Dodd), that is to say, a narrative "reflecting the literary style and interest of the individual evangelist."[28] Among the "Lucan theological motifs" that Fitzmyer identifies in the Emmaus road account is Luke's penchant for "revelatory" scenes.[29] In Fitzmyer's view, the claim that "their eyes were kept from recognizing him [the risen Jesus]" is not historically accurate but rather shows tell-tale signs of being "a literary device," a way of dramatically showing the importance of the "eyes of faith."[30] Like Green, Fitzmyer appreciates that the risen Christ, for Luke, "is now manifested . . . not only as a prophet but as the suffering Messiah, of whom Moses and all the prophets had written."[31]

Yet, the Lucan motif that stands out is the one that Fitzmyer calls "Eucharistic." He contends that the "scene with Christ reclining at table with the disciples of Emmaus, taking bread, uttering a blessing, breaking the bread, and offering it to them (v. 30), not only recalls the Last Supper (22:19), but becomes the classic Lucan way of referring to the Eucharist," specifically in Acts 2, 20, and 27.[32] Like Augustine, the meaning that Fitzmyer draws from the Emmaus road account is that Christians will now encounter the risen and ascended Christ in the communal celebration of the Eucharist. As Fitzmyer puts it, "The lesson in the story is that henceforth the risen Christ will be present to his assembled disciples, not visibly

---

[27]Ibid.

[28]Joseph A. Fitzmyer, SJ, *The Gospel According to Luke X–XXIV*, AB 28A (Garden City, NY: Doubleday, 1985), 1557.

[29]Ibid., 1558.

[30]Ibid.

[31]Ibid.

[32]Ibid., 1559.

(after the ascension), but in the breaking of the bread. So they will know and recognize him, because *so* he will be truly present among them."[33] For Fitzmyer, the
fact that Jesus interprets the Scriptures for Cleopas and his companion does not
undermine the central position of "the breaking of the bread." After all, every
encounter with the risen Christ in the Eucharist requires scriptural instruction
that awakens faith and hope in the crucified Messiah. The celebration of the Eucharist cannot rightly be separated from the proclamation of the Word and its
homiletic interpretation.

As evidenced by his willingness to use the word *Eucharistic*, Fitzmyer clearly has
the church's sacrament in view. At the same time, he seeks to avoid anachronism
by raising and rejecting a question that arose in patristic and medieval times. The
question is whether Christ himself was celebrating the Eucharist for Cleopas and
his companion. He argues that the question is anachronistic and unanswerable; no
one can know whether Christ himself actually broke "bread in the sense of celebrating the Eucharist."[34] Indeed, since Cleopas and his companion were not present
at the Last Supper, Fitzmyer suggests that their recognition of Jesus "in the breaking
of the bread" looks back to the miraculous feeding of the five thousand in Luke 9:16,
presumably since Cleopas and his companion could have been present then.
Whatever ideas Cleopas and his companion might have had, however, Fitzmyer
thinks that Luke himself is firmly aware of the Eucharistic meaning of the Emmaus
road account. Fitzmyer affirms that "Luke intended a Eucharistic connotation."[35]
For Luke at least, the claim that Christ "was known to them in the breaking of the
bread" (Lk 24:35) is a claim about how the Christian community experiences and
knows the presence of the risen Christ and the truth of his resurrection. Fitzmyer
adds that we need not take the Emmaus road account as a literal description of the
earliest Eucharistic liturgy. But he grants that the presence of the basic elements of
the Eucharistic liturgy—specifically, the proclamation of the Scriptures, the affirmation of faith in Christ's resurrection, and the breaking of the bread—"suggest[s]
clearly a relation to the Eucharist" even if they do not necessarily "reflect the *mode*
of a primitive eucharistic celebration."[36]

---

[33]Ibid.
[34]Ibid., 1560.
[35]Ibid.
[36]Ibid. In a brief note on Lk 24:35, Fitzmyer amplifies his point with regard to "the breaking of the
  bread": "E. Haenchen (*Acts*, 584) understands Acts 20:7, 11 to refer to a celebration of the Lord's
  Supper, but the other passages (2:46; 27:35) to ordinary (perhaps sumptuous) meals. Yet it is difficult
  to see a reason for the distinction. True, it is not always said that the bread was distributed, but we
  are clearly confronted here with an abstract way of referring to the Eucharist, which was current in

I. Howard Marshall. Discussing Luke 24:30, I. Howard Marshall associates Rudolf Bultmann with the view that the resurrection appearances, as narrated in the Gospels, often involve meals because the earliest Christians "expected Jesus to 'appear' at the Lord's Supper."[37] Marshall proposes that Bultmann has gotten the causal direction the wrong way around. It is because Jesus' real resurrection appearances involved meals that the earliest Christians though he would be present at the Lord's Supper. Marshall finds the Emmaus road account especially significant because it reveals how the risen Jesus will henceforth make himself present to his followers. As Marshall says, "In the reading of Scripture and at the breaking of bread [the Lord's Supper or the Eucharist] the risen Lord will continue to be present, though unseen."[38] Marshall's position thereby accords with that of Fitzmyer and Johnson, and it is no wonder that Green explicitly states his disagreement with Marshall.

Evaluation. I agree with Marshall's conclusion: "In the reading of Scripture and at the breaking of bread [the Lord's Supper or the Eucharist] the risen Lord will continue to be present, though unseen." Marshall's view fits with Fitzmyer's insistence that in 24:30-31 and 24:35, "Luke intended a eucharistic connotation."[39] This agreement retains its ecumenical significance even though what Marshall thinks the Lord's Supper involves in many ways differs from what Fitzmyer, as a Catholic, thinks is involved.[40] The key point is that the Lord's Supper, or the Eucharist, is a privileged mode in which we come to know the risen Christ and thus come to know the truth that Christ is truly risen. Like Johnson, I nonetheless agree with Green that Jesus is revealing that the fittingness of his Messianic suffering. Until the disciples appreciated the fittingness of his suffering, they could not really recognize the risen Jesus because they could not conceive of him as the true Messiah for whom resurrection was possible.

Luke's time. He [Luke] has read it back into these instances (even into this one) at Stage III of the gospel tradition (say what one might about Stage I [i.e., the actual historical events]). This is the way that Luke wants it to be understood" (Fitzmyer, *The Gospel According to Luke X–XXIV*, 1569; citing E. Haenchen, *The Acts of the Apostles: A Commentary* [Philadelphia: Westminster, 1971]).

[37] I. Howard Marshall, *The Gospel of Luke: A Commentary on the Greek Text*, NIGTC (Exeter: Paternoster, 1978), 898.

[38] Ibid., 900.

[39] Fitzmyer, *The Gospel According to Luke X–XXIV*, 1560.

[40] For Marshall's perspective on the Lord's Supper, see Marshall, *Last Supper and Lord's Supper* (Vancouver: Regent College Publishing, 2006), 155-57.

WHAT THE EUCHARIST ADDS TO THE QUEST
TO KNOW WHETHER CHRIST IS RISEN

In his recent book *The Reality of the Resurrection: The New Testament Witness*,
Stefan Alkier titles his final chapter "The Lord's Supper as a Gift of the Resurrected
Crucified One."[41] He contends that "the Lord's Supper offers participation in the
Jesus-Christ-Story as an incarnational reminder,"[42] whereas I think that a better
way to put it would be to say that the Lord's Supper (or the Eucharist) enables us
literally to come to know Jesus as the risen Christ, present in the sacrament. For
Alkier, the central step consists in allowing ourselves to move beyond the level of
empirical or historical proof and to penetrate, at our emotional core, into the very
heart of the whole biblical story, since it is there—when "our hearts burn within us"
(Lk 24:32)—that we will be able to encounter the truth of Christ's resurrection as
Luke aims to teach it to us.[43]

I agree with Alkier that "the investigation of historico-empirical reality," while
necessary and valuable since it has to do with "an ineluctable realm of the reality
we experience," cannot be the whole of the way by which Christ intends for us to
come to know the truth that he is risen from the dead.[44] Scripture makes clear that
faith in Christ's resurrection will come about not only through "historico-empirical"
evidence, important as such evidence is. Alkier remarks that historico-empirical
arguments "lead to theological and philosophical blind alleys . . . if the question of
the resurrection is (or should be) answered implicitly or explicitly with them
alone."[45] In my view, Luke 24:35's observation that the risen Christ "was known to
them in the breaking of the bread" suggests that the Eucharist is a crucial non–
historico-empirical way of knowing Christ's resurrection with certitude.

Richard B. Hays notes that Alkier's approach to the study of the historicity of
Jesus' resurrection emphasizes the need for the "transformation of the mind
brought about by the resurrection as a real event—that is, by the power of God."[46]
On this view, the questions that we have about Christ's resurrection will involve us
in historical study but will not be firmly answered without encounter with the
divine power of the resurrection itself. To Alkier's approach, I would add that this

---

[41]Stefan Alkier, *The Reality of the Resurrection: The New Testament Witness*, trans. Leroy A. Huizenga
(Waco, TX: Baylor University Press, 2013), 255.
[42]Ibid., 262.
[43]See ibid., 213.
[44]Ibid., 2.
[45]Ibid.
[46]Richard B. Hays, foreword to Alkier, *Reality of the Resurrection*, ix-xiii, at xiii.

encounter, as Luke suggests, takes place literally "in the breaking of the bread," the Lord's Supper. The Lord's Supper or Eucharist is unifying for Christians because we are unified by the power of encounter with the crucified and risen Christ. It is in the Lord's Supper or the Eucharist that we experientially have our eyes opened, in the full sense, to the truth of Christ's resurrection. We come to know the truth about Christ in and through the act of worship, or liturgical "remembrance," that he commanded us to perform.

On biblical grounds, Marshall points out that "the function of the Lord's Supper is to proclaim the death of the Lord."[47] In a Catholic manner, I would make this more concrete by stating that the Lord's Supper or Eucharist is a real participation in Christ's Passover, Christ's sacrificial death by which he restores the order of justice and embodies the offering of supreme love that joins us to the Father in the Spirit. Marshall adds that the Lord's Supper also serves as "a means of fellowship with the risen Lord," and indeed as "the place of meeting with the risen Lord."[48] He considers that the Eucharist's status as the "place of meeting with the risen Lord" is evident particularly "in the Gospel of Luke where the Emmaus story can be summed up as showing how the risen Lord 'was known in the breaking of the bread.'"[49] In my view, this insight can be fruitfully joined with Alkier's insistence that historical study is not enough, or at least is not the only mode by which Christ intends for people to know the truth of Christ's resurrection.

Yet, if we lack faith prior to taking part in the Lord's Supper or Eucharist, then we are hardly likely to recognize him. We must first hear the word of the Lord, in which Christ unfolds to us "in the scriptures the things concerning himself"

---

[47] Marshall, *Last Supper and Lord's Supper*, 148.

[48] Ibid., 150.

[49] Ibid. Marshall also points out (pp. 150-51), along lines that allow for much commonality (though certainly not complete commonality) with the Catholic position:

> The same stress is to be found in Paul. He regarded the bread and the cup as the means of participation in the body and blood of Jesus, that is to say as the means of sharing in the saving benefits of his death, but at the same time he spoke of the table of the Lord in a way which suggested that he regarded believers as taking part in a meal at which the Lord is host and they have fellowship with him. Although we have carefully differentiated between participation in the body and blood of Jesus and communion or fellowship with him, we must not regard these as completely separate experiences. It is a firmly established theological principle that Christ and his benefits are inseparable, so that it is a short step from participation in salvation to communion with the Saviour. We can find this same thought in John where believers eat the bread of life which is identified with Jesus himself; to eat the bread of life is in fact to believe in Jesus and this leads to the believer and Jesus entering into communion with one another. When the risen Lord invites believers to share in supper with him in Revelation 3:20, we may well see language that can be applied to the Lord's Supper. Thus the fact is established that the Lord's Supper is an occasion of fellowship with the risen Jesus.

(Lk 24:27) so that "our hearts burn within us" (Lk 24:32) in faith and love. If our hearts are burning already, then it seems that we come to know the truth of Christ's resurrection when he opens the Scriptures to us, and not, therefore, "in the breaking of the bread."

I agree that without faith, we will not be able to encounter Jesus in the Lord's Supper or Eucharist. As Marshall says, "It goes without saying that it is with his believing people that the Lord has fellowship in the Supper."[50] But like the faith of the Israelites as they journeyed out of Egypt to worship the Lord their God, our faith takes hold fully in worship, in sharing in the Lord's Passover by obeying his command to "do this in remembrance of me" (Lk 22:19).[51] In this sense of fully enacted and embodied faith, we know the truth of Christ's resurrection preeminently in the Eucharist, just as Cleopas and his companion finally recognized him "in the breaking of the bread."

Cleopas and his companion saw the risen Christ "in the breaking of the bread" in a unique way: he was sitting beside them in his risen flesh. Christ showed himself uniquely to his apostles. But other Christians over the centuries have continued to recognize the risen Christ "in the breaking of the bread." As an example of the fact that believers over the centuries have known the risen Christ intimately in the Eucharist, I will explore the testimony of the thirteenth-century Christian religious sister Gertrude the Great.

THE EXAMPLE OF GERTRUDE THE GREAT (1256–CA. 1302)

In her *Herald of God's Loving-Kindness* (*Legatus memorialis abundantiae Divinae pietatis*), Gertrude's theology arises from Scripture, the fathers of the church, prayer, communal fellowship (including with other important thinkers, notably her friend Mechthild of Magdeburg), and personal relationship with the risen Christ. Born in 1256, Gertrude became a child oblate of the Benedictine monastery in Helfta at age four, received a thorough education in the liberal arts and theology, and at age twenty-five experienced a profound conversion to Christ. Maximilian Marnau describes this conversion as a shift "from a life lived in a monastery and following a monastic rule, and so having God for its object but permitting other interests and

---

[50]Ibid., 151.

[51]Marshall uses the analogy of "a child who is conscious of the love which his father has for him and which is the constant atmosphere in the home; yet there can be occasions when the father takes the child in his arms and expresses his love for him in a special way" (ibid., 152). Indeed, were the father not to do this, the relationship of love between the child and the father would likely not be fully claimed or enacted on the part of the child.

motivations, to a life totally centered upon and given up wholly to God."[52] Marnau notes that "love" is Gertrude's message, a love that relies utterly upon God, so that "our powerlessness [against mortal threats] is a source not of fear but of joy."[53] On numerous occasions during the liturgy of the Eucharist, Gertrude experienced an interior encounter with the risen Christ. The frequency of her interior encounters with him during the Eucharistic liturgy is evidence of Marshall's contention that, according to the Gospel of Luke, the Lord's Supper is a special "place of meeting with the risen Lord." In what follows, I give seven examples of her interior encounters with the risen Christ, drawn from book three of *The Herald of God's Loving-Kindness*.

1. During the elevation of the chalice in the liturgy of the Eucharist, Gertrude desires to unite her own will to Christ's offering of his life for us. Spiritually, she casts herself down, expressing her willingness to follow the path of the cross if by doing so she can serve God and neighbor. In response, however, Christ does something very surprising. When she casts herself down interiorly, she finds that "the Lord immediately rose up in haste and lay down beside her on the ground."[54] In other words, he immediately joins her in the lowliest place. More than that, he draws her to himself, claiming her as his own. She responds to this action by affirming that she is his creature, the work of his hands. But he replies in a manner that again surprises her. He says that beyond the gift of creaturely existence, "A new gift is yours: that my love for you is so tightly bound up with you that without you I cannot happily live."[55] We expect to hear such words from a husband to his wife, but when Christ says such words, it surprises us because it is as though he has gone too far and placed himself in too lowly a position. As Gertrude recognizes, and as she experiences at this Eucharistic liturgy, Christ has done precisely that, casting himself down to our lowly condition out of the greatest personal love. When Christ says these words, Gertrude responds interiorly with amazement, pointing out to Christ that in his divine freedom and transcendence, he certainly does not need any specific creature (let alone her) to assure his happiness. But Christ responds that having created her, he wills to join her personally and to love her and care for her closely, refusing to lose her.

---

[52]Sister Maximilian Marnau, introduction to Gertrude of Helfta, *The Herald of Divine Love*, ed. and trans. Margaret Winkworth (New York: Paulist, 1993), 5-44, at 8.

[53]Ibid., 44.

[54]Gertrude the Great of Helfta, *The Herald of God's Loving-Kindness: Book Three*, trans. Alexandra Barratt (Kalamazoo, MI: Cistercian Publications, 1999), 35.

[55]Ibid.

2. On another occasion, just as the priest was about to consecrate the host, Gertrude receives an interior encounter with the risen Christ. She begins by speaking interiorly to Christ, telling him that she is not worthy to watch the greatness of the sacramental action by which Christ makes himself present in the Eucharist. She throws herself interiorly into an abyss of humility. Christ, however, personally insists that she participate in the liturgy of the Eucharist interiorly by uniting herself in prayer with the liturgical offering of Christ's sacrifice.[56]

3. On another occasion, during Mass, "the Lord [Christ] showed himself to her with as strong an emotion of friendship as ever friend could render friend with tender emotion."[57] However, she wants more—she wants to encounter the "consuming fire" of the charity of Christ and to become one with his love. She reaches out to the holy Trinity by praising the holy Trinity in every possible way she can conceive. Still, she had planned not to receive communion that day. The risen Christ, however, comes to her interiorly and urges her to receive communion and thereby to be united supremely with him (and with his offering of self-sacrificial love). After she has received communion, as she is thanking him joyfully, he comes to her again. The risen Lord again surprises her with the power of his love. He tells her that in her original plan not to receive communion, she had supposed that she had to serve Christ in the way that the ancient Israelites served the Egyptian pharaohs. Christ explains that Gertrude's own will sought to undertake "hard service, in mortar and brick" (Exod 1:14) for Christ. As the risen Christ tells her, however, his own will is to raise her in love to his very table, and to dine with her as with his friend and equal: "I chose you to be among those who would most sweetly take their fill of the delicacies of my royal table."[58] When we think of our relation to Christ's love, we vastly underestimate how much he loves us. Only when we understand how much he loves us can we love him with the intensity that the greatness of his love deserves. The encounter with the risen Christ gives her such a great desire for union with him that "it would not have seemed hard to her to fly to the most saving sacrament even though the midst of swords."[59]

4. During another Mass, at the time of the chanting of *Kyrie eleison* (Lord, have mercy), she encounters the risen Christ interiorly in another way. It seems to her interiorly as though an angel has caught her up and taken her to be presented to

---

[56]See ibid., 37.
[57]Ibid., 46.
[58]Ibid., 47.
[59]Ibid.

God the Father. As she stands before God the Father, though, she fears that the Father is remaining silent rather than giving her his blessing, and she begins to feel deeply unworthy and embarrassed to be standing before the divine Father. In this interior vision, however, the Son dresses her and elevates her to his own measure. The Father then blesses her, and in gratitude she offers to the Father not anything of her own, but rather Christ himself. This causes her garments to resound in praise for the Father. She sees that everything is divine gift.[60]

5. Another time, the risen Christ appeared to her during the liturgy of the Eucharist "as if all honeyed with the sweetness of divine grace, exhaling a life-giving, divine breath," the Holy Spirit.[61] In response to his appearance, she prays for those she knows. He then teaches her that to each person, he has given free will to be like a straw from which the person can draw in all graces from the heart of Christ. Christ offers to everyone the opportunity to drink deeply of the grace of the Holy Spirit, which he desires for each of us. In the interior vision, she sees that the crucial thing is to try to come "nearer to the Lord's Heart," which means to "conform and subdue" oneself "to the divine will" rather than continuing to rely upon one's own will.[62] Only in this way can a person drink of the grace of the Holy Spirit "easily, sweetly and abundantly,"[63] since in this way the person's will is aflame with the love that is a sharing in God's infinite love.

6. During another liturgy of the Eucharist, she finds herself "meditating on her lukewarmness," her lack of great thirst for Christ.[64] Again, the risen Christ comes interiorly to speak with her. Christ says that even when humans desire earthly good things, Christ does not feel offended because all these good things come from Christ. Christ is not waiting to punish us but rather desires to count everything that he can to our credit, unless we have "deliberately turned away" from Christ.[65] If Christ wants to give good gifts, Gertrude asks, why does he not give her good health? Interiorly, the risen Christ answers her that the reason he sometimes withholds such temporal gifts from his beloved people is that in his "burning love," he wishes to give them greater gifts, namely eternal ones, by drawing them to an intimate dependence upon himself.[66]

---

[60]See ibid., 89.
[61]Ibid., 102.
[62]Ibid., 103.
[63]Ibid.
[64]Ibid., 121.
[65]Ibid.
[66]Ibid.

7. At another liturgy of the Eucharist, when ill health prevents her from receiving communion, she interiorly asks to receive spiritual communion—that is, although she cannot receive communion bodily, she hopes to receive it spiritually. She fears, however, that she has not prepared herself adequately. The risen Christ interiorly comes to her, and it seems to her as though his eyes shine upon her. She receives "the gaze of the divine loving-kindness."[67] It enables her to acknowledge her faults humbly, to concentrate on God devoutly, and to trust God faithfully. Christ's gaze nourishes everything good in us. Having received Christ's gaze, she receives also an interior vision of what happens when the priest offers communion to each communicant. Namely, Christ offers himself to each communicant without thereby dispensing with the mediation of the priest. Moreover, whenever a communicant received communion at that Mass, Gertrude felt herself receiving a powerful blessing from Christ. Even when those who love the Lord cannot receive communion bodily (i.e., sacramentally), Christ wills to pour out blessing.

More examples from Gertrude could be given. It is important to note that she does not claim a miraculous appearance of the risen Christ. She simply finds herself conversing in deeply intimate and profound ways with the risen Christ during the liturgy of the Eucharist. This accords with Marshall's view, based upon the Emmaus road account, that Christians should expect the Lord's Supper to be a special "place of meeting with the risen Lord." Obviously, there are other ways of meeting the risen Lord. Even without such special interior manifestations, furthermore, a believer can encounter the risen Lord in the Eucharist or Lord's Supper. Nonetheless, Gertrude's experiences suggest that the Eucharist or Lord's Supper remains a place for having our eyes "opened" (Lk 24:31) so that we truly perceive the risen Lord and know him as the suffering Messiah in his love and humility.

CONCLUSION

In a book provocatively titled *The Resurrection*, which argues against the historicity of Jesus' resurrection, Geza Vermes concludes his summary of Luke's Emmaus road narrative by observing that "during the meal they were sharing, at the sight of some unspecified idiosyncrasy in the stranger's benediction ritual, it dawned on them that their traveling companion was Jesus, but by then he had vanished."[68] Vermes supposes that the trigger for their recognition of Jesus was an "idiosyncrasy" in his practice of the Jewish ritual of blessing and breaking the bread. This seems to me to

---

[67]Ibid., 132.
[68]Geza Vermes, *The Resurrection* (New York: Doubleday, 2008), 95.

miss the point. In the Emmaus road account we find testimony not solely to the unique experience of Cleopas and his companion but also to the fact that in the liturgy of the Eucharist or Lord's Supper, understood as an integral whole (including the opening of the Scriptures), believers can come to know the risen Christ.

Certainly, this was the experience of Gertrude the Great. Interiorly, she encountered the risen Christ frequently during the liturgy of the Eucharist. She conversed with him and received powerful experiential proofs of his wisdom, love, mercy, and goodness, as well as of his existence and personal presence. Indeed, I expect that many Christians have experienced similar presences of the risen Christ during the liturgy of the Eucharist or the Lord's Supper. Since he can make himself present, it is surely fitting that he does so "in the breaking of bread" (Lk 24:35) when we are carrying out his command to "do this in remembrance of me" (Lk 22:19).

If the unity of Christians is to increase, who better to increase it than the risen Christ himself? And where could be more fitting for this unity to be increased than in the Lord's Supper or the Eucharist, whose effect is to deepen the baptismal unity of "all the faithful in one body—the Church"?[69] Recall the words of St. Paul: "The bread which we break, is it not a participation [or 'communion'] in the body of Christ? Because there is one bread, we who are many are one body, for we all partake of the one bread" (1 Cor 10:16-17). If Marshall, Johnson, and Fitzmyer are correct, we become "one body" in and through the Lord's Supper or Eucharist not least because the risen Christ makes himself known to us "in the breaking of the bread" and unites us to himself and thus also to each other.

When Cleopas and his companion arrive back to Jerusalem, their testimony turns out not to be needed, since the eleven disciples are already aware of the truth of Jesus' resurrection: "The Lord has risen indeed, and has appeared to Simon [Peter]!" (Lk 24:34). The truth of Jesus' resurrection is knowable in other ways than through "the breaking of the bread." Historical research into the credibility of Jesus' resurrection assists in knowing its truth, as does believing in the creator God of the Old Testament. But the experience of Cleopas and his companion—reflected by later Christians such as Gertrude, notwithstanding the fact that the risen Jesus was uniquely present on the road to Emmaus—suggests that sacramental participation is also a crucial mode of knowing the truth about the risen Jesus. From the outset, Christ wills to make the full truth about himself known not merely to intellectual inquirers but through the meal of ritual "remembrance" that, in each generation, his followers share.

---

[69]*Catechism of the Catholic Church*, §1396.

10

THE ESCHATOLOGICAL DIMENSION OF SACRAMENTAL UNITY

An Orthodox Christian View

PAUL L. GAVRILYUK

THE TWENTIETH CENTURY was uniquely marked by a movement toward Christian unity. Some leaders of the Orthodox Church have been significant players in this movement from its inception, whereas others have maintained a more cautious, sometimes even antagonistic attitude. While the ecumenical movement continues to have its share of vocal detractors in the Orthodox Church, the most authoritative conciliar body to pronounce on the matter was the Holy and Great Council, which met on the island of Crete in June 2016.[1] This council issued eight documents, the most controversial of which was the document titled "Relations of the Orthodox Church with the Rest of the Christian World." The opening paragraph of this document reads: "The Orthodox Church, as the One, Holy, Catholic, and Apostolic Church, in her profound ecclesiastical self-consciousness, believes unflinchingly that she occupies a central place in the matter of the promotion of Christian unity in the world today."[2] While the representatives of the Orthodox Church have been making similar statements in various ecumenical contexts for about a century, this was the first time the "promotion of Christian unity" had received a *conciliar* endorsement.

---

[1] The council included more than 160 episcopal delegates and approximately sixty clerical and lay advisors.

[2] "Relations of the Orthodox Church with the Rest of the Christian World," 1, www.holycouncil.org /-/rest-of-christian-world.

With respect to those Orthodox who are inclined towards isolationism and sectarianism, the Council decreed:

> The Orthodox Church considers all efforts to break the unity of the Church, undertaken by individuals or groups under the pretext of maintaining or allegedly defending true Orthodoxy, as being worthy of condemnation. As evidenced throughout the life of the Orthodox Church, the preservation of the true Orthodox faith is ensured only through the conciliar system, which has always represented the highest authority in the Church on matters of faith and canonical decrees. (Canon 6 of the 2nd Ecumenical Council)[3]

This is a clear and unambiguous condemnation of sectarians who consider any participation in the ecumenical movement as compromising the purity of Orthodoxy.[4] Unfortunately, the Council of Crete itself demonstrated that the conciliarity of worldwide Orthodoxy remains deeply *wounded*, when four out of fourteen self-governing Orthodox Churches refused to send their delegations to the council at the last moment. As the grounds for their refusal, some local churches, including the Bulgarian Orthodox Church and the Georgian Orthodox Church, cited among other things their objections to the document "Relations of the Orthodox with the Rest of the Christian World."[5] It is also worth noting that these two churches withdrew from the World Council of Churches in the late 1990s. Crucially, then, the churches whose leadership exhibits the strongest isolationist tendencies tend to cave to the pressures of their anti-ecumenical lobbies. These significant exceptions notwithstanding, most Orthodox leaders worldwide appreciate the importance of the ecumenical movement, however one evaluates its success over the last hundred years.

---

[3]Ibid., 22.

[4]A few clerics in Greece and Ukraine have reacted to the "Relations" document by suspending the commemoration of their ruling bishops and even anathematizing the council itself for its promulgation of the "heresy of ecumenism." For example, a senior priest of the Greek Orthodox Church, Father Theodore Zisis, recently announced that he would cease commemoration of his ruling bishop, metropolitan Anthimos of Thessaloniki. See "Well-Known Theologian Archpriest Theodore Zisis Ceases Commemorations of the Metropolitan of Thessaloniki," www.pravoslavie.ru/101874 .html. Bishop Longin Zhar of the Ukrainian Orthodox Church (Moscow Patriarchate) anathematized the Council of Crete on March 5, 2017, on the Sunday of the Triumph of Orthodoxy. See "Episkop Longin (Zhar) predal anafeme kritskii sobor," вестник-верных.рф/mat/svrus /ochishenieoteresei/653-episkop-longin-zhar-predal-anafeme-kritskiy-sobor.html.

[5]The objections of the Georgian Orthodox Church are discussed in the article "Gruzinskaia Pravo-slavnaia Tserkov' ne primet uchastiia vo Vsepravoslavnom Sobore," www.patriarchia.ru/db /text/4536081.html. According to an official report, published at theorthodoxchurch.info/blog/news /georgian-orthodox-church-rejects-document-on-ecumenism-drafted-for-the-great-council-2016/, in February 2016, the Holy Synod of the Georgian Orthodox Church rejected the pre-conciliar draft of the document on ecumenism. The reasons for the rejection were not publicized.

EASTERN ORTHODOXY AND INTERCOMMUNION

Indeed, if the ultimate goal of the ecumenical movement is *intercommunion*, then the Orthodox Church's involvement in the movement has not produced the desired result. The reasons for this frustrated effort are multiple, having to do with intra-Orthodox politics as much as with theological disagreements with the non-Orthodox. In the realm of church politics, the fear of internal schism due to pressures from the traditionalist groups often prevails over ecumenical considerations. Thus, for example, Patriarch Kirill's meeting with Pope Francis in February 2016 was arranged in an atmosphere of secrecy, without consultation with the Holy Synod of the Russian Orthodox Church, at a rather clandestine location at the Havana airport in Cuba. The reason for this situation is that at home, Patriarch Kirill did precious little to convince his fellow bishops and educate his flock, especially certain bishops and monastics, about why such a meeting could be beneficial for the Orthodox. He avoided pomp and circumstance not out of humility but because he knew that the meeting with the Pope would generate strong opposition from the anti-ecumenical front within his own church. He was right to be cautious: seven female monasteries in Moldova and a Romanian bishop in western Ukraine went off the rails in their anti-Catholic zeal, condemning the Havana meeting and going so far as to cease commemorating Patriarch Kirill during the liturgy, which is paramount to an implicit excommunication, or perhaps self-excommunication.[6] Some Orthodox zealots had a similar reaction to the document on ecumenism ratified by the Council of Crete. For example, a small group of monastics on Mount Athos issued a statement condemning the patriarch of Constantinople for the "heresy of ecumenism" and threatening to break communion with him.[7] Their action had support among traditionalists both in Greece and the United States.[8] Faced with such actions, it is understandable why some Orthodox Church hierarchs are cautious when it comes to making any significant progress in ecumenical relations.

---

[6]Bishop Longin (Zhar) announced that he had ceased commemoration of Patriarch Kirill on March 10, 2016, on the grounds that the Havana meeting implied a recognition of the Pope as a legitimate bishop. See "V UPT (MP) bunt: episkop Longin (Zhar) obviniaet patriarkha Kirilla v otstupnichestve ot pravoslaviia," www.risu.org.ua/ru/index/all_news/orthodox/uoc/62941.

[7]See "Open Letter of the Holy Mount Athos Kinot to the Patriarch Bartholomew I," www.katehon .com/article/open-letter-holy-mount-athos-kinot-patriarch-constantinople-bartholomew-i.

[8]See Theodore Zisis, "The Recent History of Ecumenism and the Struggle for Orthodoxy," www.orthodoxethos.com/post/the-recent-history-of-ecumenism-and-the-struggle-for-orthodoxy -part-a; and Peter Heers, "The 'Council' of Crete and the New Emerging Ecclesiology: An Orthodox Examination," orthodoxethos.com/pan-orthodox-council.

ORTHODOXY AND ORTHOPRAXY

Leaving aside the political dimension, the principal theological issue is the correlation between orthodoxy ("true belief") and orthopraxy ("true practice"). The Council of Crete expresses this conjunction in the following manner: "The responsibility of the Orthodox Church for unity as well as her ecumenical mission were articulated by the Ecumenical Councils. These stressed most especially the indissoluble bond between true faith and sacramental communion."[9] The document offers no guidance in understanding the nature of the "indissoluble bond" and does not specify the content and scope of the "true faith." The most common Orthodox understanding of the "indissoluble bond" treats the "true faith" as the *necessary* condition of intercommunion. In other words, it is necessary to agree on the content of the "true faith" in order to share the Eucharist. Another possible understanding of the "indissoluble bond" is that the "true faith" and "sacramental communion" condition each other. Access to the "true faith" is rendered possible through the participation in the sacraments, and the meaning of sacramental participation is authenticated by the "true faith."[10]

The matter is additionally complicated by the fact that the scope of the "true faith" is left unspecified, although the Crete document makes a broad reference to the

---

[9]"Relations of the Orthodox Church with the Rest of the Christian World," 3.

[10]The 1987 Bari Document, "Faith, Sacraments and the Unity of the Church," of the Joint Commission for Theological Dialogue between the Roman Catholic Church and the Orthodox Church, clarifies this relationship in the following manner in the first three paragraphs: "1. After our meeting in Munich in 1982 and in accord with the *Plan* adopted by our commission during its first meeting at Rhodes in 1980, this fourth session of the commission has undertaken to consider the question of the relation between faith and sacramental communion.

"2. As was stated in the *Plan* of our dialogue, which was approved at Rhodes, unity in faith is a presupposition for unity in the sacraments, and especially in the Holy Eucharist. But this commonly accepted principle raises some fundamental issues which require consideration. Does faith amount to adhering to formulas or is it also something else? Faith, which is a divine gift, should be understood as a commitment of the Christian, a commitment of mind, heart, and will. In its profound reality it is also an *ecclesial* event which is realized and accomplished in and through the communion of the Church, in its liturgical and especially in its eucharistic expression. This ecclesial and liturgical character of the faith must be taken seriously into consideration.

"3. Given this fundamental character of faith, it is necessary to affirm that faith must be taken as a preliminary condition, already complete in itself, which precedes sacramental communion; and also that it is increased by sacramental communion, which is the expression of the very life of the Church and the means of the spiritual growth of each of its members. This question has to be raised in order to avoid a deficient approach to the problem of faith as a condition for unity. It should not, however, serve to obscure the fact that faith is such a condition, and that there cannot be sacramental communion without communion in faith both in the broader sense and in the sense of dogmatic formulation," www.vatican.va/roman_curia/pontifical_councils/chrstuni/ch_orthodox_docs/rc_pc_chrstuni_doc_19870616_bari_en.html.

teaching of the ecumenical councils. In contemporary Orthodox theology, the understandings of the scope of the "true faith" fall between what Sergei Bulgakov called "dogmatic minimalism" and "dogmatic maximalism." Dogmatic minimalism reduces the universally binding part of the Orthodox teaching to two dogmas: the Trinity and the incarnation, expressed in the Nicene Creed and the Chalcedonian Definition. Dogmatic minimalism allows for a considerable range of theological opinion in such areas of dogmatic theology as ecclesiology, sacramental theology, and eschatology. In contrast, dogmatic maximalism considerably expands the range of the doctrinal consensus necessary for intercommunion. For example, the 1984 "Agreed Statement of the Eastern Orthodox-Roman Catholic Consultation in the United States on the Lima Document" states, "Concerning the possibility of eucharist sharing, we do not find that growing consensus on eucharistic theology and practice is of itself sufficient for such sharing among our churches. The resolution of questions connected with ministry and the nature and faith of the Church are also important."[11] Such a position implies a form of dogmatic maximalism, which makes the consensus on Eucharistic theology and threefold ministry, along with other unspecified doctrines, all vitally important for the restoration of Eucharistic communion.

Methodologically, the views of most mainline Protestant ecumenists favor dogmatic minimalism or even a weaker position. The Roman Catholic doctrinal stance seems to be closer to dogmatic maximalism, although there is no precise equivalent to the Orthodox position. As recently as 2010, the participants of the North American Orthodox-Catholic Theological Consultation inquired,

> How much formal agreement on doctrine and Church structure is necessary before the Orthodox and Catholic Churches permit local communities to begin at least some degree of sacramental communion with each other? If diversity within our own Churches on theological issues is usually not seen as a barrier to Eucharistic sharing, should we allow the differences between Orthodox and Catholic Christians to overrule the substantial agreement our Churches already enjoy on most of the fundamental issues of faith, and keep us from receiving each other at the Eucharistic table, at least on some occasions?[12]

---

[11]Eastern Orthodox/Roman Catholic Consultation in the United States, "An Agreed Statement on the Lima Document: 'Baptism, Eucharist, and Ministry'" (1984), www.usccb.org/beliefs-and-teachings/ecumenical-and-interreligious/ecumenical/orthodox/statement-lima-baptism-eucharist-and-ministry.cfm.

[12]North American Orthodox-Catholic Theological Consultation, "Step Towards a Reunited Church: A Sketch of the Orthodox-Catholic Vision for the Future" (2010), 9, www.usccb.org/beliefs-and

In bilateral dialogues, it is common for the representatives of the Roman Catholic Church to appeal to the faith of the first millennium on such controversial questions as the filioque and papal primacy. On the filioque, significant progress has been made with a 2003 joint statement of the North American Orthodox-Catholic Theological Consultation (in which Fr. Brian Daley had a hand);[13] on primacy and synodality, a 2016 statement by the Joint International Commission for Dialogue Between the Roman Catholic Church and the Orthodox Church was another major step in a positive direction.[14]

As valuable as they are, these agreements have not generated any public discussion among the Orthodox leaders of the possibility of intercommunion with the Roman Catholics, despite the openness of the Catholic Church to such a practice. Such reluctance has to do as much with the history of divisions and present-day Orthodox Church politics as it has to do with theological issues. On the political side, the standoff between Moscow and Constantinople is not conducive to making progress in pan-Orthodox decisions. What impedes the dialogue theologically is the fact that the content of the "true faith" is either unspecified or specified in a manner approaching a form of "dogmatic maximalism," which makes doctrinal consensus an exceedingly difficult proposition.

SACRAMENTAL PARTICIPATION: AN ESCHATOLOGICAL ACCOUNT

Have we reached an impasse in ecumenical dialogue, or is it possible to move forward? In other words, is it possible to approach sacramental unity differently? In what follows, I will sketch out a fresh approach to sacramental participation focusing on the eschatological dimension of baptism and Eucharist.

My central claim is this: in order to appreciate the degree of unity already shared by all Christians, one needs to attend to the christological and eschatological dimensions of the sacraments. In baptism, the initiates are united with Christ. This new reality can be described in terms of "putting on Christ" (Gal 3:27) and in terms of "burial with Christ" of one's old humanity, which ensures the baptized's "new birth" (Jn 3:5) and subsequent "new life" with Christ (Rom 6:4).

-teachings/ecumenical-and-interreligious/ecumenical/orthodox/steps-towards-reunited
-church.cfm.

[13]"The Filioque: A Church-Dividing Issue? An Agreed Statement" (2003), www.usccb.org/beliefs
-and-teachings/ecumenical-and-interreligious/ecumenical/orthodox/filioque-church-dividing
-issue-english.cfm.

[14]"Synodality and Primacy During the First Millennium" (2016), www.unifr.ch/iso/assets/files/Texte
/Chieti_Document_E_final.pdf.

Baptism is incorporation into the body of Christ. The body of Christ is an eschatological reality inasmuch as it is the body of the risen Christ, who is the second person of the Trinity, fully God and fully man, and the Lord of all. To the extent to which all faithful are engrafted into the body of Christ, they draw near to each other. The unity of believers is not reducible to a moral, social, or political reality. The believers are united in a communion *sui generis*, the communion of the saints by means of God's sanctifying and reconciling action, begun in baptism, continued in the sacramental life of the church, and fulfilled in the kingdom. Since Christ is the kingdom, baptism is also the sacrament of initiation into the kingdom of Christ.

Similar to baptism, the Eucharist is an invitation to have a foretaste of the kingdom.[15] The public part of the Orthodox divine liturgy begins with the exclamation, "Blessed is the kingdom of the Father, and the Son, and the Holy Spirit, now and ever, and unto ages of ages." As Alexander Schmemann explains,

> From the beginning the destination is announced: the journey is to the Kingdom. This is where we are going—and not symbolically, but really. In the language of the Bible, which is *the* language of the Church, to bless the Kingdom is not simply to acclaim it. It is to declare it to be the goal, the end of all our desires and interests, of our whole life, the supreme and ultimate value of all that exists.[16]

It was Schmemann who rediscovered the eschatological dimension of the liturgy as a movement toward the kingdom of God, an experience of the ascent of the mountain of Christ's transfiguration. Such an ascent becomes possible because in the Eucharist Christ descends upon the congregation by becoming, in the words of the Liturgy of St. John Chrysostom, "the Offerer and the offered, the Receiver and the received." By the power of the Holy Spirit, in the Eucharist, Christ is the host and the meal. The Eucharist is a memorial not only of God's redemptive acts in the past but also, paradoxically, the commemoration of the eschatological acts of Christ's resurrection, ascension, and second coming.

Thus, the function of the Eucharist cannot be limited to the validation of an already existing unity. As an eschatological sign, the Eucharist has the potential to relativize all forms of existing human alienation; it is a purification of the fallen

---

[15]As stated in "The Nature and Mission of the Church: A Stage on the Way to a Common Statement" (Geneva: World Council of Churches, 2005), 79: "The Lord's Supper is . . . the communion of the faithful and an anticipation and foretaste of the kingdom to come."

[16]Alexander Schmemann, *For the Life of the World* (Crestwood, NY: St. Vladimir's Seminary Press, 1998), 29.

forms of unity (tribal, national, racial, political, and so on) that go against the believers' new life in Christ. According to the letter to the Ephesians, "In Christ Jesus you who once were far off have been brought near by the blood of Christ. For he is our peace. In his flesh he has made both groups into one and has broken down the dividing wall, that is, the hostility between us" (Eph 2:13-14). What applies to the first-century divisions between the Jewish and Gentile Christians may be extended mutatis mutandis to present-day Christian divisions. No matter how deeply entrenched, these divisions are dissolved as a result of incorporation into Christ. To the extent to which baptism and Eucharist connect the believers with Christ and render them participants in the kingdom of God, partial *intercommunion is already a reality*. While such a conclusion seems inescapable, this reality is often passed over in silence, preoccupied as we are by our continuing differences. But it is a reality nevertheless, because incorporation into Christ cannot be reduced to a purely individualistic communion of each believer with God separately, in splendid isolation from other Christians. Such an isolated condition is a metaphysical impossibility, for in Christ the unity of all redeemed humanity is already eschatologically realized. It is important to acknowledge the eschatological reality of intercommunion before addressing the no less significant social, historical, and psychological realities of our divisions as well as our enduring theological differences. In baptism and Eucharist we are already partially eschatologically united, despite being historically divided.[17]

My distinction between the historical and eschatological dimensions of church unity does not intend to relegate the eschatological dimension to the nebulous sphere of the non-historical. On the contrary, the eschatological dimension stands for the divine action that breaks into the confines of history in the sacramental life of the church. This mutually determining relationship between the historical and eschatological dimensions is powerfully synthesized by metropolitan John

---

[17]This point is expressed in "On Baptism: Towards Mutual Recognition" (Geneva: World Council of Churches, 2011), 57-58, www.oikoumene.org/en/resources/documents/commissions/faith-and -order/ii-worship-and-baptism/one-baptism-towards-mutual-recognition: "In baptism we are baptized into the one body and we become members of one another. The church is both the body of Christ and the people of God (1 Pet 2:9-10). Baptism in Christ, and in the Spirit, is inseparable from Christian life in community (1 Cor 12:12-27). Baptism, however, always occurs in a particular local church which shares in a specific confessional identity. Thus it is the church in which a person is baptized that determines his or her confessional identity. But the local churches are, in too many cases, not in full communion with one another. This results in a paradox: while baptism brings Christians into the unity of Christ's body, which is one, the location of baptism within a specific confessional body means that the baptized experience disunity with many other Christians."

Zizioulas regarding the question of apostolic continuity and succession. Zizioulas writes,

> In the historical approach the main components of continuity are the following: In the first place continuity means succession or survival in time, i.e. from the past to the present into the future. This succession or survival of the Church's apostolic origins can take place in different ways. It can take place by means of *transmission* of certain powers, authority, etc. It can also take place by way of normativeness, i.e. in the form of an example to be copied. In any case the historical approach creates the basis for a *retrospective* continuity with the past. . . . On the other hand the eschatological approach implies no sense of transmission or normativity. Here apostolicity comes to the Church from the side of the future. It is the anticipation of the end, the final nature of the Church that reveals her apostolic character. . . . It is the *Risen Christ* that is related to apostolicity, i.e. the final and ultimate destiny of all that exists.[18]

It is important to note that Zizioulas is far from denying the importance of the historical dimension of continuity; at the same time, he tends to subordinate the historical dimension to the eschatological dimension, or, more precisely, he sees the eschatological dimension as the ultimate completion of the continuity conveyed by the historical dimension. In other words, it is important that faithfulness to Christ is maintained through specific historical communities, offices, and texts. But it is even more significant that the church, as the living community of the faithful, maintains a sacramental communion with its Lord, who dwells in it by the power of the Holy Spirit. For Zizioulas, "true faith" does not exist as a set of dogmatic prerequisites to "sacramental communion." Rather, sacramental communion discloses the content of the "true faith," which is Christ and the communion of the Trinity.[19] Eucharistic communion anticipates the perfect union into which the faithful will be drawn in the eschaton.

EUCHARISTIC THEOLOGIES AND ONTOLOGICAL UNION

We do not have to endorse the particulars of Zizioulas's metaphysics of communion or his personalist epistemology in order to appreciate his profound synthesis of the eschatological and historical dimensions of sacramental theology. I suggest that this synthesis provides a clue for mending the historical divisions, including those

---

[18]John Zizioulas, *Being as Communion: Studies in Personhood and the Church* (Crestwood, NY: St. Vladimir's Seminary Press, 2002), 178-79.
[19]Ibid., 81.

that have involved disagreements over Eucharistic theologies (especially pertinent for the churches of the Reformation). It is not necessary to have identical Eucharistic theologies in order to enter into an ontologically identical sacramental union with the risen Christ. In fact, within the same ecclesial community, it is common for communicants to have vague, partial, or even mistaken understandings of how precisely the bread and wine mediate the reality of the body and blood of Christ. It would be odd to claim that their beliefs alter the nature of their Eucharistic communion so as to break it altogether.

Consider the following three analogies. Consider a driver who has a vague, partial, or mistaken knowledge of the mechanical equipment of his car, including the engine, transmission, steering, and so on. As a rule, such a driver would manage to reach his destination. Of course, somebody who has never driven a car, or drives it recklessly, is less likely to succeed. Or consider a patient who takes a medicine, the precise mechanism of which he does not fully understand. If the prescription is correct and taken as prescribed, such a patient in most circumstances is eventually healed. It should be noted that someone who takes the wrong medicine, or takes it inconsistently, is unlikely to have the same success as the person who takes the right medicine as prescribed. Finally, consider an act of communication between two persons. One might only vaguely remember the other person's name or have a partial or mistaken knowledge of her character. Still, despite these obvious epistemological defects, this person would still manage to refer to the other person and they would manage to communicate. It is certainly possible for us to miscommunicate if I call you by a wrong name, forget your features altogether, or misunderstand what you say or do. To cast the matter in more technical philosophical terms, the conditions for securing a reference to p are weaker than the conditions for having factual knowledge that p or even for defining p. Similarly, the scope of the knowledge required for a driver, patient, or interlocutor is narrower than the scope of the knowledge required for a car engineer, doctor, or close friend (call it "expert knowledge"). For the vast majority of people, the success of driving, healing, and communicating does not depend on expert knowledge but on partial knowledge and other, noncognitive factors such as physical aptitude and moral disposition. To apply these analogies to the Eucharistic communion, as a rule, a Christian could communicate with Christ, receive the healing grace of the sacraments, and traverse the road into the kingdom while having only a vague, partial, and even mistaken grasp of sacramental theology. (Most of my undergraduate students are in this situation.)

It could be objected that these analogies tendentiously minimize the cognitive dimension of faith at the expense of the non-cognitive dimension. It may be observed that church leaders and theologians should be less like clueless drivers and ignorant patients and more like knowledgeable engineers and doctors because they need to ensure that the cars run well and that the right medicine is prescribed. It is generally desirable to resolve the disagreements among the experts before a newly engineered car enters a construction line or a newly created medicine is sold in the drugstores.

While this objection is serious, it can be met by making three observations. First, I am not defending sheer ignorance but rather the sufficiency of *partial* knowledge of communicants, who may nevertheless succeed in communicating fully. My premise is a recognition that when it comes to the "metaphysical mechanism" of the Eucharist, our pertinent knowledge is bound to remain partial, similar to the knowledge that we have vis-à-vis the "metaphysical mechanism" of the incarnation or the Trinity.

Second, in the case of the Eucharist, the problem is compounded by the fact that in addition to the partiality of the communicants' knowledge, their "spiritual state" is fully known only by God. The problem is not just cognitive, or even primarily cognitive, but more profoundly concerns one's existential orientation God-ward, which affects the believer's will, conscience, and so on. Eucharistic communion is possible only as a gift of grace and can be received only as a gift of grace, which completes that which is lacking in the human powers of understanding, will, and affect. The Eucharistic communion, if its eschatological implications are taken seriously, is about a continuing re-creation of the new humanity, the re-creation initiated in Christ's incarnation, continued in the church, and consummated in the kingdom of God.

My third and final observation attends to the cognitive dimension, namely an ecumenical foundation for a common Eucharistic theology. Here I suggest, although I do not have the space to elaborate this point sufficiently, that we need to resuscitate an understanding of the Eucharist as a sacramental *sign*. The main function of the sign is to provide a connection for believers with the signified, namely God. The Orthodox tradition draws on a robust ontology of signs and symbols as participating in the reality of their divine archetypes. In the Anaphora of St. Basil the Great, used in the Orthodox Church in the Sunday Liturgies of Lent, before the epiclesis (the invocation of the Holy Spirit), the presiding minister prays, "We dare to approach Your holy altar and bring forth the symbols of the holy Body and Blood of Your Christ."[20] The metaphysics of participation, which we find, for example, in Pseudo-Dionysius the Areopagite, is of great help for moving beyond the medieval differentiations between a symbol and reality, and between the Reformation-era debates about the real and other forms of sacramental presence. Given the significance that Calvin attributed to *signe* in his sacramental theology, a common appeal to the sacramental sign holds promise for a future dialogue between the Orthodox, Catholic, and Reformed traditions. My proposal that a future ecumenical theology is to be built around the concept of a sacramental sign sharply parts ways with Schmemann's critique of Dionysian and later Byzantine sacramental symbolism while endorsing Schmemann's eschatological vision. By identifying the concept of a sacramental sign as a point of ecumenical convergence, I do not mean to overlook or underestimate the differences that exist between the Reformed and the Orthodox traditions in their respective metaphysics of signs. I only wish to suggest that such differences need not be church-dividing because, as I have emphasized, the epistemic conditions for identifying something correctly are much weaker than the epistemic conditions for defining or knowing something. The type of knowledge attained through communion is closer to knowledge by acquaintance than to knowledge by description, to invoke a famous distinction of Bertrand Russell.[21] It is not necessary to have the same description of the Eucharist in order to have the same experience of the Eucharistic gifts, the same communion.

It could be legitimately asked whether my emphasis on the eschatological dimension of the Eucharist entails an "open table communion" or "open communion." Let me clarify that the openness in question does not extend to the non-baptized, for the Orthodox tradition takes for granted the universal early Christian assumption that the sacrament of initiation has to precede the first communion. To draw on my earlier set of analogies, a non-baptized person receiving the Eucharist is a bit like a person who decides to drive without any driving lessons or a patient who takes her medications in the wrong sequence— or fails to take the first medication (baptism) without which the benefit of the second medication (communion) is nil.[22] With this clarification in mind, should

---

[20]"The Divine Liturgy of St. Basil the Great," www.goarch.org/-/the-divine-liturgy-of-saint-basil-the -great.

[21]Bertrand Russell, "Knowledge by Acquaintance and Knowledge by Description," in *Mysticism and Logic* (Totowa, NJ: Barnes and Noble, 1951), 152-67.

[22]The WCC's 2005 document signals that a wide divergence of practices is a problem: "It is a matter of continuing concern that not all Christians share the communion. Some churches believe that

communion be open to the members of an ecclesial community other than one's own? As it is well known, it is not a practice of the Orthodox Church to open the Eucharistic table to non-Orthodox Christians. The reason for this is that there is already enough doctrinal and moral chaos in the Christian world, and we Orthodox do not wish to contribute more than our fair share to it. In the absence of a church-wide discussion of the eschatological dimension of the Eucharist, spontaneously practiced "open communion" could lead to scandal and, most likely, more far-reaching divisions within the Orthodox Church. While it would not be wise to give in to the spiritual blackmail of all who threaten a schism, at this point in our ecumenical journey, "open communion" is problematic for pastoral reasons.

A deeper question is whether and in what sense communion can be "closed." The practice of excommunication suggests that there could be forms of belief and behavior so incompatible with the life in Christ that they render communion "in an unworthy manner" ineffectual or even harmful (see 1 Cor 11:28-30). If we set such cases aside, we have to ask whether the notion of a "closed communion" squares with the eschatological dimension of the sacrament. My argument has been that the Eucharistic communion has the potential to break down the barriers imposed by the historical divisions of the churches because the Eucharist is the in-breaking of the kingdom of God into history. Since there can be no confessional divisions in the kingdom of God, the Eucharist is meant to give a foretaste of the unity in Christ that breaks all barriers among the believers (see Gal 3:28; Col 3:11), including those created by the historical confessional divisions. In the practice of an "open communion," the seriousness and tragic reality of these divisions is ignored; a "closed communion" goes against the eschatological character of the sacrament. My view, then, is that Eucharistic communion holds the potential for completing that which is lacking in individual Christians and of opening that which is closed due to our enduring divisions. The Eucharist creates a greater unity at the same time as it manifests the already existing unity.

---

eucharistic sharing is both a means of building communion between divided churches as well as its goal; others either do not offer Eucharistic hospitality, or offer it under restricted conditions. Some churches invite all who believe in Jesus Christ to receive communion; other Churches invite only those who believe in Jesus Christ and are baptised and in good standing in their own Churches. Among still other churches eucharistic communion is understood as the ultimate expression of agreement in faith and of a communion in life. Such an understanding would make the sharing of the Lord's Supper with those outside their own tradition an anomaly. As a result, for some churches the practice of 'Eucharistic hospitality' is the antithesis of the commitment to full visible unity."

The historic motto of Wheaton College is "For Christ and His Kingdom." The christological and eschatological frames of reference are as fitting in higher education as they are indispensable in sacramental life. Baptism is the sacrament of initiation into the kingdom of God and the means of incorporation into the body of Christ. The Eucharist is a foretaste of the messianic banquet and a sacrament of communion with Christ. While both initiation and communion take place in particular Christian communities, which bear the wounds of disunity, the sacraments, to the extent to which their eschatological character is made manifest, are the vehicles of intercommunion. The reality of the eschatological intercommunion is obscured by continuing Christian divisions and quarrels; nevertheless, this reality is not a fantasy, illusion, or vague hope about the future. To the extent to which we are Eucharistically taken up into fellowship with Christ, our divisions melt away in the life of communion.

11

"FOR YOU HAVE BEEN PLANTED TOGETHER WITH CHRIST"

Sacraments and the Life of the Church

GEORGE KALANTZIS

The church gave men and women a new love,
Jesus Christ, a person who inspired their actions
and held their affections. This was a love unlike others.

ROBERT LOUIS WILKEN,
THE SPIRIT OF EARLY CHRISTIAN THOUGHT

I WANT TO BEGIN BY DESCRIBING a photograph that I took in May 2011, just a day after that year's commencement celebration at Wheaton College (fig. 11.1). Since I came to Wheaton College, it has been my custom to meet weekly with a group of students for a meal and conversation on what it means to be faithful Christians in community, bearing witness to the fact that Jesus is Lord. Each year, a number of the students are seniors who have recently returned from their Human Needs and Global Resources (HNGR) internships, a six-month program in majority world contexts where students "live, work, worship, and serve with local communities worldwide, while accompanying host partner organizations that confront poverty, challenge inequity, transform conflict, pursue justice, and seek fullness of life." This particular group, the 2010 HNGR cohort, had served in Africa, Latin America, and Asia and had been touched deeply by what they had seen and experienced. Their lives and their faith had been changed by the endless social brutality that is the consequence of colonialism and the aftermath of civil conflicts. So, as a community that had traveled together their college years, these friends asked if we

could share the Eucharist, a last meal as a group. That is what we did. We each brought the various elements and shared them together. The chalice and paten were a gift from a student when I was teaching in seminary. This set was one of Barbara Adams's early attempts at this kind of pottery, and it has become my favorite. Both chalice and paten are a bit crooked, not quite perfect, a constant reminder that so are all of us who come to the table. The V-shaped cloth on either side is a stole laid on the table. This stole came from Rwanda and was given to the HNGR cohort the year before. It was made at the Amani ya Juu women's cooperative in the Gikondo area of Kigali, a sewing, marketing, and training cooperative project of marginalized Hutu and Tutsi women who came together in the name of Christ to share life, work, and raise each other's children around their common table—literally. The multicolored covering of the table is a skirt from Senegal, made through still another women's cooperative efforts, this time of Christian and Muslim women working together around yet another table. The bread was baked by the students. The photograph is a constant reminder to me of what our life together could be.

Figure 11.1.

OF ADJECTIVES AND NOUNS

As we think about our ecclesial identities and the locus of our common life and worship, I will take it as axiomatic that Christians throughout the history of the church have longed to bear faithful witness to the true and living God. I will also take it as axiomatic that Christians understand our own reality and experience always and only as penultimate, and, regardless of our respective ecclesial identities, we recognize baptism and the Eucharist to be a foretaste of the kingdom. The previous chapters in this volume have made these claims quite well.

For my part, I want to turn the vocative in our title into a question. I want to turn from the invitation *"Come,* let us eat together!" and ask, "On what basis ought we think we have the right—or even the expectation—to come to the (same) Table?"

Since theology is biographical, in order to attempt an answer I am forced to ask the prior question of self-identity. So, in the spirit of full disclosure, I confess I am a Christian. I am an evangelical. I am a Greek evangelical in the free-church tradition. Even as I identify myself, I am driven to question which of these descriptions (self- or other-imposed) functions as the noun, the *esse* of who I am, and which one or ones are important yet secondary—adjectives, if you wish. At first glance, the question may seem trite or innocent, easy to respond to. Yet history tells us that questions of *nouns* and *adjectives* provide insight into community formation, rituals, power dynamics, and the setting of boundaries that identify the community first to itself and then to those outside. The works of Mary Douglas on purity and the development of boundaries, of Catherine Bell on rituals as identity formative, and of Pierre Bourdieu on distinction and social stratification, among others, show us how rituals function as performative identifiers of difference and as community demarcations for the initiated as well as for those outside the community.[1]

Therefore, we need to ask the question of adjectives and nouns: How do our denominational, ecclesial identities function? When I identify myself as an evangelical Christian, which one is the adjective, and which the noun? Instinctively we know which one ought to be the noun—Christian—and which the adjective, yet how do we relate to each other in practice? Isn't it our habit to reverse the order and treat our ecclesial identities as nouns? What then of "Christian"?

For the purposes of this chapter, I will concentrate on two such identifiers I consider to be primary hindrances to our possible communion and offer perhaps a modest proposal for a way forward. On the way, I will make two claims that,

---

[1]See, for example: Mary Douglas, *Purity and Danger: An Analysis of Concepts of Pollution and Taboo* (London: Routledge, 1966); Catherine Bell, *Ritual Theory, Ritual Practice* (Oxford: Oxford University Press, 1992); Pierre Bourdieu, *Distinction: A Social Critique of the Judgment of Taste* (London: Routledge, 1986). Also, my review of Allen Brent, *Cyprian and Roman Carthage* (Cambridge: Cambridge University Press, 2010) in *The Classical Review* 62, no. 1 (2011): 191-92.

on the one hand, ought to be self-evident but, on the other, appear to have captivated our religious imagination and transfixed our self-identities as particular *kinds* of Christians.

My first claim is that since history is the stories we tell of our common past, the stories we tell of ourselves and others are the means through which we make sense of the world and gain a better understanding of who we are. As such, our narratives are character formative: they help us define ourselves.[2] It is for this reason that, as Rowan Williams has argued, "good history is irreducibly a moral affair."[3] My second claim—and I limit myself to my own evangelical Protestant communion in this claim—is that our view of the sacraments forms and frames our view of our community, not the other way around.

CLAIM A: JESUS IS SO LUCKY TO HAVE US!

One more self-disclosure: by discipline and affection I am a historical theologian who makes my intellectual dwelling among the writers of the early church. This means that in everything I do, I aim to enter the narratives of the earliest church in a way that is theologically sensitive while doing "good history" at the same time, for good theology does not come from bad history.

So, what does it mean to do "good history"? How do we remember well? How are we to engage the arguments, lives, passions, questions, practices, and witness of people who are so different than us? David Bentley Hart tells us how *not* to do it. In his essay titled "The Mirror of the Infinite: Gregory of Nyssa on the *Vestigia Trinitatis*," Hart reminds us that for the most part, "in our weaker moments, [we] prefer synopsis to precision [and] find in it a convenient implement for arranging our accounts of . . . history into simple taxonomies, under tidily discrete divisions."[4] That is not history at its best. Yet, not only do we prefer synopsis to precision, most often we find our own self-identity in it. One has only to look at how we tell the history of our own denomination or ecclesial community as part of the history of Christianity from the time of Jesus and the apostles to us. How often do we draw the straight line from Jesus through the apostles to us, with other communions and groups branching off in all manner of ways? And even though

---

[2]I have developed this further in my *Caesar and the Lamb: Early Christian Attitudes to War and Military Service* (Eugene, OR: Cascade, 2012).

[3]Rowan Williams, *Why Study the Past? The Quest for the Historical Church* (Grand Rapids: Eerdmans, 2005), 1.

[4]David Bentley Hart, "The Mirror of the Infinite: Gregory of Nyssa on the *Vestigia Trinitatis*," *Modern Theology* 18, no. 4 (2002): 541.

we may accept some denominations or traditions as still somewhat connected to us and our story, we quickly identify others (usually the ones with whom our forebears quarreled) as irredeemably disconnected from the central story of the church, namely, our story.

The claim of the univocal, pure past is one of the most dangerous assertions we make about ourselves. This may appear to be self-evident, yet it seems to trip up with surprising regularity not only those who claim to be in historic continuity with the tradition of the church but also evangelical Protestants. A simple Internet search will reveal surprising results. We do not like diversity even though we thrive in it. We abhor conflict, and we shy away from nuance. Thus, we tell stories of a pure past that somehow got quickly off the proverbial rails into a Hellenized Christianity that adulterated the teaching of Jesus and the disciples, only to be restored, redeemed, rescued, protected, and/or preserved by our own tradition. Such narratives are dangerous, for they are both bad history and bad theology. They are bad history because they are simply not true, and bad theology for they put *us*—once again—at the center of the story.

As Christians in the twenty-first century we cannot continue to abide by the fictitious narratives of historical purity, unity, and continuity without serious and critical reflection. Like the Hellenization thesis, these mythopoetic narratives have outlived their apologetic usefulness.[5] Unencumbered by history, such grand narratives become dangerous when they fetishize the past and breed ahistorical Christians, uprooted from the messy, *real* lives of *real* Christians who had to make hard decisions, calling each other to account and faithfulness. For how else are we to read, *inter alia*, the Council of Jerusalem in Acts 15, or Paul's account of what preceded it, in Galatians 2:11-21? Or the numerous local, regional, and even ecumenical councils of the church? How else are we to read the countless protreptic letters and treatises of the diachronic church?

History matters because particularity matters: actual, real, lived particularity matters. For Christians, particularity matters also because there is no other way to make sense of the resurrection of Jesus. Particularity matters because it is the tomb of Mary's son, of this particular Jewish man who lived in first-century Palestine, the one who suffered "under Pontius Pilate," that is empty. Christians recognize that the *idea* of an empty tomb does not actually matter—it is simply a cipher. What

---

[5]Among a plethora of works on the hellenization thesis, see Robert Louis Wilken, *The Spirit of Early Christian Thought: Seeking the Face of God* (New Haven: Yale University Press, 2003).

matters is the particularity of *Jesus'* resurrection, for it is his resurrection that makes ours possible. As Robert Louis Wilken so eloquently puts it,

> The Resurrection of Jesus is the central fact of Christian devotion and the ground of all Christian thinking. The Resurrection was not a solitary occurrence, a prodigious miracle, but an event within the framework of Jewish history, and it brought into being a new community, the church. Christianity enters history not only as a message but also as a communal life, a society or city, whose inner discipline and practices, rituals and creeds, and institutions and traditions were the setting for Christian thinking.[6]

Particularity matters because it is there that life happens, and life is messy. And so is the church.

Telling truthfully the multiple stories of the church as people always in need of formation and *re*formation, called by God throughout the generations to be continuously *re*formed, means that we recognize ourselves as ones called to be *trans*formed into the image of the Son (see 2 Cor 3:18; Rom 8:28-30). The fiction of the pure past serves only our own agendas and fosters isolationism. The reasons for such narratives are as numerous as the protagonists of the stories, and here is neither the place nor the time to enumerate them, for we are all well aware of the plethora of historic divisions affected throughout time and accentuated by geo-politics, the rise and fall of empires and fiefdoms (both ancient and more recent), the plague of enthno-nationalism and the ethno-religion(s) it brings in its wake, of national identities masquerading as theological purity, and simple hatred of the "other."

Recognizing the history of the church as the history of *ecclesia reformata semper reformanda* means that we acknowledge the faithfulness of God calling God's people anew in every generation regardless of our own failings.

CLAIM B: DEMOCRATIZED MYSTICISM AND BOURGEOIS SACRAMENTALITY

An essay that appeared in the *New York Times* on March 8, 2010, has stayed with me. During Lent, Ross Douthat (who has spoken openly of his ecclesial journey first to charismatic Pentecostal Christianity and then to the Roman Catholic Church) wrote an op-ed piece titled "Mass-Market Epiphany." In his essay Douthat quibbles with the perception that mysticism, and religion with it, is on the path to extinction and

---

[6]Ibid., xv.

argues, "In a sense, Americans seem to have done with mysticism what we've done with every other kind of human experience: We've democratized it, diversified it, and taken it mass market." The result, as we know, is not all that pretty. Douthat argues,

> By making mysticism more democratic, we've also made it more bourgeois, more comfortable, and more dilettantish. It's become something we pursue as a complement to an upwardly mobile existence, rather than a radical alternative to the ladder of success. Going to yoga classes isn't the same thing as becoming a yogi; spending a week in a retreat center doesn't make me Thomas Merton or Thérèse of Lisieux. Our kind of mysticism is more likely to be a pleasant hobby than a transformative vocation.[7]

It is the infernal "I am not religious, I'm just 'spiritual'" slogan of the ecclesially illiterate.

For decades now many of us Protestants, whether in mainline or evangelical denominations, have shifted our attention and energy to make sure the musical and performative rhythm and beat of our services invokes the requisite emotive response that will attract the "unchurched" rather than to the rhythm and beat of the story of God through Israel, Jesus, and the church. Many evangelical churches have abandoned the liturgical year and catechesis in favor of making our churches more inviting and "seeker-oriented." In most of our churches, the reassuring "Remember your baptism!" sign, worn by the touch of countless generations, is no more. The coffee bar has replaced the baptismal font at the entry of the church building. The church barista is the new deacon and catechist.

From clown and puppet Eucharists to musical performances that drown out the voice of the congregation to "dystopia dis-service"[8] to pillows and candles for no particular reason other than to make church feel less like church and more like home, Protestants of all hues (Catholic parishes have not been immune) seem to have substituted the *sacred* in the sacraments with the moralistic therapeutic deism Christian Smith and Melinda Lundquist Denton so amply describe in *Soul*

---

[7]Ross Douthat, "Mass-Market Epiphany," *New York Times*, March 8, 2016. I have mentioned this argument before, in my epilogue to George Kalantzis and Andrew Tooley, *Evangelicals and the Early Church: Recovery, Reform, Renewal* (Eugene, OR: Cascade, 2011), 246.

[8]I invite the reader to look these up and explore how such expressions—yes, clowns and puppets have presided over the Eucharistic celebration—became part of liturgical practices in churches in recent decades. I remember vividly clowns with red noses and in full costume stabbing the Eucharistic bread at the table with a knife as two hand-puppets from behind the altar imitated Sesame Street's Cookie Monster and took the bread in their mouths to break it, inviting the congregation to come forward and receive the body and blood of Christ. Somehow it did not seem appropriate to come forward.

Searching: The Religious and Spiritual Lives of American Teenagers.[9] Yet, lest we claim these are rare aberrations and blame a momentary lapse in judgment, we ought to take a good look at the ever-increasing use of liturgical simulacra in our services, divorced from the proper, time-consuming education of the congregants on how to read symbol and narrative, icon and story, significance and signification, and thus distinguish the sacred from the ephemeral.

It seems to me that in our more recent attempts to rediscover how to work together and be in worshiping community with our sisters and brothers from across traditions, many of us Protestants have adopted a view of unity (and, by extension, of the sacraments) that is derived from the prevalent experiential expressivism that dominates our cultural norms and sees doctrines as statements derived from internal feelings, attitudes, and spiritual experiences.[10] Because many of us are convinced that doctrines are not truth statements but mere attempts to put into words what we know to be true based on private experience, we can weave our way through a variety of ecclesial communions without much difficulty or commitment—as long as it feels good. We are all liberals after all.

I often question what appears to have become the default in contemporary Western Christianity (dare I say, Anglo-dominated, Enlightenment-formed, post-Christendom) for Roman Catholics and Orthodox no less than Protestants (of every variant). Namely, those of us who are eager to enter community and communion, Eucharist, liturgy, passion, art, and even beauty in all its multifaceted splendor more often than not do so as mere spectators, as sincere visitors to the "event," as ones who keep our return ticket—our "right" to disagree, "leave," and join another communion—tucked safely in our breast-pocket.[11] For how often are liturgy, sacraments, and church order relegated to the *adiaphora*, to matters of opinion and preference? Aren't they? How could they be anything else? If they were not merely your opinion and mine, what else could they be?

In his brilliant piece on discerning the divine in contemporary culture, Rodney Clapp warns us,

> Opinions are cheap and come easy. A conviction, on the other hand, is a "persistent belief" that "cannot be relinquished without making its holder a significantly different"

---

[9]Christian Smith and Melinda Lundquist Denton, *Soul Searching: The Religious and Spiritual Lives of American Teenagers* (Oxford: Oxford University Press, 2005).

[10]George Lindbeck, *The Nature of Doctrine: Religion and Theology in a Postliberal Age* (Louisville: Westminster John Knox, 1984).

[11]Literature on this abounds, but I am thinking particularly of Rodney Clapp's *A Peculiar People: The Church as Culture in a Post-Christian Society* (Downers Grove, IL: IVP Academic, 1996).

person or community. Our convictions define us. They are beliefs we hold as highly probable or even certain, out of some considerable experience and reflection. To change a conviction is to change as a person, to fundamentally alter an identity— [to no longer be something or someone, but something or someone else instead]. So convictions are costly and come hard.[12]

The commemoration of the five-hundredth anniversary of the Protestant Reformation reminds us again that 1517 was about convictions, not opinions. It is conviction that Scripture calls *faith*. It is conviction that the Fathers talked about. And this is what the great tradition is about: *conviction*, not *opinions*. By entering into worship with our sisters and brothers from communions different than ours, by participating in the sacraments together, by allowing God's gifts to enact God's grace in us, on us, through us, and among us, we allow God to change us slowly from whatever and whoever we were to something and someone completely different. Since sacraments and the sacramental life fundamentally alter our identity, such discussions cannot be relegated to the realm of *adiaphora*. Whether we recognize our everyday life as sacramental or not, Christians affirm St. Paul's claim that there is something fundamentally different, something new, in the Christian's lived reality (Gal 2:20). A sacramental life is a life of conviction, not ephemeral opinions.

OF MOTHERS AND CHILDREN

This new birth, however, is not an individual endeavor to be pursued in isolation. This is a new birth through faith and baptism to a new family of God through Jesus (see Jn 3:5-7; Rom 6:3); a family that transgresses national identities and gender and societal constructs through the realigning effect of baptism (Gal 3:28; Eph 2:14), a family that brings all into a new kingdom (Rom 6:1-3; Gal 3:27-29).

Even from the very beginning, the Protestant Reformers insisted on the importance of this new reality. John Calvin devoted the whole of book four of the *Institutes of the Christian Religion* to ecclesiology—the doctrine of the church. Calvin titled the first chapter of book four "The True Church with Which as Mother of All the Godly We Must Keep Unity." And his subtitle for the opening section is "The Holy Catholic Church, Our Mother [quia priorum omnium mater est]."

Calvin begins book four this way: "God . . . first of all instituted sacraments, which we who have experienced them feel to be highly useful aids to foster and

---

[12]Rodney Clapp, "God Is Not 'A Stranger on the Bus': Discerning the Divine in Popular Culture," in *God Is Not . . . : Religious, Nice, "One of Us," an American, a Capitalist*, ed. Brent Laytham (Grand Rapids: Brazos, 2004), 37.

strengthen faith." Throughout book four Calvin returns to the work of Cyprian of Carthage (ca. 200-258 CE) to find language and imagery to describe the church. Borrowing from Cyprian's *On the Unity of the Catholic Church*, where the bishop of Carthage famously declared, "He cannot have God as his Father who does not have the Church as his Mother," Calvin develops the analogy further, showing its implications:

> I shall start with the church, into whose breast God is pleased to gather his [children], not only that they may be nourished by her help and ministry as long as they are infants and children, but also that they may be guided by her motherly care until they mature and at last reach the goal of faith, . . . so that, for those to whom he is Father the church may also be Mother.[13]

It is well established that the Protestant Reformers valued Cyprian for his focus on the close union between Christ and church members and considered him a vital source.[14] In the 1559 edition of the *Institutes*, Calvin references Cyprian thirty-one times—most often on the subject of the church. Calvin cites *On the Unity of the Catholic Church* three times, always with approval, and quotes extensive portions of the famous *On Unity* 5 twice.[15] In this arresting passage, Cyprian draws upon

---

[13]Calvin uses *sinum* for "breast" in the Latin edition of 1559, which is carried over as *sein* in French in the 1560 edition. Translating *sinum/sein* as *breast* instead of *bosom* carries better the idea of feeding/breastfeeding, to which Calvin returns often in this section. Here, Calvin's *ut quibus ipse est Pater, ecclesia etiam mater sit* explicitly invokes Cyprian, *On the Unity of the Catholic Church* 6.7: "He cannot have God as his Father who does not have the Church as his Mother [*Habere non potest deum patrem qui ecclesiam non habet matrem*]." In *St Cyprian of Carthage, On the Church: Select Treatises*, trans. Allen Brent (Crestwood: St. Vladimir's Seminary Press, 2006), 157.

[14]See, Aza Goudriaan, "Cyprian's *De ecclesiae catholicae unitate*: Why Did the Reformed Theologians Consider It a Useful Book (1559-1665)?," in *Cyprian of Carthage: Studies in His Life, Language and Thought*, ed. Henk Bakker, Paul van Geest, and Hans van Loon (Leuven: Peeters, 2010), 227-28. For a discussion on the relevance of Cyprian for Lutherans in particular, see also Robert J. H. Mayes, "The Lord's Supper in the Theology of Cyprian of Carthage," *Concordia Theological Quarterly* 74 (2010): 307-24.

[15]In *Reading Christian Theology in the Protestant Tradition*, ed. Kelly M. Kapic and Hans Madueme (London: T&T Clark, 2017), Amy Brown Hughes and I have shown how both Protestants and Roman Catholics turned to Cyprian to find support during the sixteenth and seventeenth centuries. There are two sets of manuscripts of *On Unity* 4-5, each containing differing versions of Cyprian's exegesis of Mt 16:18-19 and Jn 20:21. While both versions of *On Unity* demonstrate a similar conclusion on Cyprian's part—that Christ commands the unity of the church—his emphasis does shift to accommodate contextual needs. The earliest version is referred to as the *Primacy Text* (*PT*) because it speaks of a primacy given to Peter by Christ. The later *Received Text* (*RT*) refers to the version that was believed to be the only version of *On Unity* until the *PT* was rediscovered in 1563. Since each version offers a different take on the authority of the local bishops in relationship to Peter, there was considerable debate during and after the Protestant Reformation regarding what Cyprian does or does not say about the primacy of the bishop of Rome. In 1896 Anglican E. W. Benson claimed that the "papalist" version (*PT*) of *On Unity* 4-5 was a forgery. While Dom John Chapman called the

various images from nature to locate the maternal source of life in the church as the body of Christ:

> Thus also the Church, when the light of the Lord is poured forth, though she sheds her rays of light throughout the whole world, nevertheless the light is one that is spread everywhere, but the unity is not cut off from the body. She extends her boughs into the whole world with an abundance of fruitful growth, she opens wide her streams that flow forth bountifully, nevertheless one is her head and source, and the one Mother is rich with the offspring of her fertility. From her womb we are born, by her milk we are nurtured, by her spirit we are given life.[16]

Calvin appropriates and reintroduces Cyprian's principle in *Institutes* 4.1.4:[17]

> But because it is now our intention to discuss the visible church, let us learn even from the simple title "mother" how useful, indeed how necessary, it is that we should know her. For there is no way to enter into life unless this mother conceive us in her womb, give us birth, nourish us at her breast, and lastly, unless she keeps us under her care and guidance until, putting off mortal flesh, become like the angels [Mt 22:30]. Our weakness does not allow us to be dismissed from her school until we have been pupils all our lives. Furthermore, away from her bosom one cannot hope for any forgiveness of sins or any salvation, as Isaiah [Isa 37:32] and Joel [Joel 2:32] testify.[18]

For Cyprian, the unity of the church is life. The church is the body of Christ, its source unwavering, its unity unbroken, and its fruitfulness unceasing.[19] Cyprian's

---

forgery thesis into question and was the first to establish the existence of alternative texts, the Protestant Ulrich Wickert also called the *PT* fraudulent based on his rendering of how Cyprian viewed Peter. The text-critical work of Maurice Bévenot, however, brought about consensus that both versions were indeed written by Cyprian, the first (*PT*) in 251 CE (at the time of *Letter* 55) and the second (*RT*) at the time of his dispute with Stephen of Rome, around 256 CE (at the time of *Letters* 72-73; see, Allen Brent, *St. Cyprian*, 150). Karl Shuve notes that Bévenot's conclusion relies "largely on philological analysis of *primatus* . . . which should be understood to denote the symbolic 'starting point' of unity rather than the absolute priority of the Roman bishop above all others" ("Cyprian of Carthage's Writings from the Rebaptism Controversy: Two Revisionary Proposals Reconsidered," *Journal of Theological Studies* 61 [2010]: 638). The language of the *Received Text* is therefore edited to downplay the emphasis on the primacy of Peter for obvious reasons.

[16]Cyprian, *On Unity* 5 (Brent, *St. Cyprian*, 155). Later, Cyprian contrasted the fertility of the church, which results in the birth of life and salvation, with those who are born of the devil, that is, those who give birth to heresy and schism (*On Unity* 12 [Brent, *St. Cyprian*, 164-65]), and who have no access to the truth or promises of God (*On Unity* 11 [Brent, *St. Cyprian*, 162-63]).

[17]Citing Cyprian's *Ep.* 72.19.

[18]Calvin, *Inst.* 4.1.4. See also *Inst.* 4.1.20. and *Com. on Isa.* 33:24.

[19]Cyprian, *On Unity* 23 (Brent, *St. Cyprian*, 178). The *Primacy Text* affirms that bishops have equal power and honor but that their unity begins from the "starting point" that is Peter. The bishop is under the "foremost obligation to grasp tightly this unity and to assert our title to it, with the object of proving that the episcopate in itself is one and indivisible," and the church member faithfully

concern here is less about the importance of Peter than it is about how the unity of the church is revealed to the world. He identifies the common ancestor of the episcopal family tree in Peter so that the Holy Spirit's preservation of the oneness of the familial legacy is recognizable and accessible in one's bishop, regardless of geographical location. For Cyprian, unity is a cooperative and familial endeavor. Accordingly, there is no conception of the church as divided; "one body and one Spirit, one hope of your calling, one Lord, one faith, one baptism, one God" (see Eph 4:4-6) admits no division. For our purposes, it is important to note here that in the later revision of *On Unity* (ca. 256 CE) Cyprian moved away from a singular ecclesiological reliance on Rome as the guarantor of the unity of the church. He saw Peter's chair instead as representing the diffuse but unified authority of any bishop who manifests the "widespread increase of [the church's] fruitfulness" that characterizes the many boughs of the firmly rooted episcopal tree.[20] Snapping a bough from the tree only succeeds in cutting off any hope of its fruitfulness; it does not fundamentally hurt the tree.

OF FAMILY AND BODY

If this new life is, as Scripture attests, based on a new birth, then it must be a new reality of a new family, so as to do life together. John Milbank has argued that the church is not primarily an institution but rather a body formed by the Eucharist and the celebration of the Eucharist. Milbank identifies the church as "the dissemination of love which is the repetition of the occurrence of complete love in the world, a bearing of evil and death within humanity to the point of exposure of their predatory unreality by the divine Logos itself."[21] Since the church is the instrument and dispenser of grace, the Eucharist is what constitutes the continuity of the church through time and space.[22] As a result, like Cyprian, Milbank shows us that in some sense disunity is an illusion—for we are already united in the Eucharist at

---

participates in this oneness (Cyprian, *On Unity* 5 [PT]). In the shorter *Received Text* (*RT*) version of *On Unity* 4, Cyprian omits much of the direct Petrine primacy language. He quotes Jesus after his resurrection charging Peter to "Feed my sheep" (Jn 21:17) and lodges the construction of the church and the establishment of the source of episcopal authority (the "one Chair") with Christ: "Upon [Peter] [Christ] builds his Church, and to him he hands over in trust his sheep to be fed and, although he might assign to all the apostles equal power, he however established one Chair and ordained by his own authority that Chair as the source of unity and its guiding principle."

[20]Cyprian, *On Unity* 5 (Brent, *St. Cyprian*, 155).

[21]John Milbank, *The Future of Love: Essays in Political Theology* (Eugene, OR: Cascade, 2009), 166.

[22]See John Milbank, *Theology and Social Theory: Beyond Secular Reason*, 2nd ed. (Oxford: Blackwell, 2006); and *Being Reconciled: Ontology and Pardon* (London: Routledge, 2003). See also Medi Ann Volpe, *Rethinking Christian Identity: Doctrine and Discipleship* (Oxford: Wiley-Blackwell, 2013).

a more fundamental level. I want to push the argument, however, and claim that Scripture compels us to look at baptism as the antecedent that reveals disunity to be an illusion, a fact the Eucharist reminds us.

To many of us who are attracted much more to the *idea* of the one, holy, catholic, and apostolic church than to the lived reality of the body of Christ and the persistent work of reconciliation and mutuality that such body-politics demands, the scriptural analogies of family and body sound anachronistic. Yet the most common analogy of the church in the New Testament is that of family (Mt 12:49-50; 2 Cor 6:18; Eph 2:19; Gal 6:10; 1 Tim 5:1) and body (Rom 12:4-5; 1 Cor 10:17; 12:12, 17; Eph 4:12; 5:30; Col 1:24).[23]

Why? Because in the church we experience the effects of the liberating *conviction* that we are not alone, we come from another (God the Holy Spirit), we belong to another (the church), and we are for another (the world). This is how Paul puts it in Galatians 3:26-28: "For in Christ Jesus you are all children of God through faith. As many of you as were baptized into Christ have clothed yourselves with Christ. There is no longer Jew or Greek, there is no longer slave or free, there is no longer male and female; for all of you are one in Christ Jesus. And if you belong to Christ, then you are Abraham's offspring, heirs according to the promise" (NRSV).

Scripture tells us time and again that we are one body because of the one Spirit who called us and grafted us into the one Lord. It is the testimony of the New Testament that Jesus' literal, physical, Jewish body precedes our being constituted—grafted, if you will, into him.

Cyprian and Calvin echoed Paul in Ephesians 4:4-6: "There is one body and one Spirit, just as you were called to the one hope of your calling, one Lord, one faith, one baptism, one God and Father of all, who is above all and through all and in all" (NRSV). The order of Paul's argument matters: Christ comes first; we derive from him. His humanity redeems, restores, and reveals ours. His completeness makes ours possible. His oneness is manifested in us. We do not constitute his body; we are constituted by his body through baptism.

PLANTED TOGETHER

As he was preparing catechumens for baptism, Cyril, the fourth century bishop of Jerusalem, turned to Paul in Romans 6 to explain to them what Christian baptism

---

[23]Of course, the church is also described by various other analogies, such as bride, vine, temple, and building/house, but the main images invoked by both Jesus and the apostolic witness are in familial terms.

is. In Romans 6:3-5 St. Paul declares this baptism to be a *participation* in Christ's death and resurrection. "Do you not know that all of us who have been baptized into Christ Jesus were baptized into his death? Therefore we have been buried with him by baptism into death, so that, just as Christ was raised from the dead by the glory of the Father, so we too might walk in newness of life. For if we have been united with him in a death like his, we will certainly be united with him in a resurrection like his" (NRSV).

Most English translations use an expression like "united with him" to render the meaning of the word *symphytoi* (σύμφυτοι, lit. "planted with"), which Paul uses in v. 5 to describe what happens to us in baptism. Cyril shows the beauty of the picture Paul paints and keeps the organic relationship of Paul's metaphor: "If we have been '*planted together* in the likeness of his death, we shall be also in the likeness of his resurrection.' Well has he said, *planted together*. For since the true Vine [see Jn 15:5] was planted in this place, we also by partaking in the Baptism of death, *have been planted together with Him*."[24] We are not *united* to Jesus in an additive relationship but rather bloom from him. We receive our very life and being from him. If we have been planted with him, it is out of him that we bloom to life. We come to be because of him.

Like Cyprian before him, Cyril recognized the scriptural idiom that is central to the Christian life, namely, being a Christian is not a singular, punctiliar event, a moment in time, but rather a process of becoming, just like a bough: "When you are counted worthy of this Holy Chrism, you are called *Christians*, verifying also the name by your new birth. For before you were vouchsafed this grace, you had properly no right to this title, but were advancing on your way towards being Christians."[25] Baptism, insisted Cyril, "is a ransom to captives; the remission of offenses; the death of sin; the regeneration of the soul; the garment of light; the holy seal indissoluble; the chariot to heaven; the luxury of paradise; a procuring of the kingdom; the gift of adoption."[26] For Cyril, there are no "Christ-followers," only Χριστιανοί, "little Christs," organically brought forth from the vine itself.

Unlike the democratized mysticism Douthat describes, a sacramental life is a life of conviction. God is the Lord of history. As a result of that conviction, our very identity changes, and our life bears witness to the One Lord.

---

[24]St. Cyril of Jerusalem, "On the Rites of Baptism: Rom 6:3-14," *Mystagogical Catechesis* 2.7, in *Lectures on the Christian Sacraments: The Procatechesis and the Five Mystical Catecheses*, ed. F. L. Cross, trans. R. W. Church (Crestwood, NY: St. Vladimir's Seminary Press, 1986), 62.

[25]St. Cyril of Jerusalem, "On the Holy Chrism: 1 Jn 2:20-28," *Mystagogical Catechesis* 3.5, in *Lectures on the Christian Sacraments*, ed. Cross, 66.

[26]St. Cyril of Jerusalem, *Procatechesis* 16, in *Lectures on the Christian Sacraments*, ed. Cross, 50.

OF BRANCHES AND LIFE TOGETHER

What Cyril of Jerusalem describes to those who seek Christian baptism is the life of costly conviction. It is the life that does not come easily, for *in* the church, we are no longer this thing or that one but something or someone altogether different (see Gal 2:20; 3:27-28). We are conceived by the Holy Spirit in faith, gestated and formed by catechesis, birthed through baptism into the church, which, like a mother, nourishes us into the faith to be received by a family that eats together at the Lord's Table so as to have life.

The natural outflow of such an understanding of our common life together ought to manifest itself in at least three distinct but interdependent proposals I would like to present as a way forward. The first principle is our common understanding that particularity matters. Yet, particularity is adjectival; it describes how I live my life, how I *experience* who I am. It does not define who I *am,* serving as a noun. I am a Christian (noun) because I am planted with Christ, organically connected to the long history of the vine itself and the boughs that bloom from him throughout the life of the historic church. *Evangelical* is the adjective; it describes how I experience this life in Christ, with its own particularities, its own scents and sights.

Second, based on this first concept of the noun, it ought to be clear that the language of "conversion" between ecclesial communions ought to be recognized for the harm it has caused, and it should be abandoned among Christians. Language matters, for it is identity formative. There is abundant literature on the damage effected by modern missionary movements into historically Christian cultures where the language of conversion has been used to undermine the faith handed down through generations of Christians and relegate its local instantiation to the sphere of superstition, idolatry, and even paganism. Disrespectful of the work of the Spirit through countless generations and the witness (often in blood) of Christians of past generations as this is, such phenomena are by no means limited to the mission fields abroad. How often do we hear the infernal, "When I was a Catholic (or Orthodox, or Episcopalian, or Lutheran) . . . but now that I am a Christian . . . " even among Christians in the North American context? Until and unless we recognize that even though God the Holy Spirit may call us to worship within this particular ecclesial communion or that, and that one is not "converted" from Catholic to Orthodox or Protestant, we will continue to deny the noun *Christian.*

Blooming takes time. Our task is neither to romanticize unity nor to resign to its lack, for as Fr. Weinandy challenges us, "One cannot be united to Christ in the Eucharist without being united to one another." The serious business of family demands that we recognize our differences, not dismiss them, and that we lament our brokenness and not enforce an ephemeral unity based either on rights or sentiments. We work through our differences; we do not ignore them—or one another—for that is the hard work of family. Born through the same water, can we sit at the same table and receive life from the same Lord?

If there is an order to physical life progressing from conception to gestation to birth and reception to be part of a family, then—and this is my third proposal—there is an order to the sacramental participation in the life and faith of the church. In faith we are conceived, and in baptism we are given life to be gestated in our Mother's womb, nurtured by her catechesis and fed at the table, formed as a family that bears witness that "there is one body and one Spirit, just as you were called to the one hope of your calling, one Lord, one faith, one baptism, one God and Father of all, who is above all and through all and in all" (Eph 4:4-6 NRSV).

In the meantime, we lament.

12

WHO INVITED THE BAPTIST?

The "Sacraments" and Free Church Theology

MARC CORTEZ

MY GOAL IN THIS CHAPTER IS SIMPLE. I would like to speak *to* people who may find it difficult to appreciate what this entire discussion is about given certain reservations about the whole idea of "sacraments," and I would like to speak *for* those same people given that these discussions can sometimes unfold in ways that often make it seem as though their perspective has been marginalized from the beginning. My own journey toward serious theological reflection on this subject began years ago with apple juice and Oreo cookies. But more on that in a moment.

WHAT DO WE DO WITH THE BAPTISTS?

In his study of the relationship between Eucharist and ecumenism, George Hunsinger claims that any "ecumenically viable" view of the Eucharist must be able to affirm Christ's bodily presence both in heaven and in the elements of the supper.[1] Without at least this much common ground, he argues, the major Christians traditions will remain irremediably divided over the table. Yet he also recognizes that any such affirmation constitutes a significant challenge for substantial elements of the Christian church, admitting, "what to do about those churches rooted in the Anabaptist traditions, including charismatics and Pentecostals, is beyond me."[2] In

---

[1]George Hunsinger, *The Eucharist and Ecumenism: Let Us Keep the Feast* (New York: Cambridge University Press, 2008), 47.
[2]Ibid., 11.

other words, since those traditions are generally associated with more symbolic and memorialist views of the Eucharist, he simply does not see how they could develop the kind of common ground necessary for meaningful dialogue with other traditions. So he proceeds to develop the rest of his study without reference to those traditions. As a Baptist theologian, it's hard not to feel just a tad marginalized by that. To be fair, it's not like he hung a "Baptists need not apply" sign on the front of his book. It was more like a "Baptists are weird and we don't know what to do with them" sign. But the end result is the same.

Having said that, it's easy to understand the problem. Growing up in largely Baptist, or at least baptistic, contexts, I routinely heard the clear message that Communion involves nothing more than a set of symbols and symbolic actions that remind us of God's saving action in the past. We participate in them regularly as an act of faithful obedience to the Lord's command, which is why the Baptist preference is for the term *ordinance* over that of *sacrament*.[3] Indeed, pastors would often go out of their way to emphasize that these are "nothing more" than symbols, as though afraid that some quasi-Catholic or crypto-Presbyterian had slipped in among them unnoticed. Instead, they wanted to make sure we understood that baptism and Communion were nothing more than expressions of our faith as a witness to what God has already done.

Of course, this emphasis on a purely symbolic view of the sacraments was not unique to my experience. Baptists have long been known for their resistance to sacramentalism, which they often associate with unwarranted attempts to control God's free grace through the manipulation of material elements. Instead, Baptists commonly maintain that rites like baptism and Communion do not effect any change in the Christian, being particularly clear that practices do not involve any infusion of grace into the believer. Thus, for example, *The Baptist Faith and Message* (2000) stipulates that baptism is "an act of obedience symbolizing the believer's faith."[4] Likewise, Communion is "a symbolic act of obedience" in which we "memorialize" the Lord's death. Thus, as Dallas Roark argues, "These rites do not strengthen grace in the heart of man; they speak of faith and commitment on man's part."[5]

---

[3] Although I will use the terms *Communion, Eucharist,* and *Lord's Supper* interchangeably throughout this paper, I will privilege *Communion* both because it was the term that has been used most often in my own Baptist contexts, even more so than the historically predominant *Lord's Supper,* but also because it seems unlikely well-suited for the broader topic of ecclesial unity.

[4] Southern Baptist Convention, "Baptist Faith and Message, 2000," www.sbc.net/bfm2000/bfm2000 .asp.

[5] Dallas Roark, *The Christian Faith* (Nashville: Broadman, 1969), 289.

Indeed, this view of the ordinances is so pervasive in contemporary Baptist churches that many think any attempt to introduce the sacramental ways of thinking into Baptist theology would result in a theology that hardly merits the label "Baptist."

APPLE JUICE AND OREO COOKIES

This is the theological framework that led to my experience with apple juice and Oreo cookies. I was a twenty-year-old youth director on a retreat with a couple of volunteers and eight high school leadership students. Coming to the end of a great weekend of prayer, worship, and fellowship, I decided that it would be great to conclude our retreat by celebrating Communion together. Of course, as is often the case in youth ministry, this thought occurred to me at the last possible minute with neither planning nor preparation. To make matters worse, since it was the end of the retreat, pickings were slim. The beverage choices were either apple juice or Coca Cola, and our only "bread" options were a not-quite-yet-stale bag of Oreo cookies, and, if I remember correctly, leftover pizza. I remember thinking that apple juice was a better stand-in for the "wine" since at least it comes from a fruit, but I don't recall what made me think Oreos should trump pizza. Regardless, you can see where this is going.

Now, my plan did not go entirely unchallenged. One of my volunteer leaders, who was not then but somehow eventually came to be my wife, and who was raised Catholic, had more than a few questions about the wisdom of having a non-ordained youth director lead Communion for a handful of high school students, outside the context of the gathered church, in which the elements were represented by apple juice and Oreo cookies. According to the theology I thought I had received growing up, however, the logic of my position seemed to follow rather inevitably. You just take a symbolic view of Communion, mix in some priesthood of all believers and a healthy dash of "where two or three are gathered together," and voilà: instant Communion. Granted, I was going to have to work a bit harder to explain the significance of apple juice and Oreo cookies so that the ritual had the requisite symbolic aspect, but I was a youth worker. We can turn pretty much anything into an analogy.

Now, to be fair to my tradition, many good Baptist theologians would be horrified at this line of thinking, rightly pressing on the *unique* symbolism of bread and wine in Communion and the inherently *ecclesial* nature of Communion as starting points for thinking that this might not have been such a good idea. Yet I think that a rather extreme example like this helps illustrate what it means to say that Communion is merely a symbolic expression of the believer's faith, and why someone like George Hunsinger might find it so difficult to find any common ground between that view of Communion and the views held by other Christian traditions. Indeed, Hunsinger's dialogue requires that any tradition that would like to participate must be able to affirm a rather robustly sacramental understanding of Communion, which is precisely what the Baptist seems unable to do.[6] However, I think it is worth asking whether that is necessarily the case.

YOU KEEP USING THAT WORD

The key question at this stage thus seems to be whether Baptists can have a sacramental view of things like baptism and Communion. Yet that raises the perplexing question of what precisely we mean by the adjective *sacramental*. Definitions are challenging enough as it is, but we increase the difficulty level significantly when we take something that used to be a noun (*sacrament*), turn it into an adjective (*sacramental*), and then pretend like everyone knows what we're talking about. And I'll admit that I was kind of hoping that someone would already have provided a fairly robust definition of *sacramental* by this point so that I wouldn't have to. Since that hasn't happened, it seems that we're going to let the Baptist try to define what *sacramental* means to a bunch of non-Baptists. That should go well.

Part of the problem, of course, is that each tradition has its own understanding of what *sacrament* means, presumably with a correspondingly unique definition of what it means for something to be adjectivally related to the sacraments. Consequently, there is no way to offer a single, all-encompassing definition by which to determine if a particular view qualifies as sacramental without biasing the discussion irretrievably from the outset. Rather than try to develop a comprehensive definition of the term, then, I will instead see if I can just capture some of the shared assumptions at work when people describe something as "sacramental." In other words, the following is an attempt to identify some principles that might be *necessary* for a particular view to qualify as sacramental, even if they are not *sufficient* for a view to qualify as sacramental according to any particular tradition.

Divine agency. First, it seems to be that such a view must affirm that God himself is somehow the primary agent at work in the sacrament. Of course, no one would deny that the sacrament is also a human action. After all, humans are clearly doing

---

[6]Hunsinger, *Eucharist and Ecumenism*, 60.

something when they consecrate and consume the elements. Yet it seems likely that any properly sacramental view would maintain the primacy of divine action. As important as human action might be, it is only divine action that makes these things true sacraments.

Real efficacy. The next principle maintains that a sacramental view must think that something important is actually happening in the sacramental action. This follows closely from the first point. If God is the primary agent in the sacramental action, he must be doing *something*. And God's actions are always efficacious. Additionally, when God acts, change happens. We may not always be able to see or articulate the details of the change, but God's actions make a difference. Consequently, to qualify as sacramental, any view must affirm that God is doing something in the sacrament that is real, effective, and transformative, even if we continue to differ about precisely what that entails.

Uniqueness. Our third principle emphasizes that a sacrament must somehow be distinct from other ways in which God works efficaciously in the world. I realize that some use sacramental language in ways that deemphasize the uniqueness of the classic sacraments, arguing for a more thoroughly sacramental universe. And I don't think we need to take this principle so far as to say that a sacramental view has to deny that God can and does work efficaciously through all kinds of material realities. Yet it seems to me that most sacramental views would still want to affirm that there is something unique about sacraments like baptism and Communion, along with others, depending on your tradition.

Necessity. I cannot imagine any truly sacramental view that would present the sacraments as somehow optional additions to the Christian life. Instead, to qualify as sacramental, it seems important that we view the sacraments as somehow necessary for Christian life and ministry. The "somehow" in that sentence is important since it still allows us to have interesting discussions about the kind of necessity we have in mind. Most would affirm that they cannot be strictly necessary since we have to allow for those circumstances where someone becomes a Christian without access to the sacraments. Yet we should be able to acknowledge those exceptional circumstances while maintaining that the sacraments are not optional for normal Christian living.

Presence. This fifth principle cheats just a bit, since it focuses more on what it means to say that a view of Communion in particular qualifies as sacramental. Since I'd like that to be the primary focus of what follows, though, it will help to add this as a fifth qualifier. For a view to be sacramental, it must in some way emphasize divine presence in the rite, and, drawing on the earlier point about uniqueness, this divine presence must somehow be different from God's presence elsewhere. Having said this, I will admit that I am not entirely certain how far to press the *presence* principle. Many would probably prefer not to use sacramental language to describe any view of Communion that fails to assert in rather straightforward ways that Christ is somehow present to the worshiping community in his humanity. Yet others routinely use sacramental language when talking about views that emphasize more the presence of the Spirit or the presence of Christ as mediated by the Spirit. I will let others wrestle with such details. For our purposes, though, I think we can stop with affirming that "sacramental" applies only to those views that can affirm God's unique presence in and through these particular sacraments.

If we put these five principles together, we end up with the conclusion that something qualifies as a *sacramental* view of Communion if it understands communion to be a unique and necessary occasion in which God acts on his people in such a way as to effect their real transformation by making himself present to his people. As I said earlier, this definition leaves room for considerable debate about each of these principles, and none of the traditions is likely to see this as an adequate description of sacramental realities as they understand them. Nonetheless, I hope this gives us enough to get started with the process of thinking about whether a Baptist view of Communion can play any meaningful role in ecumenical conversations about Eucharistic unity.

And, at first glance, it's not a very promising start. After all, as we saw earlier, at least some Baptist statements about Communion explicitly identify it as a *non-efficacious, human* action in which Christ is *not* truly present. While such a view might continue to maintain that Communion is *necessary*, this would only be the necessity of obedience. In other words, Communion is not necessary because of what it does for the believer. Instead, its necessity is grounded entirely in the fact that the believer cannot be an obedient believer without participating in this ritual. Focusing on obedience in this way, then, such a view also cannot maintain Communion's uniqueness, since we cannot truly differentiate it from other obedient actions commanded by our Lord Jesus. Given this view of Baptist theology, and given this definition of "sacramental," we again seem to be at an impasse.

THE RISE AND FALL OF BAPTIST SACRAMENTALISM

To help with this apparent dilemma, we turn to the Baptist tradition. Many scholars have recently argued that there is an explicitly sacramental stream within the Baptist heritage itself.[7] Indeed, although there has always been a memorial tradition as well, these scholars contend that the sacramental emphasis dominated in the earliest periods of Baptist history and that the Zwinglian—or, as some prefer to say, sub-Zwinglian—view did not become the primary Baptist understanding of communion until the nineteenth century. If this is the case, Baptists may have more resources for engaging sacramental conversations than they realize.

In an influential historical analysis of early Baptist theology, Stanley K. Fowler demonstrated that sacramental theology was a prominent feature of Baptist thought in the sixteenth, seventeenth, and eighteenth centuries.[8] Looking at some of the earliest Baptist confessions, we see quite a number that either imply or explicitly affirm something more than the merely symbolic view so pervasive in modern Baptist circles. One of the earliest, the *Short Confession of Faith* (1610) refers to the two "sacraments" instituted by Christ.[9] Here we need to be careful. Merely noting that a particular author or confession uses the term *sacrament* is not sufficient to warrant the claim that they are affirming some kind of sacramental view. Even today many Baptists use the term interchangeably with *ordinance*, often meaning nothing more than the standard memorialism. Early Baptists also viewed these two terms as virtual synonyms, meaning that we need to press beyond the mere use of *sacrament* to discern the underlying theological framework. Similarly, we should not draw hasty conclusions from the *non*-use of the term by a particular confession or theologian. Even if they restrict themselves entirely to the language of *ordinance*, we should not conclude that such a view is non-sacramental.

---

[7]Particularly important in this regard are two sets of collected essays: Anthony R. Cross and Philip E. Thompson, eds., *Baptist Sacramentalism*, Studies in Baptist History and Thought (Milton Keynes, UK: Paternoster, 2003), and Anthony R. Cross, ed., *Baptist Sacramentalism 2* (Eugene, OR: Wipf & Stock, 2009). Other important studies include Michael John Walker, *Baptists at the Table: The Theology of the Lord's Supper Amongst English Baptists in the Nineteenth Century* (Didcot: Baptist Historical Society, 1992); Philip E. Thompson, "A New Question in Baptist History: Seeking a Catholic Spirit Among Early Baptists," *Pro Ecclesia* 8, no. 1 (1999): 51-72; Anthony R. Cross, "Dispelling the Myth of English Baptist Baptismal Sacramentalism," *The Baptist Quarterly* 38, no. 8 (2000): 367-91; Stanley K. Fowler, *More Than a Symbol: The British Baptist Recovery of Baptismal Sacramentalism* (Milton Keynes, UK: Paternoster, 2002); Brian C. Brewer, "'Signs of the Covenant': The Development of Sacramental Thought in Baptist Circles," *Perspectives in Religious Studies* 36, no. 4 (2009): 407-20; Paul W. Goodliff, *Ministry, Sacrament and Representation: Ministry and Ordination in Contemporary Baptist Theology and the Rise of Sacramentalism* (Oxford: Regent's Park College, 2010); Scott W. Bullard, "James William McClendon Jr., the New Baptist Sacramentalists, and the Unitive Function of the Eucharist," *Perspectives in Religious Studies* 38, no. 3 (2011): 267-88.
[8]Fowler, *More Than a Symbol*.
[9]William L. Lumpkin, *Baptist Confessions of Faith* (Valley Forge, PA: Judson, 1969), 60.

With that caveat in place, we can press further and notice that the *Short Confession* goes on to describe baptism and the Lord's Supper as signs in which God is truly present and active. While baptism involves an "outward" sign (water) that witnesses to the inward reality of Spirit baptism, the confession identifies the former as the occasion on which God effectively accomplishes the latter. Thus "the baptism of water leadeth us to Christ, to his holy office in glory and majesty" and serves as a "holy prayer to mount upward, and to beg of Christ the good thing signified."[10] Likewise, Communion involves "the outward visible supper" that provides the occasion for God to nourish his people on Christ's "heavenly being," which is "the alive-making bread, meat, and drink of our souls."

The *Second London Confession* (1677), an early expression of Calvinist Baptist theology, likewise affirmed that "worthy receivers, outwardly partaking of the visible Elements in this Ordinance, do then also inwardly by faith, really and indeed, yet not carnally, and corporally, but spiritually receive, and feed upon Christ crucified & all the benefits of his death."[11] Here again we have a clear distinction between the outward sign and the inward reality alongside an emphasis on Communion as an event in which God's people truly, albeit spiritually, feed upon the crucified Christ. Elsewhere the confession affirms that baptism and the Lord's Supper are both "means appointed by God" for the purpose of increasing and strengthening the faith of the church.[12]

Lest we think that the sacramental language of these early creeds was merely expressing the Calvinist sympathies of certain strands of Baptist theology, we should notice that the Orthodox Creed (1678) of the General Baptists affirmed a similarly sacramental stance. According to this creed, "The supper of the Lord Jesus was instituted by Him . . . for the confirmation of the faithful believers in all the benefits of His death and resurrection and spiritual nourishment and growth in Him; sealing."[13] Here again we have a view of the sacraments that argues for more than just a symbolic re-enactment of already existing truths or a testimony of personal faith. Instead, the Lord's Supper is the occasion on which the believer actually is confirmed in "all the benefits" bestowed through the death and resurrection of Christ, including "spiritual nourishment and growth." It would be difficult to argue that such early statements are doing anything other than identifying these sacraments as occasions in

---

[10]Fowler, *More Than a Symbol*, 12.

[11]Brewer, "Signs of the Covenant," 413.

[12]Philip E. Thompson, "Sacraments and Religious Liberty: From Critical Practice to Rejected Infringement," in *Baptist Sacramentalism*, ed. Cross and Thompson, 40.

[13]Lumpkin, *Baptist Confessions of Faith*, 321.

which God actually and effectively brings about realities necessary for the spiritual well-being of his people.

Fowler goes on to identify a broad range of Baptist theologians from the seventeenth and eighteenth centuries who maintained similarly sacramental views. From the seventeenth century we have figures like Robert Garner (1640–1650), Henry Lawrence (1600–1664), Thomas Grantham (1634–1693), and William Mitchell (1662–1705), while the eighteenth century sees the impact of thinkers like John Gill (1697–1771), Abraham Booth (1734–1806), Anne Dutton (1692–1765), Andrew Fuller (1754–1815), and John Ryland Jr. (1753–1825). Among these are some of the most notable thinkers of early Baptist theology, each affirming in their own way that baptism and Communion are more than just acts of human obedience.[14]

Philip Thompson offers another important window into early Baptist views of the sacraments by focusing on the theology expressed in their worship life.[15] As Thompson claims, "The theology Baptists sang, prayed, and performed ritually was churchly and sacramental (even if sacramental terminology was not widely utilized)."[16] For example, one baptism prayer clearly highlights the significance of Christ's presence in the waters of baptism: "O let us find the messiah here! Thou that comest by water and art witnessed to of the water come by this water, . . . and afford us communion with thee in thy baptism; for in the water and in the floods thy presence is promised."[17] In another hymn, the congregation would echo that same thought, singing, "When in the water they descend, there they meet the sinner's friend."[18] Yet another clearly highlights both the prominence of the Spirit in the baptistic rite and the intimate union of both "substance" and "sign":

> Eternal Spirit, heavenly Dove,
> On these baptismal waters move;
> That we through energy divine,
> May have the substance with the sign.[19]

---

[14]Fowler, *More Than a Symbol*, 20-32.

[15]Philip E. Thompson, "Re-Envisioning Baptist Identity: Historical, Theological, and Liturgical Analysis," *Perspectives in Religious Studies* 27, no. 3 (2000): 287-302. Throughout this section, I will be relying on Thompson's excellent account of sacramental motifs in early Baptist worship.

[16]Ibid., 290.

[17]Morgan Edwards, *The Customs of Primitive Churches -or- A Set of Propositions Relative to the Name, Materials, Constitution, Power, Officers, Ordinances, Rites, Business, Worship, Discipline, Government, &c. of a Church; to Which are Added Their Proofs from Scripture, and Historical Narratives of the Manner in Which Most of Them Have Been Reduced to Practice* (Philadelphia, 1774).

[18]Andrew Broaddus, *The Dover Selection of Spiritual Songs* (Richmond: R. I. Smith, 1829), 50.

[19]Eleazar Clay, *Hymns and Spiritual Songs, Selected from Several Approved Authors* (Richmond: John Dixon, 1793), 260.

Moving on from liturgical expressions regarding baptism, the worship life of these early Baptists expressed a similarly sacramental understanding of Communion. One description of an early Baptist Communion service instructed the pastor to say the following when distributing the elements: "Thus (giving the bread/wine) did Christ give his body/blood for you. And thus he now tendereth the benefits of it to you." Their hymns similarly focused on the real benefits experienced by God's people in the event of Communion:

This holy bread and wine
Maintains our fainting breath,
By union with our living Lord,
And int'rest in his death.[20]

In other words, Communion instantiates a real union with the Lord that provides sustenance for Christian life. Even more explicitly, another hymn claims,

Here at thy table Lord, we meet
To feed on food divine;
Thy body is the bread we eat,
Thy precious blood the wine.
He that prepares this rich repast,
Himself comes down and dies;
And then invites us thus to feast
Upon the sacrifice.[21]

Throughout the period, then, we have a consistent witness to a thoroughgoing sacramentalism that shapes not only Baptist theology but Baptist life and worship.

However, many see a significant shift beginning to take place in the nineteenth century as Baptists became increasingly hesitant to talk about ordinances in sacramental terms. Many of the confessional statements of this period explicitly limit the meaning of baptism and the Lord's Supper to their purely "commemorative" aspects,[22] and we have already seen the outworking of this symbolic turn in later Baptist declarations.

People have offered various explanations for this move, and we do not need to trouble ourselves with those arguments in any detail. Some have focused on

---

[20]Andrew Broaddus, *The Virginia Selection of Psalms, Hymns, and Spiritual Songs* (Richmond: Smith, Drinker, and Morris, 1846), 164.

[21]Staunton S. Burdette, *Baptist Harmony* (Philadelphia: E. W. Miller, 1842), 302.

[22]See especially the widely influential *New Hamphsire Confession* (1833) in Lumpkin, *Baptist Confessions of Faith*, 366.

the rise of individualism in American Christianity, which, when joined with the Baptist emphasis on personal faith, contributed to a declining interest in communal actions like the sacraments.[23] Additionally, the advent of the great evangelical awakenings may have caused some to downplay the uniqueness and normativity of the sacraments given that the Spirit seems perfectly capable of working transformatively without sacramental practice.[24] Still others emphasize a heightened concern about Catholic views of the sacraments, brought about largely by a reaction to the Oxford Movement, which caused Baptists to draw lines more sharply than before.[25] One or more of these may also have contributed to what looks like an increased tendency to downplay the spiritual significance of the material world, what one author referred to as the "scorning of creation."[26] Not only does the Spirit not *need* to work through material elements in order to transform his people, but there is an increasing sense that there is something inappropriate about thinking that he *does* so. Emphasizing the Spirit's immediate influence in the life of each individual believer, the idea that the work of the Spirit would need to be mediated through material objects became increasingly troubling.

Regardless of the particular explanation, the end result is the same. In this period, we begin to see a notable shift away from this earlier openness to sacramental ways of thinking to a more pervasively symbolic understanding of baptism and Communion, becoming, as we have seen, the dominant paradigm of modern Baptist theology.

In the first part of the twentieth century, however, we begin to see yet another shift as an increasing number of Baptist thinkers began embracing far more sacramental views of baptism and Communion, as well as things like prayer, preaching, ordination, and the material world itself.[27] The most influential figure in the rise of this new Baptist sacramentalism was H. Wheeler Robinson.[28] Concerned about the "Zwinglianism" that dominated in Baptist circles, Robinson argued that central aspects of Baptist faith and practice pointed in a different direction. He argued, for

---

[23]Curtis W. Freeman, "'To Feed Upon by Faith': Nourishment from the Lord's Table," in *Baptist Sacramentalism*, ed. Cross and Thompson, 194-210.

[24]E.g., Thompson, "New Question in Baptist History," 53.

[25]E.g., David F. Wright, *What Has Infant Baptism Done to Baptism? An Enquiry at the End of Christendom* (Milton Keynes, UK: Paternoster, 2005), 87-88.

[26]Thompson, "Re-Envisioning Baptist Identity," 296.

[27]See esp. Brewer, "Signs of the Covenant," 408.

[28]Anthony R. Cross, "The Pneuatmological Key to H. Wheeler Robinson's Baptismal Sacramentalism," in *Baptist Sacramentalism*, ed. Cross and Thompson, 151-76.

example, that instead of rejecting the possibility that God can and does work transformatively through material elements, Baptists should draw on their own doctrine of Scripture to see that this is precisely how God works in the world. "The Bible itself is no more than a collection of ancient documents till it becomes . . . a sacrament, that is, something which is a means by which the divine Spirit becomes active in the heart of reader or hearer."[29] Just as the Bible is a material object through which the Spirit acts transformatively in the life of the believer, so also should we understand the sacraments of baptism and Communion. Rather than being mere symbols of an already experienced transformation, these become pneumatologically transformative events in their own right. This does not mean Robinson downplayed the importance of faith or the role of the believer in the sacrament. Instead, with respect to baptism he contended that we need to affirm both that it is a *believer's* baptism and that it is the believer's *baptism*.[30] In other words, this sacrament involves a twofold dynamic in which the believer both acts and is acted upon by the Spirit. This allowed Robinson to retain the Baptist emphasis on the necessity of personal faith while also refusing to reduce the sacrament to an expression of faith alone.

A number of prominent Baptist scholars picked up on many of these same themes, including R. E. O. White and George Beasley-Murray. White expressed deep concern about contemporary Baptist views that present an ordinance as if it were only "an attenuated parable-rite in which noting vital is even expected to happen."[31] In his influential *The Biblical Doctrine of Initiation*, White echoed Robinson by arguing for a view of the ordinances that includes both divine and human action, which he referred to as "dynamic" sacramentalism:

> The dynamic, or existential, sacramentalism of the New Testament seizes upon the fact that divine activity and human response meet in sacramental *action*. The sacramental effect—enduement, gift, remission, reception, incorporation, death-resurrection—occurs within the personal relationship which the act expresses. Thus efficacy belongs strictly neither to the element, nor to the rite, but to the action of God within the soul of the baptised who at that time, in that way, is making his response to the grace offered to him in the gospel.[32]

---

[29]H. Wheeler Robinson, *The Christian Experience of the Holy Spirit* (London: Nisbet, 1928), 190.
[30]Cross, "Pneuatmological Key to H. Wheeler Robinson's Baptismal Sacramentalism," 156.
[31]R. E. O. White, *The Biblical Doctrine of Initiation: A Theology of Baptism and Evangelism* (Grand Rapids: Eerdmans, 1960), 305.
[32]Ibid., 308.

Here again we have an emphasis on both "divine activity and human response" in which the sacrament involves a real change in the believer. Beasley-Murray agreed, pointing out that although the biblical authors routinely use symbolic language to describe sacramental action, "they go further and view the act as a symbol with power, that is, a sacrament."[33] Indeed, he contends that "the extent and nature of the grace which the New Testament writers declare to be present in baptism is astonishing for any who come to the study freshly with an open mind."[34] For Beasley-Murray, the sacraments involve "no impersonal influence, injected through material substances, but the gracious action of God himself."[35]

By the latter part of the twentieth century, a whole host of Baptist thinkers had begun making similar arguments, including people like James William McClendon Jr., Christopher Ellis, Paul Fiddes, John Colwell, Anthony Cross, and Philip Thompson. Each of these have argued in their own way that there is space in Baptist theology for a view of the sacraments in which we continue to maintain Baptist distinctives like the emphasis on personal faith, along with the corollary rejection that the sacraments work *ex opere operato*, while emphasizing that the ordinances involve more than mere acts of obedience or the symbolic communication of information. Scott Bullard has labeled this increasingly influential movement the "new Baptist sacramentalism,"[36] yet we have seen that it is only "new" in the sense that it presents itself as a correction to *contemporary* Baptist thought and practice. In light of the foregoing, it is actually more of a retrieval of an important stream that has always been present within Baptist theology.

SACRAMENTAL SIGNS THAT REMEMBER AND RE-MEMBER

To press a bit further into the theological form that such a Baptist sacramental view might take, let us consider briefly how James William McClendon Jr. used this newly recovered sacramental framework to develop a more robust while still thoroughly Baptist view of the sacraments. To begin, we should acknowledge that McClendon himself remained hesitant to use the term *sacrament*. Although he recognized the importance of retaining the biblical idea of "mystery" in our understanding of these rites, and he also appreciated the covenantal and promissory ideas conveyed by the Latin term *sacramentum* in its original context, he worried

---

[33] G. R. Beasley-Murray, *Baptism in the New Testament* (London: Macmillan, 1962), 263.
[34] Ibid.
[35] Ibid., 265.
[36] Bullard, "James William McClendon Jr."

that the term now carried too much historical and theological freight to be of much use. Nonetheless, his overall theological framework was still clearly sacramental as I have defined it.

Focusing specifically on his view of Communion, McClendon contended that we need to understand it as an "effectual sign" that involves both "remembering" and "re-membering."[37] Let's take those pieces one a time. First McClendon views all the ordinances as effectual signs. Here he draws on modern research into the nature of religious practices and the idea of actions as "speech acts" to present liturgical actions like baptism and Communion as more than merely communicative. "In the prophetic and Baptist heritage baptism is not merely a symbol but a *sign*, for it is the nature of signs not only to betoken but to do something, to convey something. I put a sign on my office door: 'Students are welcome.' It employs some symbols, namely letters and words, in order to *do* something, in this case, to *welcome* the students who read it."[38] Drawing primarily on the speech-act theory of J. L. Austin, McClendon thus concludes that there is nothing "merely" about symbolic action. Such actions are performative and person-forming.[39]

Second, when McClendon focuses on the specific kind of action involved, he unsurprisingly deals first with the idea that communion involves an act of remembrance. Consistent with his conviction that these are effectual signs, though, he emphasizes that there is nothing mere about remembering, particularly not when what we are remembering involves God's own historical acts of redemption. Some of the chapters in this book rightly focus on the nature of the *anamnēsis* that Paul says is part of the communion meal: "Do this in *remembrance* of me" (1 Cor 11:24). Yet I think we all know that such memory is anything but trivial. Many modern thinkers have addressed the significance of memory and historical narrative for shaping personal and corporate identities. And we could easily point to the many instances in which God calls his people to remember their own history specifically because that history is what constitutes them as the particular people they are. The *anamnēsis* of communion is just such a constitutive action. We simply could not be the people that God has called us to be if we did not regularly participate in this *anamnētic* action.

---

[37]James William McClendon Jr., *Systematic Theology,* vol. 2, *Doctrine* (Nashville: Abingdon, 1994), 382.
[38]Ibid., 388.
[39]James William McClendon Jr., "Baptism as a Performative Sign," *Theology Today* 23, no. 3 (1966): 403-16.

Third, McClendon emphasized that communion acts as a "re-membering" sign in which we are incorporated into one body in a very tangible sense. For McClendon, Communion is fundamentally an act of solidarity in which we are joined together in one body with one another. This brings to mind yet another of Thompson's Baptist hymns from the eighteenth century. There they sang,

With Jesus in the midst,
We gather round the board;
Though many, we are one in Christ,
One body in the Lord.[40]

For McClendon, Communion thus functions as a kind of counter-practice to the many ways in which the practices of the world dis-member and dis-unite God's people. "Such union with Jesus is re-membering, it is reconstitution, being made part of the whole. In it we are re-united, we are re-membered one to another as his members. Thus as in baptism there is here not only *reference* to God's great historic sign; here again is a (re-membering) sign from God in its own right."[41]

However, as important as all three of these principles might be for developing a more robust account of what is happening when God's people perform the particular actions of baptism and Communion, nothing about what I have just said requires any robust notion of divine agency in these liturgical actions. Indeed, the fact that signs, memories, and practices all play a key role in constituting personal and corporate identity is something that has been embraced in many fields of study. Yet McClendon precludes any such conclusion, maintaining that God himself must be at work in these signs and practices for them to be the kinds of effectual signs he intends them to be. In other words, although McClendon does not tease out this implication, apart from the Spirit, these practices would still shape our identities, but they would no longer do so as Spirit-empowered signs and with Spirit-intended effects. Indeed, as Amy Peeler's essay demonstrates with regard to the Corinthian churches, left to our own devices, we will take the very practice intended to re-member God's people and turn it into an occasion for dis-memberment.[42] McClendon contends that even the simple act of remembering God's historic actions in the past requires divine agency to function properly. "God acts to make these *remembering signs* effectual, just as God originally acted in the great historic

---

[40]Thompson, "Re-Envisioning Baptist Identity," 298.

[41]McClendon, *Doctrine*, 402.

[42]See Amy Peeler, "The Supper of the Lord: Goodness and Grace in 1 Corinthians 11:17-34," chap. 1 in this volume.

signs themselves."[43] Consequently, as we saw with Robinson, here as well we need to affirm that in any true sacrament, "human action and divine action converge."[44]

At the very least, then, I think we would need to supplement this explanation with a strong emphasis on the Spirit's work in and through these realities. While it is true that we can form our own identities through memory, action, and symbol, we will only be formed rightly as God's people, even in and through the sacramental actions instituted by the Lord Jesus, as our memories, actions, and symbolic imaginations are rightly shaped through the work of the Spirit. Otherwise, as we have already discussed, we will take these same sacramental actions and distort them for our own sinful and sectarian purposes.

McClendon's hesitation with the term *sacrament* itself alludes to the fact that he remained committed to a distinctively Baptist view. Yet he also emphasizes that God himself is present and active in particular signs such that they work efficaciously to transform us into the people he desires us to be. Indeed, I would argue that something like this lurks beneath the surface of the Baptist theology I grew up on. Though I was not aware of it at the time, there was an odd incongruity in the Baptist approach to Communion. On the one hand, they emphasized that Communion was no more than a symbolic expression of personal faith, which technically should have made it no different from doing my chores at home without complaining. On the other hand, though, I have never been in a Baptist service that did not approach Communion as an event in which they expected the Spirit of God to be powerfully present and active. Regardless of what Baptists say about the meaning of the elements themselves, I think it is clear that Baptists do *not* believe that the event of Communion involves a merely human action. Instead, Communion is the event in which the Spirit of God takes up our human actions and uses them to shape us transformatively as the people he has called us to be.

Thus, when Stanley Grenz worries that many Baptists view such acts "as having no real importance beyond serving as a personal statement of faith,"[45] I think the worry is slightly misplaced. Most Baptists have a real and lively sense that something important is happening in Communion, but they often lack the theological and conceptual tools necessary to articulate *what* is happening, and they often suspect that any attempt to explain the *what* of Communion will inevitably slide toward a

---

[43]McClendon, *Doctrine*, 382.
[44]Ibid., 389.
[45]Stanley J. Grenz, "Baptism and the Lord's Supper as Community Acts: Toward a Sacramental Understanding of the Ordinances," in *Baptist Sacramentalism*, ed. Cross and Thompson, 83.

non-Baptist view of Communion. As we have seen throughout this overview of Baptist thought, and particularly in the theologies of Robinson and McClendon, this does not have to be the case.

With this emphasis on the Spirit's action in Communion, we can affirm everything necessary to describe this view as sacramental in some meaningful sense. This view clearly emphasizes the importance of *divine agency* and *real efficacy* in the pneumatological event. At the same time, I think we can maintain the *uniqueness* principle by affirming that the Spirit works in this way only, or at least normatively, through these particular sacraments. Such an account may struggle to *explain* why the Spirit works uniquely through these particular actions, but we could always appeal to the principle that "the Spirit blows where it wills" and cry mystery. From this, it would be easy to conclude that the Spirit's work in and through these sacramental actions is also necessary for the proper formation and transformation of God's people. As I indicated earlier, questions will remain about whether this pneumatological account of divine presence is adequate for understanding what is happening in Communion, but that is a task for another time.

THE CLOSED/OPEN TABLE

I cannot end without making two observations regarding the implications of all this for the idea of a shared supper: one optimistic and one less so. Thus far, we have established that there is nothing inherent to the Baptist tradition that precludes Baptists from engaging in sacramental ways of thinking or participating in ecumenical dialogue about the sacraments. Or at least, Baptists do not seem to face any inherent challenges that are not shared by the other Christian traditions as well. Some might even be inclined to think that a view like McClendon's has particular advantages for ecumenical dialogue since it may offer a helpful way of thinking about what is happening in the Eucharistic practices of other traditions. Rather than baldly denying that *anything* is happening in those celebrations other than an act of remembrance, a claim that those other traditions would almost certainly find objectionable, this kind of Baptist sacramentalism would allow us to talk about a myriad of ways in which the Spirit is transformatively at work in the community of believers without needing to engage the many details that continue to separate their respective faith traditions. All Christians, insofar as they are guided by texts like 1 Corinthians 11, will still be shaped by the same Spirit using the same practices to re-member us into the one body of Jesus Christ. You might think that something is happening in the Eucharist *in addition* to this basic fact, and you are within your rights to think so, but this allows the Baptist to affirm far more about what is significant in our shared Eucharistic practices than is possible for any purely memorial view.

In addition, some might think that such a view creates possibilities for actually sharing in the table together. While a Baptist would probably still have difficulties attending a Catholic service and sharing in the "amen" that we have already discussed, it is not clear that this kind of sacramental view inherently precludes anyone from another faith tradition from participating in a Baptist Communion service. And it also seems at least possible that the greater common ground established by this kind of Baptist sacramentalism would make such participation more likely. So, we might conclude from this that while I might not be welcome at your table, you are welcome at mine.

Alas, however, things are never quite as simple as they appear. Any such argument would inevitably find itself mired in the difficult and often passionate debate surrounding open or closed Communion. In other words, should Communion be open to all Christians as a witness to our unity in Christ, or even to all people as an expression of the free grace of the gospel? Or should participation in Communion be limited in some way, typically by contending that Communion should be limited to the baptized, thus linking the sacraments together as a unified work of God's grace? It is the connection between baptism and Communion that creates particular challenges for Baptists in this conversation given their consistent rejection of infant baptism as a legitimate form of baptism. In other words, if Communion should only be for those who have been baptized, and if infant baptism does not qualify as a legitimate baptism, then those who were baptized as infants should not be permitted to take Communion. The logic follows rather straightforwardly.

Faced with this challenge, the Baptist seems to have only a few options. First, she could adopt the increasingly common practice of open Communion, allowing at least anyone who is a Christian to participate in Communion. Yet this seems to have two unfortunate consequences. First, in so doing she is actually creating even greater distance between her position and that of many historic Christian traditions who have always maintained the inseparable unity of baptism and Communion. Second, by severing this link, she needs to address how she will continue to maintain the importance of baptism. Open Communion at least raises questions about how important the initiatory rite of baptism can possibly be if a person can participate fully in the ongoing rite of Communion.

Second, she could simply drop the Baptist rejection of infant baptism, maintaining the validity of both paedobaptism and credobaptism despite the stark differences in their respective theologies of baptism. However, although this would solve the ecumenical problem, it would seem to do so by requiring her to drop a fundamental Baptist conviction. As Father Weinandy so powerfully demonstrates in his essay, whatever we mean by sacramental unity, we cannot proceed as though theological distinctives can or should be casually dismissed.

This would seem to leave only the option of retaining the commitment to credobaptism and the inseparable unity of baptism and Communion, along with an understanding of the table that would seem to preclude the participation of non-Baptists. I will not even attempt to untie the knot I have created here at the end of my chapter. My point is really to establish that even if we develop a more robust understanding of the Baptist view of the sacraments, one that allows Baptists to participate meaningfully in ecumenical conversations about shared ground regarding the nature and function of the sacraments, we need to recognize that Baptists do not come to that conversation unencumbered by theological convictions of their own, convictions that create unique challenges for the possibility that we might all eat together. We cannot allow any kind of Baptist triumphalism that believes this entire problem to result from the sacramental views of other traditions. For the Baptist as well, considerable work remains to be done before we can fully embrace the invitation to eat together.

13

SACRAMENTS AND (DIS-)UNITY

A Constructive Ecumenical Proposal Toward Healing the Divisions and Facilitating Mutual Recognition

VELI-MATTI KÄRKKÄINEN

A VISION FOR RESPONDING TO THE SCANDAL OF DISUNITY

It "strangely warms my heart" that the Wheaton Theology Conference chose the question of the unity of the church as its topic. This is an important and urgent issue for all Christians but particularly so for evangelicals. I agree with the late Lutheran systematician Wolfhart Pannenberg that "for the first time . . . the scandal of divided Christendom has reached such a head that it has become intolerable for the faith consciousness of countless modern Christians." Rightly, Pannenberg raises this important question: "How can we recognize and treat one another as Christian brothers and sisters united by faith in the one Lord and its trinitarian exposition in the church, yet at the same time say nothing about full communion with one another?"[1]

Indeed, so much is at stake with the issue of divisions and unity that, to further cite Pannenberg, only "[if] Christians succeed in solving the problems of their own pluralism, they may be able to produce a model combining pluralism and the widest moral unity which will also be valid for political life."[2] This is a badly needed

---

This essay is based on chap. 14 of my *Hope and Community*, vol. 5 of *A Constructive Christian Theology for the Pluralistic World* (Grand Rapids: Eerdmans, 2017). Used by permission.

[1]Wolfhart Pannenberg, *Systematic Theology*, trans. Geoffrey W. Bromiley (Grand Rapids: Eerdmans, 1998), 3: 411.

[2]Wolfhart Pannenberg, "Christian Morality and Political Issues," in *Faith and Reality*, trans. J. M. Maxwell (Philadelphia: Westminster, 1977), 38.

call for the religiously pluralistic and secular world of ours. Indeed, if we Christians are not able to constructively deal with the plurality and diversity among us, how can we ever fulfill our mission to the world?

In this essay, I propose the possibility in the current theological milieu—building on a half century of ecumenical work and reflection—of tackling the scandal of disunity in a new constructive manner—indeed, in a manner that would allow major Christian families to recognize the full ecclesiality (the full "churchliness") of other Christian communities even with regard to the most contentious issues related to sacraments and ministry. I believe that this does not require us to compromise our distinctive identities but that it would require us to imagine the sacramental and ministerial markers and borderlines in a new, constructive manner.

Boldly and simply stated, my vision is no less than this: that the catholic traditions (both Eastern Orthodox and Roman Catholic), the Anglican and Protestant traditions, and the free churches and independents could come to a place of mutual recognition as churches of the one and same church of Christ, a communion of communions. If this sounds like a grand and bold vision, it is!

Since no ecumenical proposal comes from nowhere, let me locate my own position and the perspective it comes from. I take the mainline Protestant rule, to be more precise, the Lutheran "rule of ecclesiality" (as expressed in the Augsburg Confession [*Confessio Augustana*]) as the defining guideline and seek to find commonalities with both older and younger ecclesial traditions. An ordained Lutheran minister (Evangelical Lutheran Church in America), I also have deep affinities with Pentecostal-Charismatics and other independents and wish to engage them in a way that has not happened much in the past. This means that although my approach is particular and perspectival, it does not have to be exclusively so. The ecumenist may also build on one's tradition self-critically and attempt to transcend it for the sake of inclusivity and the unity in diversity of the whole church. If I have learned anything during more than two decades of intense ecumenical work at regional, national, and international forums, it is this: only proposals that are specific and particular further the effort to resolve ecumenical problems, but those proposals have to be specific and particular with a view toward inclusivity rather than cementing already existing hard walls.

Having now briefly laid out my ultimate goal and having reminded us of the grave scandal of disunity, the rest of the presentation follows in this way: first, I will outline more specifically what the ecumenical impasse of lack of mutual ecclesiastical recognition is all about. I do so by outlining three main positions and how deeply differing understandings of the role and meaning of sacraments and ministry lie behind them. Second, I will take a critical look at a debate at the center of this dispute about ecclesiality, namely, how do we discern the presence of Christ in a Christian community? While all churches agree that the presence of Christ (and indeed, the whole Trinity) is church-constitutive, they differ on how that can be decided in a definitive manner. The third major section takes me to the constructive proposal itself: taking a lead from the Augsburg Confession, I lay out as clearly and transparently as possible my tentative ecumenical vision for mutual recognition. Fourth—and in this last section I have to paint with very broad strokes—I recommend some new and fresh resources and tools to continue this ecumenical work. Some of these resources are emerging and in the process of development in international ecumenical theology even now.

THE BASIC ECCLESIOLOGICAL-ECUMENICAL DILEMMA: THREE DEFINING POSITIONS

The most basic ecumenical dilemma and scandal facing the church of Christ has to do with the deeply and radically differing positions concerning the ecclesiality of the church—that is, what makes the church, church. The underlying problem is simply this: the continuing impossibility of mutual recognition of the ecclesiality (the "churchliness") of other Christian communities. In other words, some churches do not consider others as churches but as something "less" or "defective," such as "Christian communities." This wound is particularly deep between the "older" (Roman Catholic and Orthodox) and "younger" churches (free churches and various types of independent churches), but it also relates to Protestant and Anglican communities. My own Lutheran Church is not considered a "full church" in the theological sense of the word by some important ecclesiastical counterparts; hence, Lutheran sacraments are not fully valid; neither is our ministry.[3]

The problem of ecclesiality has to do with the radically different ways of conceiving what makes the church, church. The key debate relates to the role of sacraments, episcopacy, and personal confession of faith. For the sake of clarity and pedagogical usefulness, let us name three main positions.

---

[3]According to the Vatican (*Lumen Gentium* 15, 26), Protestants, Anglicans, and free churches are not "churches" but rather ecclesial communities.

First, for Orthodox and Catholic ecclesiology, not only does the church carry out the sacraments, but the sacraments first and foremost make the church. This means that only where there is the celebration of the sacrament of the Eucharist (whose attendance requires water baptism), there is the Christian church. And for that celebration to be ecclesiologically valid, there needs to be a bishop whose standing is considered to be linked with the first apostles (somewhat differently defined in those two traditions, a topic into whose details there is no need to delve here). In sum: this is the "sacramental" and "episcopal" (lowercase) rule of ecclesiality.[4]

Second, for the youngest Christian family, the free churches, the presence of personal confession of faith is decisive for men and women who then gather together as the church. Faith is mediated directly through the preaching of the Word, as it were, and does not necessarily require mediation by the sacraments or office. The celebration of the sacraments of water baptism and the Lord's Supper is an important part of the church's life, but they are not considered ecclesiologically constitutive and, where personal faith is missing, might even be taken as something formal and useless. Furthermore, among those free churches that have an ecclesiastical office by the name of "bishop,"[5] it does not have any ecclesiologically determinative function.

Third, there is the Protestant mainline definition of the church's "foundation" in terms of the preaching of the gospel and administration of the sacraments (baptism and Eucharist). Although for Anglicans and many Protestants (all Lutherans and some Reformed) the theology (of salvation) is sacramental in the sense that one comes to the faith and is sustained in it by the sacraments (when integrally linked with the Word), neither sacraments nor ministerial patterns are considered ecclesiologically constitutive after the manner of Orthodox and Catholic theology. As a result, even if they have a bishop (as a large number of Lutherans do), that office is not constitutive for the being of the church and can also be otherwise.[6]

---

[4]Hence, in what follows, the word *episcopal* (as distinct from the proper name of the Episcopal, i.e., Anglican, Church) is used in that technical theological sense.

[5]This is common among most African American churches in the United States, as well as in a large number of Pentecostal and other free churches all over the world, particularly in Africa but also in the former Soviet Union and elsewhere.

[6]A materially similar presentation (limited to Orthodox/Catholics and free churches) can be found in Miroslav Volf, *After Our Likeness: The Church as an Image of the Trinity* (Grand Rapids: Eerdmans, 1998), 130-35. For details, see my "Unity, Diversity, and Apostolicity: Any Hopes for Rapprochement Between Older and Younger Churches?," in *Believing in Community: Ecumenical Reflections on the Church*, ed. Peter de Mey, Bibliotheca Ephemeridum Theologicarum Lovaniensium (Leuven: University of Leuven Press, 2013), 487-506.

Now, the ecumenical and ecclesiastical implications are simply these: for Orthodox and Catholics, neither Protestant/Anglican communities, regardless of their sacramentality, nor free churches qualify as churches. That is because they lack episcopal and sacramental validity for the reasons explained above. Even the Anglican and Protestant celebration of the sacraments (particularly the Eucharist) is invalid because of the episcopal deficit. On the other hand, for free churches, particularly in the beginning years of the movements, no amount of appeal to episcopacy or sacraments had any church-constitutive meaning; indeed, putting them in the forefront often elicited a response against mere formal religion. The mainline Protestants (and Anglicans, I suppose) come closest to not having binding reasons for nonrecognition of either free churches, as long as they also honor the sacraments (and they do appreciate the preaching of the Word, after all), or Orthodox and Catholics (without endorsing their exclusive appeal to episcopal succession).

This impasse over mutual recognition is an open wound for ecclesiology and ecumenism. If we were not so used to it, it would seem unbearable, excruciating. And it is! Neither theologically nor in terms of common sense—let alone Christian love!—can it be tolerated anymore. By it Christian churches who claim the presence of one and the same Lord continue to refuse to grant the same to other Christian communities with similar claims![7] Taken seriously, the implications of nonrecognition lead to conclusions and implications that are simply absurd and bizarre. We gather around the table of the Lord and the baptismal font with full assurance of the presence of the triune God among us—while at the same time denying the same for other Christian churches.

After this outline of the main positions, let me now advance to a critical scrutiny of the "art of the ecclesiality discourse" and assess the conditions and promises of a constructive proposal.

HOW DO WE DISCERN THE PRESENCE OF CHRIST IN THE CHURCH?

There is an ecumenical consensus about the presence of Christ (and therefore, of the Spirit and the triune God) as ecclesiologically constitutive. This rule goes back to the church fathers and is solidly based in the New Testament witness. The theologically pregnant Matthean passage affirms: "For where two or three are gathered in my name, there am I in the midst of them" (Mt 18:20). Ignatius taught that "wherever Jesus Christ is, there is the Catholic Church," and Irenaeus expressed the same with reference to

---

[7]Similarly Volf, *After Our Likeness*, 133-34.

the Spirit's presence.[8] Tertullian's oft-cited maxim states: "But where three are, [there] a church is."[9] This issue is not contested. What is debated has to do with the way Christ's (and the Spirit's) presence can be determined, as it is hardly self-evident.[10] It is widely agreed that whatever instruments one may employ to determine Christ's ecclesiologically constitutive presence, they cannot be so external to the task that they fail to disclose something essential about the church. In other words, they cannot be arbitrary—and yet, obviously, they also have to be externally perceivable.[11]

It is here that the Anglican (formerly Pentecostal) Miroslav Volf takes up the task in an important ecclesiological proposal searching for a minimalist yet significant principle of ecclesiality. He does so by seeking to develop a theology of the church based on the best and "redeemable" elements of congregationalist–free church traditions in dialogue with Catholic and Orthodox ecclesiologies.[12] Building on the above-mentioned programmatic passage from Matthew 18:20, Volf puts forth his tentative description of what makes the church, church: "Where two or three are gathered in Christ's name, not only is Christ present among them, but a Christian church is there as well, perhaps bad church, a church that may well transgress against love and truth, but a church nonetheless." Volf claims that this definition expresses what Ignatius, Irenaeus, Tertullian, and others argued, and that it is also in keeping with the rule of ecclesiality propounded by the seventeenth-century English founder of the Baptist movement, John Smyth:[13] "A visible communion of Saincts is of two, three, or moe Saincts joyned together by covenant with God & themselves, freely to use al the holy things of God, according to the word, for their mutual edification, & God's glory. Mat. 18 20 Deut. 29, 12. &c Psal. 147, 19 & 149, 6–9. Rev. 1. 6."[14]

Volf takes several steps toward a promising and ecumenically fruitful position by suggesting that even the free church traditions join the ecumenical consensus according to which the two sacraments, water baptism and Eucharist, serve the task of identifying Christ's presence. That is a tentative but also important response to the question of how to discern Christ's (and the Spirit's) church-constitutive

---

[8]Ignatius, *To the Smyrnaeans* 8; Irenaeus, *Against Heresies* 3.24.1.

[9]Tertullian, *On Exhortation to Chastity* 7.

[10]So also Volf, *After Our Likeness*, 129.

[11]Ibid., 129-30.

[12]For an exposition and useful comments, see Graham Hill, *Salt, Light, and a City: Introducing Missional Ecclesiology* (Eugene, OR: Wipf & Stock, 2012), chap. 12.

[13]Volf, *After Our Likeness*, 135-37 (here 136; emphasis removed).

[14]John Smyth, *Principles and Inferences Concerning the Visible Church,* in *The Works of John Smyth, Fellow of Christ's College 1594–1598,* vol. 1, ed. W. T. Whitley (Cambridge: Cambridge University Press, 1915), 252.

presence. Furthermore, important particularly to the mainline Reformation churches, the sacraments are tightly integrated with the Word of God, the gospel, as the sacraments left alone can hardly mediate Christ's presence.[15] As much as the Baptist Smyth underscored the unmediated presence of Christ in the church, even he considered necessary the use of "the holy things of God," namely, "the meanes of salvation . . . : the word, Sacraments, prayers."[16]

So far all churches are most likely to follow my argumentation, even if for Orthodox and Catholics this is not yet enough. Indeed, where Volf's free church–driven (but mainline Protestant church–sympathetic) proposal differs strongly from the Roman Catholic and Orthodox ecclesiologies is that it does not accept their claims for the necessity of a specific kind of office, namely episcopacy, for the validity of the sacraments.[17] As a Protestant theologian, I agree with Volf's refusal to make a bishop the absolute requirement for the sacraments' validity.[18] But instead of leaving the issue there and so living with the impasse, I wish to bring to the discussion table the ecumenically pregnant definition of ecclesiality from the mainline Protestant traditions, particularly from Lutheran ecclesiology, with the hope that several important steps toward rapprochement could be had in relation to Orthodox and Catholics.

TOWARD A MUTUAL RECOGNITION OF THE ECCLESIALITY OF THE CHURCH: A CONSTRUCTIVE PROPOSAL

Locating the proposal. I will take as a starting point the description of the ecclesiality of the church from the "middle" of the ecclesiality debate spectrum, namely mainstream Protestantism. According to the Lutheran Augsburg Confession (article 7), the church

> is the assembly of all believers among whom the gospel is preached in its purity and
> the holy sacraments are administered according to the gospel. For it is sufficient for
> the true unity of the Christian church that the gospel be preached in conformity with
> a pure understanding of it and that the sacraments be administered in accordance
> with the divine Word.

---

[15]Volf, *After Our Likeness*, 152-54.

[16]Smyth, *Principles and Inferences*, 254. For a highly useful discussion, see, Roger Haight, SJ, *Christian Community in History*, vol. 2, *Comparative Ecclesiology* (New York: Continuum, 2005), esp. 251-53.

[17]Volf, *After Our Likeness*, 133-34, 152. I will not go into the details of differences as to how Orthodox ecclesiology distinctively expresses this condition; see Volf, *After Our Likeness*, 130-31.

[18]Let me hasten to mention that Volf's position is not historically convincing because he overlooks the fact that for Ignatius (at least), the rule of ecclesiality as the presence of Christ is conditioned on the presence of the bishop as the presider at the Eucharist; Ignatius, *To the Smyrnaeans* 8.

In other words, as long as the gospel and sacraments are there, it "is not necessary for the true unity of the Christian church that ceremonies, instituted by men, should be observed uniformly in all places."[19] Clearly, the theological and ecumenical cash value of *CA* 7 lies in that as long as the gospel and sacraments are there, most everything else can be named a matter of *adiaphora*, including church structures and ministerial patterns.[20]

Hence, the ecumenical potential of *CA* 7 runs wide and deep. Before reaching out to Roman Catholics and Orthodox with this position, though, let me register some additions to the two conditions (Word and sacraments) among some Protestants and free church advocates. They have to do with "discipline" (ethical and "behavioral" criterion) and the question of whether some particular structures (like offices) might be divinely sanctioned or not (i.e., governance). This is the case with the Reformed counterpart: in Calvin's ecclesiology, "discipline," that is, obedience, is listed as a necessary condition and there is also a claim for divinely sanctioned structures and offices.[21] The same applies to the first and formative free church tradition, the Baptist movement. While materially agreeing with the Lutheran definition, it added, similarly to the Reformed, fixed structures and obedience as conditions.[22] When it comes to the Radical Reformation, the additional elements are even more numerous. While the 1527 Swiss Brethren's Schleitheim collection of Seven Articles contains, importantly, baptism and the Lord's Supper, it also lists the ban, separation from the world, pacifism, and refusal to take an oath.[23]

---

[19]*Confessio Augustana* (=Augsburg Confession [henceforth *CA*]), art. 7, in *The Book of Concord: The Confessions of the Evangelical Lutheran Church*, trans. Theodore G. Tappert (Philadelphia: Fortress, 1959), 32.

[20]For useful comments, see Risto Saarinen, "Lutheran Ecclesiology," in *Routledge Companion to the Christian Church*, ed. Gerard Mannion and Lewis S. Mudge (New York: Routledge, 2012), 171-73.

[21]John Calvin, *Institutes of the Christian Religion*, trans. Henry Beveridge (Grand Rapids: Eerdmans, 1957), 4.1.9. Note that even the current Presbyterian Church (USA)'s *Book of Order* devotes the largest section to discipline (rather than, say, to worship or government). Calvin (*Institutes*, 4.3.1) begins his consideration of offices: "We are now to speak of the order in which the Lord has been pleased that his Church should be governed." For Reformed orthodoxy's fixation on a certain order following the fourfold office based on Eph 4:11, namely, pastors, teachers, presbyters, and deacons, see Pannenberg, *Systematic Theology*, 3:385.

[22]Smyth, *Principles and Inferences*, 252, 253, respectively.

[23]The articles (also called the Schleitheim Confession) can be found, e.g., at the Anabaptist website, www.anabaptists.org/history/the-schleitheim-confession.html. Menno Simmons's marks of the true church include pure doctrine, baptism, the Lord's Supper, obedience to the Word, love, confession of Christ, and suffering for God; Menno Simons, *Reply to Gellius Faber (1552)*, in *The Complete Writings of Menno Simons (c. 1496-1561)*, ed. H. S. Bender (Scottsdale, PA: Herald, 1956), 752; for similar kinds of descriptions, see also 744, 755.

Now, what to do with these Protestant and free church additions? On what basis is it not self-contradictory on my part to reject the Catholic and Orthodox requirement of episcopacy for ecclesiality while overlooking the other kinds of additions by the Reformed, Baptists, and Anabaptists? My response is that the additional requirements by the Reformed and the free churches are merely that—*additions*—and are not meant to necessarily discredit or reject the foundational claim for ecclesiality by the Lutherans; if they were forced, I assume, not only the Reformed but also (at least most of) the free churches would be willing to negotiate the additions and live with the *CA* 7 definition. That is markedly different from the categorical rejection of the ecclesiality of all other churches (but the Orthodox) by Roman Catholics.

The ecumenical promise of the gospel and sacraments as ecclesial rule. Ecumenically, it is of utmost importance that, notwithstanding serious challenges to the acknowledgment of full ecclesiality to Protestant (and Anglican) communities, the Catholic Hans Küng notes this: "Catholic theology has never had any positive objection to raise against the two classic Protestant signs: without the preaching of the gospel in accordance with Scripture and the administering of the sacraments as divinely ordained there can be no true Church according to the Catholic view either; both are absolute prerequisites for the Catholic Church too."[24]

This robust statement is definitively endorsed by Vatican II's *Lumen Gentium*: "This Church of Christ is truly present in all legitimate local congregations . . . [in] which the faithful are gathered together by the preaching of the Gospel of Christ, and the mystery of the Lord's Supper is celebrated." So, what is the problem from the Roman side? It has to do with placing the preaching and sacraments in the context of a certain kind of episcopal ministry, as only a "bishop [is] marked with the fullness of the sacrament of Orders," and therefore, "every legitimate celebration of the Eucharist is regulated by the bishop."[25] As long as that claim is taken as a final statement from the Catholics, I see little hope for rapprochement. But what if it could be placed in a slightly different context?

I find useful Küng's note that at the core of the Catholic objection to the sufficiency of the *CA* 7 principle of ecclesiality lies the fear that "these two characteristics

---

[24]Hans Küng, *The Church* (Garden City: Doubleday, 1976), 346; materially similarly, Jürgen Moltmann, *The Church in the Power of the Spirit: A Contribution to Messianic Ecclesiology*, trans. Margaret Kohl (London: SCM, 1977), 341.

[25]*Lumen Gentium*, 26.

of the true Church are not truly distinguishing features" and hence do not fulfill the required task of identifying where the true church really is.[26] If that is the case, I think there is some hope of bringing the divergent viewpoints closer together if we consider the issue in light of the marks of the church, classically taken as the identifying distinctives of or pointers to the true church. I think it is an ecumenical consensus that the two defining features of the ecclesiality of CA 7 are integrally and irreconcilably linked with the four marks: unity, holiness, catholicity, and apostolicity. Indeed, Küng himself, as a Catholic theologian, contends that the marks "do not mean anything if they are not based on the pure Gospel message, valid baptism, and the proper celebration of the Lord's Supper. Always and in every case the Church must be certain it is in essential agreement with the original New Testament message."[27] Isn't there some kind of real mutuality between the two "marks" of CA 7 and the four "marks" of the creed? Neither set of requirements alone is specific and concrete enough to help us discern where the presence of the triune God may lie in an ecclesiologically constitutive manner. When linked together, however, they help us be more confident. Rather than a vicious circle of trying to prove what one presupposes, this linking can be seen as a *mutuality* of enrichment, information, and specification.

The legitimate fear among the Catholics and Orthodox concerning the challenge of being able to discern Christ's community-forming presence may also be eased by the following observation concerning the Protestant Reformers. As much as the Reformers emphasized the immediacy of believers to Christ (to defeat what they saw as the destructive human-made, hierarchy-related, and institutional obstacles), in no way could CA 7 be made a matter of a "community of believers" merely coming together as individuals to be the church. That would of course make the claim for ecclesiality random and release it from all traditional safeguards. Indeed, that liability should be carefully minded by free churches, as they at times tend to emphasize problematically the mere unmediated access to Christ by all.

The community's ecclesiality depends on the preaching and sacraments, which both represent apostolicity as they go back to Jesus and the institution by the apostles. Recall the *Large Catechism* (on the third article of the creed): "It is the mother that begets and bears every Christian through the Word of God."[28]

---

[26]Küng, *Church*, 346.
[27]Ibid., 347.
[28]Martin Luther, *Large Catechism* 2.42, in *The Book of Concord*, 416; Calvin, *Institutes*, 4.1.4; see Pannenberg, *Systematic Theology*, 3:100-101. For the rediscovery of the idea in contemporary evangelical

Referring to sacraments in this regard, Pannenberg rightly notes that the idea of the church as a "mother" begetting and nurturing believers alone would defeat the mistaken interpretation of Christian gathering as arbitrary. I think this is a highly important criterion for the Orthodox and Catholics.

Furthermore, it seems to me that sticking with the two foundational standards, *pure* gospel and *right* administration of sacraments—as much as it is true that the Protestant Reformation failed to provide any specific criteria for their discernment—also leads toward unity in faith and love for all communities committed to them. Whatever else purity and correctness may mean, they must stand in continuity with the apostolic Scriptures and creeds (again, as much room as there may be for differences in details of formulations). Rather than pushing toward exclusivity, isn't their embrace instead compelling the Christian community to consider as true church any community bound by and committed to the same ecclesiastical criteria? Pannenberg succinctly argues, on that basis, that the universal unity of the church across the ages finds manifestation in the worship of the local congregation that exists in virtue of its apostolic basis, having fellowship with past saints and martyrs. For the pure teaching of the apostolic gospel and administration of the sacraments that is faithful to their institution constitute the church's unity across the centuries and at the same time characterize each local congregation of believers as the church of Christ.[29] And, as Küng helpfully reminds us, believing the church to be one, holy, catholic, and apostolic for ourselves, we "want to believe and hope for others too."[30]

Having now considered the criteria for the "observable" ecclesiologically constitutive forms of Christ's presence—with hope for an ecumenical rapprochement—we note that Christ's presence is not of course limited to that function alone. Moltmann importantly reminds us that on the basis of the New Testament texts we should expect Christ's presence in many forms and places. "Christ is present in the apostolate, in the sacraments, and in the fellowship of the brethren." The term *apostolate* here denotes "the medium of the proclamation through word and sacrament, as well as the persons and community of the proclaimers." There are a number of New Testament assurances, such as "he who hears you hears me"

---

ecclesiology, see Brad Harper and Paul Louis Metzger, *Exploring Ecclesiology: An Evangelical and Ecumenical Introduction* (Grand Rapids: Brazos, 2009), 11-12.

[29]Pannenberg, *Systematic Theology*, 3:101.

[30]Küng, *Church*, 53-59; so also Moltmann, *Church in the Power of the Spirit*, 337-38.

(Lk 10:16) and "I am with you always, to the close of the age" (Mt 28:20), to those going out to share the gospel by preaching and baptizing. Similar promises of Christ's presence are attached to the celebration of the Eucharist (1 Cor 11:23-27). The baptized will be sharing death and life with Christ (Rom 6:1-12). Second, Christ has pledged his presence in the children, the poor, and other "little ones." Matthew 25:31-36 is an extended exposition of that theme. And so forth.[31]

If this proposal set forth here briefly in skeleton form has any value in itself, it calls all ecumenically minded to work together toward the common goal. What kind of resources and tools might be available for such a work? This last section briefly taps into a set of new and emerging ecumenical paradigms and developments.

NEW RESOURCES, TOOLS, AND PERSPECTIVES

Let me first list the kinds of resources and tools I have in mind and then briefly introduce them. Clearly this is nothing close to a comprehensive listing. Rather, it is suggestive and also related to the projects and enterprises I myself am involved with.

- Ecumenical recognition
- Receptive ecumenism
- Partial communion and provisionality
- Ethnography as ecumenism
- Ecumenism as comparative theology

"Recognition" in philosophical, interdisciplinary, and ecumenical perspective.
Those of you among us who are philosophically trained know that the concept of "recognition" (*die Anerkennung* in German) is a long-lived and long-debated concept. Behind it is this simple and profound question: On what basis would it be possible for the human person or group to fully recognize the other and her identity in the midst of differences, divergences, and even potential conflicts? The current pluralistic, multicultural, and multireligious world has brought those questions back to the center of attention. Issues related to negotiating between the "one" and "many," "we" and "they," or "unity" and "diversity" have been on the menu of thinkers from the ancient Greek philosophers all the way up to leading modern thinkers.

---

[31]Moltmann, *Church in the Power of the Spirit*, 121-32.

Among the modern philosophers, no thinker scrutinized the problematic of recognition with greater influence than Hegel.[32] His sustained reflections on the intersubjective concept of recognition, particularly through the lens of the master-slave analogy, have continued to inspire generations of thinkers.[33] At the heart of Hegel's conception are reciprocal recognition and the idea that in a real sense, one receives one's own personhood from the other—and commensurately, helps the other to have the same.[34] The space of the other, so to speak, is not so foreign a territory that one could not inhabit it in some sense, and that is likewise true from the other's perspective.

In contemporary philosophy, a programmatic recognition scholar is the Canadian philosopher Charles Taylor. He rightly argues that "nonrecognition or misrecognition can inflict harm, can be a form of oppression, imprisoning someone in a false, distorted, and reduced mode of being."[35] In political science, the most noted recognition theorist is the German Axel Honneth. His theory of recognition consists basically of three parts: love, respect, and esteem. What can be called "emotional recognition" emerges in the early years of one's life at home in an intimate relationship of love and worth. "Rights-based" recognition is related to learning to respect and receive respect in the legal structures of society. Esteem is related to a "community of values" in a society that values one's accomplishments. Honneth's conviction is that only through recognition from the most important social groups and communities can our personal being emerge and develop. This puts the obligation to love, respect, and show esteem—or solidarity, as he also calls it—to others in relevant contexts in the society, or else denial of recognition or misrecognition takes place.[36] Honneth's conviction is that only through recognition

---

[32] The main locus for Hegel's philosophy of recognition is in his *Phenomenology of Spirit* (1807), also known as the *Jena Lectures on the Philosophy of Spirit* (available in English in various versions, alternatively titled as *The Phenomenology of Mind*; the one used here is G. W. F. Hegel, *The Phenomenology of Mind*, trans. J. B. Baillie [San Francisco: Harper, 1967]). The master-slave analogy is in B.IV; "The True Nature of Self-Certainty" ("Self-consciousness" in other translations). Of course, Descartes and Kant (especially) contributed to what became a full-scale philosophy of recognition in Hegel; see Timothy T. M. Lim, "Ecclesial Recognition: An Interdisciplinary Proposal" (PhD diss., School of Divinity, Regent University, 2014), 46-53.

[33] Sybol Cook Anderson, *Hegel's Theory of Recognition: From Oppression to Ethical Liberal Modernity* (London: Continuum, 2009); from a theological perspective, see Martin J. De Nys, *Hegel and Theology* (New York: T&T Clark, 2009), chaps. 1-2 particularly.

[34] Hegel, *Phenomenology of Mind*, 126.

[35] Charles Taylor, "The Politics of Recognition," in *Multiculturalism: Examining the Politics of Recognition*, ed. Amy Guttmann (Princeton: Princeton University Press, 1994), 25.

[36] Axel Honneth, *The Struggle for Recognition: The Moral Grammar of Social Conflicts* (Cambridge: Polity, 1995); *The I in We: Studies in the Theory of Recognition*, trans. Joseph Ganahl (Malden, MA:

from the most important social groups and communities can our personal being emerge and develop.

Now, based on these and related contributions, ecumenical recognition "focuses on the possibility of recognizing the other [church] as a true church," and as such it is a key "part of a conscious process of changing the identification of the other [church]."[37] This is exactly what *The Church: Towards a Common Vision* (2013) does: "Visible unity requires that churches be able to recognize in one another the authentic presence of what the Creed of Nicea-Constantinople (381) calls the 'one, holy, catholic, apostolic Church.'"[38] In other words, ecumenical recognition "examines whether churches may accept the legitimacy and authenticity of other churches as the Church in the dialogical process towards fuller communion."[39] It includes recognition of each other's baptism, ministry, worship/liturgy, and so forth.

Recognition has nothing to do with cancelling out particular identities. Take a lesson again from Küng:

> As long as these Churches recognize one another as legitimate, as long as they see one another as part of one and the same Church, as long as they are in fellowship as Churches with one another and hold common services, and especially celebrate the Eucharist together, and as long as they are helping one another, working together and standing together in times of difficulty and persecution, there can be no objection to their diversity. All the differences, however profound, between the individual Churches are then swallowed up by the certainty that all are one in the unity of the Church of Christ.[40]

The promise of "receptive ecumenism." The new paradigm of "receptive ecumenism" is related to the standard ecumenical term *reception*, although it also goes beyond it. By *reception* is meant "the process by which the churches make their own

---

Polity, 2012); see also *Disrespect: The Normative Foundations of Critical Theory* (Malden, MA: Polity, 2007).

[37] Minna Hietamäki, "Recognition and Ecumenical Recognition—Distinguishing the Idea of Recognition in Modem Ecumenism," *Neue Zeitschrift für systematische Theologie und Religionsphilosophie* 56 (2014): 458. The term *recognition* had also been employed in ecumenism earlier; for this see Harding Meyer, "Anerkennung—ein 'Ökumenischer Schlüsselbegriff,'" in *Dialog und Anerkennung: Hanfried Krüger zu Ehren*, ed. Peter Manns (Frankfurt am Main: Lembeck, 1980), 25-41. For the current state of the discussion, see Risto Saarinen, "Anerkennungstheorien und Ökumenische Theologie," in *Ökumene—Überdacht*, Quaestiones Disputate 259, ed. Thomas Bremer (Freiburg: Herder, 2013), 237-61.

[38] *The Church: Towards a Common Vision*, Faith and Order Paper 214 (Geneva: World Council of Churches, 2013), 9.

[39] Lim, "Ecclesial Recognition," 7.

[40] Küng, *Church*, 356-57.

the results of all their encounters with one another, and in a particular way the convergences and agreements reached on issues over which they have historically been divided."[41] Reception is already present in the New Testament—just think of the Pauline words of institution of the Eucharist (1 Cor 11:23). Reception was also a key issue in the early centuries, particularly with regard to the ways the churches embraced and understood the pronouncements of ecumenical councils.[42] No wonder the question of reception has received a lot of attention in the modern ecumenical movement.[43] Not only doctrinal reception but also "the broader process by which churches can receive elements such as liturgy, spirituality and forms of witness from one another's traditions" relates to this task.[44] Reception, if it really is true and genuine, does not leave the church the same; it may lead to renewal and change.[45] This is exactly what happened in the historic agreement on justification between the Vatican and Lutherans in 1999 as both parties' self-understanding and way of embracing a formative doctrinal stance were impacted.[46]

Now, the leading idea behind the new approach named "receptive ecumenism" stems from the collaborative work of the British Catholic theologian Paul D. Murray of Durham University. Its main premise is simple and profound, stating that "the primary ecumenical responsibility is to ask not 'What do the other traditions first need to learn from us?' but 'What do we need to learn from them?'"[47] The impetus behind receptive ecumenism

is to take seriously both the reality of the contemporary ecumenical moment— wherein the hope for structural unification in the short to medium term is, in general,

---

[41] "The Nature and Purpose of Ecumenical Dialogue," in *The Joint Working Group Between the Roman Catholic Church and the World Council of Churches: Eighth Report, 1999-2005* (Geneva: World Council of Churches, 2005), 59 (appendix D; 82-83); for background, see William G. Rusch, *Reception: An Ecumenical Opportunity* (Philadelphia: Fortress, 1988).

[42] See Gerard Kelly, "A New Ecumenical Wave," National Council of Churches Forum, Canberra, July 12, 2010; www.ncca.org.au/index.php/faith-and-unity/46-a-new-ecumenical-wave/file.

[43] The most recent ecumenical document is *Reception: A Key to Ecumenical Progress*, Joint Working Group Between the Roman Catholic Church and the World Council of Churches (Geneva: World Council of Churches, 2014); available at www.oikoumene.org/en/resources/documents/commissions/jwg-rcc-wcc/ninth-report-of-the-joint-working-group.

[44] *Reception*, 2.

[45] Ibid., 13.

[46] See "Joint Declaration on the Doctrine of Justification by the Lutheran World Federation and the Catholic Church" (1999), 7 (in the preamble); available at www.vatican.va/roman_curia/pontifical_councils/chrstuni/documents/rc_pc_chrstuni_doc_31101999_cath-luth-joint-declaration_en.html.

[47] This definition can be found, e.g., in "About Receptive Ecumenism," on the webpage of the Durham University Department of Theology and Religion, Centre for Catholic Studies, Projects & Research Interests; www.dur.ac.uk/theology.religion/ccs/projects/receptiveecumenism/about/.

now widely recognized as being unrealistic—and the abiding need for the Christian churches precisely in this situation to find an appropriate means of continuing to walk the way of conversion towards more visible structures and sacramental unity.[48]

For that to happen, receptive ecumenism recommends the following kinds of attitudes and postures: willingness to change oneself rather than the other; "to learn *from* and *across* our denominational differences in a mutually enriching way that fosters growth *within* traditions by finding the beauty of another tradition's focus"; and openness to continuing growth and change of tradition.[49]

"Partial communion" and "provisionality": Modest and humble goals. A differently formulated goal of ecumenical work—"partial" rather than full communion—can be linked with the tactics of recognition and mutual reception explained above. It also sticks with the concept of "provisionality" of ecclesiastical traditions and communities on this side of the eschaton. In the spirit of receptive ecumenism, in that kind of approach one would be willing to have one's own identity and self-understanding be transformed rather than working from an assumption that only fully arriving according to one's ready-made plan would qualify as a result.

The partial communion paradigm starts with this obvious question, What if full communion were unattainable as a goal? Without cynicism or an attempt to "lower standards," most all ecumenists agree that full communion seems to be too ambitious a goal of unity—at least for the time being.[50] If so,

> why not seek a partial communion? That is a more modest and realistic standard to begin with. Partial communion "means mutual recognition despite substantial or significant differences or disagreements."
>
> This notion of communion admits many degrees. Consider the principle of partial communion in relation to one of the defining aspects of ecclesiality, apostolicity, which is also the foundation for the church's missionary nature. According to the American Jesuit R. Haight, "The apostolic character of common ecclesial existence

---

[48]Paul D. Murray, "Introducing Receptive Ecumenism," *The Ecumenist: A Journal of Theology, Culture, and Society* 51, no. 2 (2014): 1; see further Paul D. Murray, ed., *Receptive Ecumenism and the Call to Catholic Learning: Exploring a Way for Contemporary Ecumenism* (Oxford: Oxford University Press, 2008); for an assessment, see Clive Barrett, ed., *Unity in Process: Reflections on Receptive Ecumenism* (London: Darton, Longman & Todd, 2012).

[49]"About Receptive Ecumenism," emphasis in original.

[50]See O. C. Edwards Jr., "Meanings of Full Communion: The Essence of Life in the Body," *Speaking of Unity* 1 (2005): 11. This and the following two paragraphs draw directly from my "Growing Together in Mission," in *Called to Unity for the Sake of Mission*, ed. John Gibaut and Knud Jørgensen (Oxford: Regnum, 2014), 69.

provides the grounds for partial communion. . . . As a common apostolic dimension in all the churches, this ecclesial existence contains the possibility to serve as a basis for partial communion among the churches. Indeed, it urges such communion and even demands it."

In keeping with the modest call of partial communion, ecumenism could envision flexible, creative, and diverse processes and structures in the service of seeking unity. That kind of imagination, rather than rigid structures, better fits the mosaic of the Christian church at both local and global levels.[51]

That would allow for new kinds of ecumenical players, such as the Global Christian Forum,[52] to be engaged as a full partner. It would also allow free churches, emerging communities, Christian coalitions, and similar groups to have a stronger voice. Flexible structures and processes with partial communion as the goal would much better fit the diverse and globalized church than rigid and fixed agendas. Partial communion as the goal is based on the conviction that diversity in itself is not the problem; exclusivity is.

Partial communion goes alongside the concept of the "provisionality" of Christian traditions and denominations. Indeed, all denominational identities and claims for the ecclesiality of any particular church (family) are by definition provisional. This is the case for two reasons. First of all, on this side of the eschatological consummation, each communion is but an anticipation of the final gathering of all people and churches in eschatological consummation. As an *anticipation*, each church is provisional. Second, each local community, each local church, while a full church, is always partial and provisional in relation to other local churches. Under one head (Christ), there cannot be "bodies" so independent that they are not members of the body of Christ. This same provisionality also characterizes the ecclesial category of "denomination," which in itself is an intermediary concept, denoting something between the local church and the final eschatological gathering of all people under one God.

On top of theological reasons, provisionality is also called for by the complexity and diversity of the contemporary global church. No doubt that as inevitable as it may be that denominational markers will be with us "until the end," there is also a widespread and increasing loosening or fluidity of those markers, particularly due to the constant emergence of new ecclesial structures and experiments. Regrettably,

---

[51]Kärkkäinen, "Growing Together in Mission," 69. Quotations from Roger Haight, SJ, *Ecclesial Existence*, vol. 3, *Christian Community in History* (London: Continuum, 2008), 277, 286.

[52]See their official website: www.globalchristianforum.org.

the contemporary ecumenical movement at large is still blind and deaf to these trends. Modern (and contemporary) ecumenism is still focused on negotiating merely between solid identities; it is blind to the emerging hybrid identities of local communions, networks of communions, and even more recent denominations.[53] Even worse, contemporary ecumenism also operates as if "denominations" were composed only of established mainline communities and provides little room for the significance of many free churches, Pentecostal/charismatic groups, emerging churches, and other newcomers.[54]

"Ethnography as ecumenism." Too often ecclesiological and ecumenical discourse loses touch with the realities of church life and becomes speculative and abstract. Instead of merely theoretically reflecting on ecclesiology and church life, an ethnographic approach seeks to find some empirical, grassroots-level information and observations concerning the church. Such sociological, psychological, phenomenological, and other empirical studies were first named "Ethnography and Ecumenism," and it is currently a transatlantic research program. I have tweaked it to "Ethnography as Ecumenism." Somewhat similarly to congregational studies, it believes that ecclesiology needs "supplementation by judicious narratives" as correctives to an overly formal ecclesiology that stays away from "real" church life.

"Ecumenism as comparative theology." The phrase "ecumenism as comparative theology" obviously builds on the wider concept of comparative theology, an emerging theological subdiscipline that engages other faith traditions with regard to specific, detailed themes and topics. Building on but also going farther than the more abstract and general theology of religions, it seeks to engage in an interfaith comparative work that is specific and deep. With regard to ecclesiology and ecumenism, it focuses on religious communities, whether the church, ummah, synagogue, sangha, or similar. It looks at the being and nature of the community, its "liturgy" and rites, its mission, and so forth, and it does so by delving deeply into specific scriptural, historical, and contemporary authoritative and defining texts.

Ecumenism as comparative theology focuses on the questions of divisions and unity within one faith tradition and in relation to others. To give an obvious example: Why, how, and for what reasons is the Islamic ummah divided into two major—and innumerably smaller—denominations and groups, and why are they not able to recognize each other? Put that in a comparative Christian perspective, and you are doing ecumenism as comparative theology.

---

[53]See further Volf, *After Our Likeness*, 19-20.
[54]So also ibid., 20-21.

It is amazing how this kind of exercise can help clarify, put in perspective, and foster reconsideration of internal Christian divisions and reasons for them. It may resource and empower the search for mutual recognition for the sake of the pluralistic world in a way that getting stuck with intra-Christian resources may not allow. My *Hope and Community* takes many steps towards that direction, and I hope it can serve as a call for many such enterprises.

CONTRIBUTORS

Marc Cortez is professor of theology at Wheaton College.

Paul L. Gavrilyuk holds the Aquinas Chair in Theology and Philosophy at the University of St. Thomas.

George Kalantzis is professor of theology and director of The Wheaton Center for Early Christian Studies at Wheaton College.

Veli-Matti Kärkkäinen is professor of systematic theology in the School of Theology at Fuller Theological Seminary.

Matthew Levering holds the James N. and Mary D. Perry, Jr. Chair of Theology at the University of Saint Mary of the Lake.

D. Stephen Long is the Cary M. Maguire University Professor of Ethics at Southern Methodist University.

Matthew J. Milliner is associate professor of art history at Wheaton College.

Bradley Nassif is professor of biblical and theological studies at North Park University.

D. Zac Niringiye is a retired assistant bishop of the diocese of Kampala, Church of Uganda, and a fellow at the School of Law, Makerere University, Uganda.

Cherith Fee Nordling is associate professor of theology at Northern Seminary.

Amy Peeler is associate professor of New Testament at Wheaton College.

Katherine Sonderegger holds the William Meade Chair in Systematic Theology at Virginia Theological Seminary.

Thomas G. Weinandy, OFM, Cap. has served as the warden of Greyfriars Hall, Oxford, a tutor and lecturer in history and doctrine at the University of Oxford, and the executive director for the Secretariat for Doctrine at the United States Conference of Catholic Bishops.

AUTHOR INDEX

SUBJECT INDEX

SCRIPTURE INDEX

Wheaton College

For Christ and His Kingdom

SINCE 1992, the Wheaton Theology Conference at Wheaton College has enabled Christian wisdom and reflection to be heard on a range of issues relevant to both current theological scholarship and the contemporary church. InterVarsity Press has cosponsored the theology conference since its inception, and it has regularly published an edited volume based on the conference lectures.

With the Wheaton Theology Conference Series, readers can now benefit by collecting all of the available volumes based on past theology conferences. Each conference and subsequent volume addresses a particular topic such as the theology of N. T. Wright, the role of beauty in the Christian faith, spiritual formation through the Holy Spirit, global theology, the relationship between theology and psychology, the doctrine of justification, racial dynamics in the church, and the role of women in ministry.

Collectively, the volumes include contributions from renowned scholars and church leaders such as Dallas Willard, Mark Noll, Kevin Vanhoozer, Amos Yong, Jeremy Begbie, Stanley Hauerwas, Mark Labberton, Scot McKnight, Soong-Chan Rah, Philip Jenkins, Deborah van Deusen Hunsinger, James Kombo, Timothy George, Ellen Charry, Bruce McCormack, and many more.

ALSO AVAILABLE

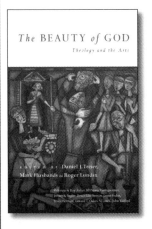

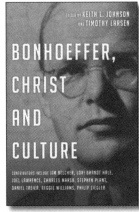

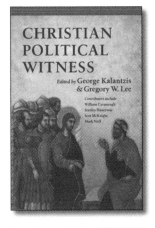

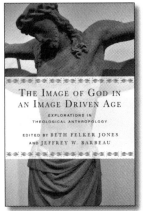

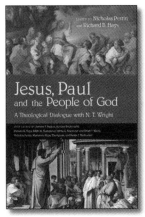

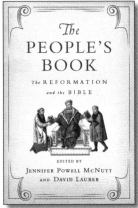

For more titles in the WTC series, go to
ivpress.com/wheaton-theology-conference-series.

Finding the Textbook You Need

The IVP Academic Textbook Selector
is an online tool for instantly finding the IVP books
suitable for over 250 courses across 24 disciplines.

ivpacademic.com